THE WHITE NILE

THE
WHITE NILE

ALAN MOOREHEAD

—

HARPER & ROW, PUBLISHERS
NEW YORK · EVANSTON
SAN FRANCISCO · LONDON

The White Nile
First published 1960
Revised edition 1971
© Alan Moorehead 1960, 1971
All rights reserved

This book was designed and produced by George Rainbird Ltd
Marble Arch House 44 Edgware Road London w.2

Picture Research: Joy Law
House Editor: Raymond Kaye
Designer: Ronald Clark
Maps: Tom Stalker-Miller
Index: Irene Clephane

Text set in Monophoto Imprint
Printed and bound by Jarrold & Sons Ltd Norwich
Colour plates and jacket originated and printed by
Westerham Press Ltd Kent

A substantial portion of the
contents of this book appeared
originally in *The New Yorker*.

Library of Congress Catalog Card Number: 78-160663
ISBN: 06-013049-0

Printed and Bound in England

TO FREYA STARK

NOTE. The first edition of *The White Nile* was published in England in 1960. Since then many things have changed in Africa, but nothing has happened to match the extraordinary courage and determination of the explorers of the last century, and their discoveries which opened up the whole hidden continent.

This new illustrated edition, revised and slightly shortened, is designed to give the reader a closer idea of the world these men found, and a more revealing view of the men themselves; it can perhaps be compared to the early illustrated productions, now hard to find, of the books written by the explorers themselves. The illustrations, both in monochrome and in colour, are mostly from contemporary sources. They have been collected and assembled with remarkable aptness and imagination by Mrs Joy Law, to whom I wish to express my thanks.

ACKNOWLEDGMENTS. The original plan for this book was suggested to me by Mr Ralph Dreschfield QC, and I cannot sufficiently express my gratitude to him. Among others who generously helped me were Sir Richard Turnbull, Professor Kenneth Ingham, Mr Rennie Bere, Sir Edwin Chapman-Andrews, Sir John Gray and Mr H. B. Thomas.

I am indebted to the Zanzibar Museum and the British Universities Mission to Central Africa for allowing me to see their records. Mr G. S. Holland of the Royal Geographical Society prepared a map which enabled me to follow the explorers' routes inland from Bagamoyo to Lake Victoria and thence down the Nile into the Sudan.

I also owe a particular debt to Mr L. P. Kirwan, the Director of the Royal Geographical Society; to Mr G. R. Crone and to Mrs Dorothy Middleton, who allowed me to see a number of unpublished letters written to the Society by Burton and Speke, and who read this book in typescript; to Mr Richard Hill and Mrs Mary Bull who also checked the manuscript; and to the London Library, who supplied most of the books listed in the Bibliography.

Dr John R. Baker, Mr Richard Stanley, Mr James Maconochie, Mr Rodney Searight, Mr D. H. Simpson, the Librarian of the Royal Commonwealth Society, and Mr G. S. Dugdale, the Librarian of the Royal Geographical Society, have most generously helped with the illustrations.

Finally I must acknowledge with gratitude the great assistance given me by my wife and by Mr Richard Brain in editing the text, and I am grateful to Sir Laurence Grafftey-Smith for his kindness in reading the proof of this revised edition.

A.M.

Contents

PART THREE

THE MOSLEM REVOLT

PART FOUR

THE CHRISTIAN VICTORY

Colour Plates and Maps

ABOVE *The Nile in flood in Nubia.* BELOW *The parched earth of Egypt.*

Prologue

No unexplored region in our times, neither the heights of the Himalayas, the Antarctic wastes, nor even the hidden side of the moon, has excited quite the same fascination as the mystery of the sources of the Nile. For two thousand years at least the problem was debated and remained unsolved; every expedition that was sent up the river from Egypt returned defeated. By the middle of the nineteenth century – barely 100 years ago – this matter had become, in Harry Johnston's phrase, 'the greatest geographical secret after the discovery of America'.

The scope of this book is limited to the years between 1856 and 1900, and so we need do no more here than mention very briefly the early history of the river. Almost certainly the ancient Egyptians knew the Nile valley from the Mediterranean as far as the present city of Khartoum, where the Blue Nile comes in from the Ethiopian mountains. Probably they knew something of the Blue Nile as well. But the further course of the parent stream, the White Nile, south of Khartoum, remained a matter of endless speculation, and it interested every distinguished geographer of his age.

This was something more than an ordinary field of exploration. In these deserts the river was life itself. Had it failed to flow, even for one season, then all Egypt perished. Not to know where the stream came from, not to have any sort of guarantee that it would continue – this was to live in a state of insecurity where only fatalism or superstition could reassure the mind.

But there is no record of the river's ever having failed. The great brown flood came pouring out of the desert for ever, and no one could explain why it was that it should rise and flow over its banks in the Nile Delta in September, the driest and hottest time of the year on the Mediterranean littoral; nor how it was possible for the river to continue in its lower reaches for well over a thousand miles through one of the most frightful of all deserts without receiving a single tributary and hardly a drop of rain.

About 460 B.C. Herodotus ascended the Nile as far as the first cataract at Assuan before turning back, having found it quite impossible to obtain definite information about the source of the river. There existed merely a vague notion that it arose from 'fountains' somewhere in the interior of Africa. The Emperor Nero sent two centurions with an expedition into the wastes of Nubia, as the Sudan was then called, but they returned unsuccessful, saying that they had been blocked in the far interior by an impenetrable swamp. Through the centuries that followed China became known to Europe; America and Australia were discovered, and the land masses and the oceans of the world were mapped and charted very much as they are today. But still, in 1856, the centre of Africa and its inner mystery, the source of the White Nile, remained almost as much an enigma as it was in the time of Herodotus.

James Bruce traced the course of the shorter Blue Nile from its source to Khartoum in the seventeen-seventies, but by 1856 even the most determined of explorers on the White Nile had not been able to get beyond the neighbourhood of the present township of Juba, on latitude 5 degrees north. At that point they were still nowhere near the source of the river. Cataracts, vast forests of papyrus reeds, malarial fever, the fierce tropical heat, the opposition of the pagan tribes – all these combined to prevent any further progress south. By now that impenetrable blank space in the centre of the continent had become filled in imagination with a thousand monstrosities, dwarf men and cannibals with tails, animals as strange as the fabulous griffin and the salamander, huge inland seas, and mountains so high they defied all nature by bearing on their crests, in this equatorial heat, a mantle of perpetual snow.

There was at least a little tenuous evidence to support some of these speculations. One of the most persistent legends about the source of the Nile concerned itself with a journey that had not been made upon the river at all, but overland, from the east coast of Africa a little to the north of Zanzibar. According to this legend a man named Diogenes, a Greek merchant, claimed that in the middle of the first century A.D. he was returning home from a visit to India and had landed on the African mainland at a place called Rhapta (which might have been the site of the present settlement of Pangani in Kenya). From Rhapta, Diogenes said, he had 'travelled inland for a 25-days' journey and arrived in the vicinity of two great lakes, and the snowy range of mountains whence the Nile draws its twin sources'.

This, at all events, is the story as it was recorded at the time by the Syrian geographer Marinus of Tyre, and it was from the records of Marinus that Ptolemy, the greatest of geographers and astronomers of his time, produced in the middle of the second century A.D. his celebrated map. It shows the course of the Nile reaching directly southward from the Mediterranean to the Equator, and the river is made to arise from two round lakes. The lakes in turn are watered from a high range of mountains, the *Lunae Montes*, the Mountains of the Moon.

For 1,700 years Ptolemy's map remained a geographical curiosity, endlessly disputed yet seldom absolutely discredited. But then in 1848 Johann Rebmann, one of the earliest missionaries in East Africa, came forward with a sensational report that he himself, like the ancient Diogenes, had journeyed inland from the East African coast and had seen a vast mountain called Kilimanjaro with snow on its summit. In the following year another missionary, Johann Ludwig Krapf, claimed that he had seen from a distance a second snow-capped peak, Mount Kenya, some-what to the north of Kilimanjaro. Still another missionary, J. J. Erhardt, produced a map which showed a large inland lake which he called the 'Sea of Uniamesi'. By the early eighteen-fifties there was other evidence as well that led to a renewal of interest in Ptolemy's map: the Arab slave and ivory traders, returning to Zanzibar from the far interior, spoke of two great lakes there, one the Ujiji and the other the Nyanza. In addition there were reports of a third lake, the Nyasa, further to the south.

All this was extremely vague and confusing. Were all these lakes in reality one lake? Were Kilimanjaro and Kenya the legendary Mountains of the Moon, or was there another range further inland? And how did both lakes and mountains fit into the supposed pattern of the Nile?

It was in order to find the answer to these questions that two explorers, Richard Francis Burton and John Hanning Speke, set off for Africa in 1856. They rejected the route that followed the Nile upstream from Egypt, and decided instead to strike westward from Zanzibar into the dark interior where no white men had ever been before.

With this new expedition the great age of Central African exploration began.

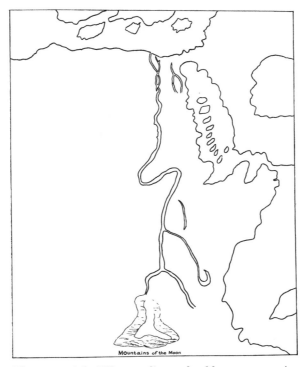

Mountains of the Moon

The course of the Nile according to the oldest extant version
of Ptolemy's map.

PART ONE

THE EXPLORATION

The Murchison Falls, about 120 feet high, from the Victoria Nile or Somerset River, to the level of Lake Albert. (Baker)

1

Zanzibar 1856

The Zanzibar that Burton and Speke first saw at the end of 1856 was a much more important place than it is today; indeed, it was almost the only centre of overseas commerce worth the name along the whole East African seaboard. The attempts of the Portuguese to found an empire on the mainland opposite the island had long since come to nothing, and all the country inland, the territories we now know as Tanganyika, Kenya, Uganda, South Sudan and the Congo, was very largely an unmapped, unknown void.

In a vague and general way the Sultans of Zanzibar laid claim to a part at least of this vast area, but in point of fact their power was restricted to the coastline and was not really effective even there. During the dry seasons slave and ivory caravans found their way into the wilderness that lay beyond and were gone for a year or more, perhaps for ever, but that was all one ever heard of Central Africa. It was almost as remote and strange as outer space is today.

The island of Zanzibar, however, was something of a name in the world, a regular port of call for the sailing vessels plying the Indian Ocean; and it was in one of these, a British sloop, that Burton and Speke came in on the north-east monsoon from Bombay on December 19, 1856.

Their first view of the island cannot have been so very different from the scene one sees at the present time. Then, as now, a whiff of cloves and tropical spices came out to greet the traveller from the shore, and on the shore itself a slow, oily sea of mar-vellous blue washed up on to white coral beaches. The jungle that began at the water's edge was green with a hectic greenness, and although occasional rainstorms and even tornadoes swept the island it was oppressed throughout the year by a soporific heat.

Seen from the sea Zanzibar port was an uneven silhouette of earthen hovels and large four-square buildings made of greyish coral, the only building stone on the island. One descried very easily the palace of the Sultan, the houses of the consuls and the merchants, and then the minarets rising from the mosques in the town beyond. It was to one of these houses, close to the foreshore, that of Lieutenant-Colonel Atkins Hamerton, the British Agent, that Burton and Speke proposed to make their way.

The anchorage before the town was much congested. Burton counted upwards of sixty Arab dhows which, like his own sloop, had been blown across the Indian Ocean by the monsoon, and they were similar to those one sees in Zanzibar now, solid wooden hulls of anything between 50 and 500 tons with a single mast, a great lateen

The Sultan's palace, Zanzibar.

sail and a bowsprit that projected so far it almost doubled the vessel's length. In addition there were half a dozen square-rigged merchantmen in port, Americans from Salem, Frenchmen and Hamburgers that had sailed round the Cape from Europe. All these had come to pick up cargoes of copal, coconuts, ivory, hides, tortoise-shell, red pepper, ambergris, beeswax, hippopotamus teeth, rhinoceros horn, cowrie shells (that were called blackamoor's teeth) and anything else that was going in the bazaar. Rubbish of every kind floated by along the foreshore, and it was not unusual for a dead body to be seen among the debris. 'Here and there,' Burton wrote later, 'a giant shark shoots up from the depths and stares at the fisherman with a cool, fixed and colourless eye that makes his blood run cold.'

There was worse to come when they got ashore. The population of Zanzibar Island was about 100,000 at this time, and most of the people were living in the town itself. In the crooked dirty streets, barely 20 feet wide, a teeming procession went by of half-naked negroes, Arabs, Indians, Persians, Swahilis and many others. Cattle and donkeys thrust their way into the crowd. Merchants, sitting cross-legged in holes in the walls, called out their wares, beggars reached up their hands to the passers-by, and over all in the stifling air hung the devastating smell of copra and decaying fish. In the bazaars piles of tropical fruits and vegetables were laid out on straw mats for sale.

In short, it was the sort of scene that is still familiar to any visitor to the East, and the only basic difference here in Zanzibar in 1856 – a difference so great that it makes one feel that one is looking into another age and another world – was provided by the presence of the slaves. They roamed through every street, men, women and children, those who had been domesticated by years of captivity, and those who had just arrived from the interior and who were half mad and half dead through hunger and maltreatment – naked, bewildered creatures with teeth filed into points and cicatrices on their bodies, their whole appearance closer to that of a trapped animal than of a normal human being.

The scene had already been effectively described by Thomas Smee, the commander of the British research ship *Ternate*, which visited Zanzibar in 1811.

'The show,' Smee wrote, 'commences about four o'clock in the afternoon. The slaves, set off to the best advantage by having their skins cleaned and burnished with cocoa-nut oil, their faces painted with red and white stripes, which is here esteemed elegance, and the hands, noses, ears and feet ornamented with a profusion of bracelets of gold and silver and jewels, are ranged in a line, commencing with the youngest, and increasing to the rear according to their size and age. At the head of this file, which is composed of all sexes and ages from 6 to 60, walks the person who owns them; behind and at each side, two or three of his domestic slaves, armed with swords and spears, serve as a guard.

'Thus ordered the procession begins, and passes through the market-place and the principal streets; the owner holding forth in a kind of song the good qualities of his slaves and the high prices that have been offered for them.

'When any of them strikes a spectator's fancy the line immediately stops, and a

OPPOSITE *Starving slaves abandoned on the march.* OVERLEAF *The Slave Market in Zanzibar. 'Slavery begets slavery. The ethnologist need only go to Zanzibar to become acquainted with all the different tribes to the centre of the Continent on that side or to the Congo.' (Speke)*

process of examination ensues, which, for minuteness, is unequalled in any cattle market in Europe. The intending purchaser having ascertained there is no defect in the faculties of speech, hearing, etc., that there is no disease present, and that the slave does not snore in sleeping, which is counted a very great fault, next proceeds to examine the person; the mouth and the teeth are first inspected and afterwards every part of the body in succession, not even excepting the breasts etc. of the girls, many of whom I have seen handled in the most indecent manner in the public market by their purchasers; indeed there is every reason to believe that the slave-dealers almost universally force the young girls to submit to their lust previous to their being disposed of.

'The slave is then made to walk or run a little way, to show there is no defect about the feet; and after which, if the price be agreed to, they are stripped of their finery and delivered over to their future master. I observed they had in general a very dejected look; some groups appeared so ill-fed that their bones seemed as if ready to penetrate the skin. From such scenes one turns away with pity and indignation . . .'

In the forty-five years that had intervened between Captain Smee's report and the arrival now of Burton and Speke in Zanzibar a great deal had been achieved by the conscience of the world. By the eighteen-thirties slavery had been abolished in the British Empire, and the trade on the Atlantic west coast of Africa, the chief reservoir of negroes, was already dying out. In 1845 the Sultan of Zanzibar had declared that the export of slaves was forbidden (though slavery within his dominions continued to be legal). British and French men-of-war patrolled the coast in search of Arab dhows bringing negroes from the mainland.

A mid-nineteenth-century British sloop, by H. J. Vernon.

But none of this had made any real difference. With a tradition of at least two thousand years of slaving behind them none of the east coast Arab dealers had as yet dreamed of giving up the trade. Slaving was in the Arab blood: no Arab regarded the trade as any more evil or abnormal than, presumably, a horse-dealer regards as evil or abnormal the buying and selling of horses today.

And so the caravans were still raiding into the interior; the dhows, with their cargoes close-packed beneath the decks, were still successfully running the blockade of the warships; and Zanzibar market was as crowded as ever. Prices varied a good deal according to the season of the year and the supply, but in 1856 a dealer could still count on obtaining £4 or £5 for an adult slave in Zanzibar and somewhat more for a female. Between twenty and forty thousand slaves were still imported into the island every year, about one-third of these being reserved for work on the plantations (which was still legal), and the remainder being destined, illegally, for export to Arabia, Persia, Egypt, Turkey and even further afield. There was tremendous wastage even among those slaves who had survived the journey from their villages inland to the coast: some thirty per cent of the males died of disease and malnutrition every year in Zanzibar and had to be replaced. Moreover the attempt to control the export trade had increased the hardships of the slaves. Prices were going up, and consequently it paid the dealer to cram more and more of his victims into the dhows: if just one vessel in four got through it was enough to make a profit. The ships were now built, Burton says, 'with 18 inches between the decks, one pint of water a head was served out per diem and five wretches were stowed away instead of two'.

The most desperate devices were used to keep up the supply. In Zanzibar harbour

The port of Zanzibar.

natives would be enticed on board a dhow with a bottle of rum or a decoy girl and then clapped under the hatches. A child worth a pound or two in Zanzibar would fetch up to £20 in Persia, and it was no difficult matter to hide the slaves in caves in the jungle until the dhows were ready to take them off by night. The highest prices were paid for Abyssinian girls and Circassians, who had been brought down from the north, but these last were very rare and seldom left the island: they were reserved for the harems of the rulers.

The sea front at Zanzibar showing the Sultan's palace, the customs house, the British consulate and the
British mission.

Burton's description of the market-place in 1856 indicates how little things had changed for the better since Captain Smee's day. 'Lines of negroes,' he says, 'stood like beasts, the broker calling out "*bazar khush*" – the least hideous of the black faces, some of which appeared hardly human, were surmounted by scarlet night-caps. All were horribly thin, with ribs protruding like the circles of a cask, and not a few squatted sick on the ground. The most interesting were the small boys, who grinned as if somewhat pleased by the degrading and hardly decent inspection to which both sexes and all ages were subjected. The woman-show appeared poor and miserable; there was only one decent-looking girl, with carefully blacked eyebrows. She seemed modest, and probably had been exposed for sale in consequence of some inexcusable offence against decorum. As a rule no one buys adult domestic (as distinct from wild) slaves, male or female, for the sufficient reason that the masters never part with them till they are found incorrigible. . . . The dealers smiled at us and were in a good humour.' Then there was the prostitutes' quarter where the women had 'faces like skinned apes and lean legs encased in red silk tights'.

It was the wild slaves from the interior who, though saleable, caused most of the lawlessness in Zanzibar. They roamed the streets in search of food like packs of hungry dogs and were prepared for any violence, any form of robbery. No one went about unarmed in the town and at night every door and shutter was barred against marauders in the deserted streets.

Domestic slaves, on the other hand – those who had been born or trained in Zanzibar and were more or less civilized – presented other problems. They were the laziest, the dirtiest, the most dishonest of servants; yet their Arab masters could not conceive of life without them. Often such slaves were incorporated into the family and not unkindly treated: if a concubine bore a child by her master it was at once declared free and adopted as a son or a daughter of the house. Yet drunkenness and petty thieving remained the rule among the domestics in most households, and slaves and masters alike were caught in a web of mutual distrust and even hatred.

There were at this time some 5,000 Arabs in Zanzibar, and some of them owned as many as 2,000 slaves in addition to large plantations of cloves and coconut palms, three-storey wooden houses with fine carved doorways and wardrobes of embroidered gowns and turbans. Together with the Indian dealers, they controlled the ivory trade, owned ocean-going ships, loaned money at fantastic rates of interest and financed expeditions into the interior. And yet it was a listless and torpid sort of life, turning upon a monotonous and limited routine that hardly varied from one month to another. The Arab master rose at dawn, performed the morning prayer, and after a light breakfast proceeded to the bazaar. Eleven o'clock found him in his house again for lunch, followed by an hour of prayers in the mosque and a sleep. At three in the afternoon he rose, washed and again prayed. Then more visits abroad, evening prayers, dinner, a walk through the streets or a visit to the harem. Finally, towards midnight, he retired to bed. Except for the annual observance of Ramadan, a family festival or a journey, this eastern habit of life remained as steady as the heavy tropical weather itself.

Among almost all the residents of the island there was a natural tendency towards drinking and the taking of drugs, either opium or hemp, a natural decline into voluptuousness. Burton remarks that the Arabs objected to the importation of jasmine into Zanzibar on the ground that 'the scent depresses the male sex and unduly excites the feminine'. He also records that the Arabs preferred negresses to their own wives, while their wives preferred negroes for reasons which, he says, were 'somewhat too physiological for the general reader'.

In the eighteen-fifties the legitimate seaborne trade of Zanzibar was chiefly in the hands of the Americans, who in 1839 were the first foreign nation to set up a consulate in Zanzibar, and then, in diminishing importance, came the British, the Germans from Hamburg and the French. In exchange for the ivory and other products they took away, the foreign traders brought in 'merikani', the coarse American cotton cloth which was an article of barter everywhere in East Africa, firearms and ammunition, coloured beads manufactured in Venice, china, cereals, and a haphazard range of gadgets and machines from the western world.

If we are to take Burton's word, the tiny white community stationed in Zanzibar lived a miserable life. The Europeans were forever quarrelling among themselves: 'All is wearisome monotony: there is no society, no pleasure, no excitement; sporting is forbidden by the treacherous climate and strangers . . . soon lose the habit of riding and walking.

'Every merchant hopes and expects to leave Zanzibar forever, as soon as he can realize a certain sum; every agent would persuade his employer to recall him.'

The drinking water of the island was poisonous or at any rate dangerous, venereal disease was endemic, everyone was in constant danger of contracting cholera and malaria, and doctors were unknown. In consequence of this, very few white women lived at Zanzibar, most of the residents being 'contented with an Abyssinian or Somali girl'.

'I am surprised,' Burton went on in his best ironic manner, 'at the combined folly and brutality of civilized husbands who, anxious to be widowers, poison, cut the throats or smash the skulls of their better-halves. The thing can be as neatly and quietly, safely and respectably effected by a few months of African air at Zanzibar.'

He was not altogether exaggerating. One required either great fatalism or a great love of money and power to live willingly in this beautiful and exotic place. Even Hamerton, the British Agent, the one European who had outlived all the others on the island, was beginning to succumb at last. At the time of Burton and Speke's arrival he had already been for fifteen years at Zanzibar and to a very large extent the social and political life of the island revolved around him. It is extraordinary that, in an atmosphere which was remarkable for quarrels and petty jealousies, so few of his contemporaries have a word to say against this warm-hearted and genial Irishman. He was the intimate friend and adviser of the Sultan Seyyid Said, who had created this new Arab empire in the Indian Ocean; he smoothed and calmed every crisis that beset the island and he wrote very sensible dispatches to his superiors in India and London. The British Consulate under Hamerton became the recognized point of rendezvous among the foreign community. 'He kept the whole town alive,' Speke wrote, and his hospitality, like his joviality and good spirits, was remarked upon by every visitor to the island.

More than once Hamerton had been on the point of asking for his recall. His health had been undermined by malaria and other illnesses, but in this case it was neither fatalism nor money that kept the consul at Zanzibar, but rather a sense of duty, perhaps also a feeling that the island and the people in it were now his life; it was too late to make a change. Seyyid Said had died in the previous year, and had been succeeded by his third son, Majid, but still Hamerton kept on. He was now so ill that he barely survived the hot day and lived only for the night. But this did not prevent him from carrying off Burton and Speke to stay at his house, nor from busying himself with the utmost enthusiasm in launching their expedition.

There was much to do. Caravans setting off for the interior at this time usually counted on being away for a year or even two years, and all supplies had to be carried on the porters' heads. A caravan of 100 men, plus an armed guard, was regarded as quite a modest affair, and Burton actually proposed to take a complement of 170 with him. These were to be recruited partly in Zanzibar and partly on the coast, and were to be under the general direction of the headman or guide, a half-caste Arab named Said bin Salim who was in the employ of the Sultan but had been loaned to the expedition. In addition there were two gunbearers, Sidi Bombay and Mwinyi Mabruki, who served more or less in the capacity of non-commissioned officers, and who were soon to become considerable figures in East African exploration; two Goan personal servants who cooked for Burton and Speke; and the guard which was made up partly of armed slaves and partly of Baluchis in the Sultan's service – about a score of them in all.

For the most part the caravan proposed to live off the country, either by the shooting of wild game or by the purchase of cattle, goats, milk and grain from the tribes. All other supplies (with the exception of scientific instruments, guns, medicines and so

Sidi Bombay. He was engaged as factotum by Speke on the basis that he was to be paid $60 a year, in advance: '. . . he then bound himself to follow me wherever I chose to lead him in Africa.'

forth which were brought from England or India) had to be obtained from the Indian and Arab merchants in Zanzibar, and the list was formidable. Among many other items Burton mentions 3 rifles, 2 smooth bores, a Colt's carbine, 3 revolvers, all with spare parts, 3 swords and ammunition sufficient to last two years; a number of chronometers, prismatic compasses, thermometers, a portable sundial, sextants, barometers, a telescope, a box of mathematical instruments and '1 pocket pedometer by Dixie' for measuring, by their paces, the number of miles they marched each day.

In their camp furniture the two explorers did themselves well. They had a tent, camp beds, a portable table and chairs, 3 mats to be used as carpets, blankets, mattresses, mosquito nets, air pillows, a canteen of knives and forks, and cooking utensils. Their clothing consisted of the normal jackets, trousers and boots in which men go shooting, in addition to turbans and thick felt caps for the head. 'N.B.,' Burton adds, 'not looking forward to so long a journey, we left Zanzibar without a new outfit; consequently we were in tatters before the end, and in a climate where flannel fights half the battle of life against death, my companion was compelled to invest himself in overalls of American domestics, and I was forced to cut up blankets into coats and wrappers. . . .'

There was a small library of scientific books, stationery of every kind, sealing wax, ink, a table of the stars, sketching and painting materials, but no camera. They had a carpenter's and blacksmith's outfit, and other tools with which they hoped to assemble and rig a small portable boat on the lakes. Among the provisions were '1 dozen brandy (to be followed by 4 dozen more); 1 box cigars; 5 boxes tea (each 6 lbs.); a little coffee; 2 bottles curry stuff, beside ginger, rock and common salt, red and black pepper, one bottle each, pickles, soap and spices; 20 lbs. pressed vegetables; a bottle vinegar, 2 bottles oil; 20 lbs. sugar (honey is procurable in the country).'

Morphia and quinine were included in the medicine chest, but at this time very little was yet known about malaria – and malaria was a governing factor in all these journeys; indeed, the success of every expedition depended very largely on the explorers' resistance to the fever. Quinine had long since been discovered, but there was much uncertainty about the size of the correct dose. Burton himself preferred to place his faith in Warburg's Drops, which were compounded of sloes, quinine and opium, and in this he made an error.

The remaining miscellaneous items in the baggage included 4 umbrellas, 2,000 fishing hooks and line, 2 lanterns (police-man's bull's eye and common horn), 2 canisters of snuff, 10 steels and flints, a Union Jack and a large cargo of cloth, brass wire and beads to be used in paying the porters and in trading with the tribes. All these things were either encased in boxes or tightly wrapped in a sort of bolster which could conveniently be carried upon the porters' heads.

There was one other aspect of the expedition, and it was to play a vital part in all the unknown hazards that lay ahead. This was the personality of the two explorers themselves.

Burton, despite the plethora of books that have been written either by or about him, still remains beyond the range of ordinary definition. Above all else he was a romantic and an Arabist; he belongs decidedly to that small perennial group of English men and women who are born with something lacking in their lives: a hunger, a nostalgia, that can be set at rest only in the deserts of the East. Whatever the reason may have been – whether it was a natural revulsion from the narrow horizons and the wet and cloudy climate of England, or from the constricting Victorian code of manners there – it was the tinkling of the camel bell that beckoned him until the day he died. And yet with all his amazing concentration and intelligence he remains an amateur of the Islamic world, a devoted dilettante, more Arab than the Arabs, but never absolutely one of them. He returns to the East again and again like a migratory bird, never at peace when he is away, yet never able to stay for long without succumbing to an overmastering restlessness. There are moments in his career when it seems that nothing in the world can appease his almost insane hunger for fulfilment and excitement. Wilfrid Scawen Blunt remembers meeting Burton once in Buenos Aires at the end of one of his debauches, when he reappeared collarless and in filthy clothes. He had, Blunt says, 'a countenance the most sinister I have ever seen, dark, cruel, treacherous, with eyes like a wild beast'. It was his eyes – the 'questing panther eyes' – that everyone remembered. Swinburne, who knew him well, speaks of 'the look of unspeakable horror in those eyes which gave him at times an almost unearthly appearance'. 'He had,' the poet adds, 'the brow of a god and the jaw of a devil.' Burton's wife, who was certainly not one to criticize, describes him as being five feet eleven inches tall, and muscular, with very dark hair, a weather-beaten complexion, an enormous black moustache, large, black, flashing eyes, long lashes and a fierce, proud, melancholy expression.

Yet beneath all this drama Burton was an intensely fastidious and scholarly man. No one else has chronicled a journey through Africa with such erudition as he has. Nothing is beyond his observation: the languages and customs of the tribes, the geography of the land, its botany, geology and meteorology, even the statistics of the import and export trade at Zanzibar. No other explorer had such a breadth of reference, or had read so much or could write so well; none certainly was graced with such a touch of sardonic humour. His *Lake Regions of Central Africa* remains, possibly, not only his best book but also, in a field of writing that was remarkably good, one of the best explorer's journals ever written.

At this time he was just 36 years of age, and we are not here concerned with the second half of his life, with all its tumultuous journeys, its quarrels and humiliations, its fantastic outpourings of books and translations, which in the end, with the publication of his *Thousand Nights and One Night* and other Eastern erotica, were to earn for him the reputation of being a sort of intellectual rake.

Yet at 36 he was already a famous man, though not a very popular one. After an education in France and Italy and at Oxford he had served seven years in the Indian Army, had made his famous journey to Mecca and a second hardly less perilous expedition to the forbidden city of Harar in Abyssinia, and had written his books about these adventures. Never at any point in his army career in India had he proceeded in a normal, orthodox way; his way was through the interior lines and the endless subtleties and aberrations of Eastern life. He was forever disguising himself in Eastern clothes, even dyeing his face and hands, and visiting low bazaars which would have been extremely distasteful to the ordinary British officer. In consequence he knew a great deal more about Indians and their way of life than the authorities cared to know. They were no more amused by his account of vice in Karachi than by his prediction that the Indian army was on the point of mutiny. As an officer he was irascible, impatient of discipline and highly critical of his colleagues. Yet he was not altogether to be dismissed as just another British eccentric, for he was a swordsman of note, he was incontestably brave, and in his command of languages and dialects there had been few to equal him. It was said that he had discovered a system by which in two months he could learn a new language, and at the end of his life he was believed to speak and write no less than twenty-nine. At one stage he lived with thirty monkeys in order to study the noises they made, and he even succeeded in putting together a short monkey-vocabulary.

Almost too much was contained here in one man. One has the feeling that he lived in a state of continual conflict within himself, the intellectual warring with the man of action, the methodical scholar grating against the poet and the romantic, the fastidious hypochondriac fighting a losing battle with the libertine. But then he recoils from his own unorthodoxy and struggles back to a respectable show of things; and it was in one such recoil that, just before the opening of this new African adventure, he entered into an engagement of marriage with the doting and carefully nurtured Isabel Arundell, in England. Having become engaged to her, however, he at once abandoned her – a thing he was to do again more than once in the long married life that lay before them – and now he had involved himself in another relationship which was even more singular. That this brilliant, courageous, highly-strung adventurer should have adopted as his close companion a man who was so complete an opposite as John Hanning Speke is, surely, as ironic a phenomenon as anything Cervantes contrived with his Don Quixote and Sancho Panza.

Not that Speke was in any way servile to Burton. Indeed, he was the very reverse, and this in the end was to be Burton's undoing. Burton needed a disciple and instead he got a rival. Speke was 30, some six years younger than Burton, and although a story was put about at one time that he was an Anglo-Indian with mixed blood there was no truth in it; he came from a West Country family that dated back to Saxon times. He was tall and slender and his blue eyes and fair hair gave him rather a Scandinavian appearance. Moreover he looked after himself; he ate a great deal but drank very little and never smoked. The ordinary relaxations and dissipations of a young man of his age were not for Speke; his life was in the open air, and to fit himself for that life he was prepared to go to great lengths. Once in Africa he even discarded his boots and walked barefoot so as to toughen himself. He planned ahead, he set himself definite objectives, and having once made up his mind he proceeded with great prudence and determination. In short, he measured up very well to the Victorian notion of what a young man ought to be: steady, abstemious, methodical in his habits, and respectable. But he was not entirely humourless and he had the gift of friendship. Underneath that cool and rather prosaic exterior there was a certain charm. Even Burton was prepared to admit this, though as is usual with most of Burton's judgments of people, his summing up of Speke carried a violent sting in the tail. He wrote: 'To a peculiarly quiet and modest aspect – aided by blue eyes and blond hair – to a gentleness of demeanour, and an almost childlike simplicity of manner which at once attracted attention, he united an immense fund of self-esteem, so carefully concealed, however, that none but his intimates suspected its existence.'

Like Burton, Speke had entered the Indian Army, though at an earlier age and as a cadet, and had fought in the Punjab. Like Burton, he had a taste for solitary expeditions in India, though of a very different kind; he used to go shooting in the distant Himalayas. Speke had a mania for shooting – few specimens in India and Tibet, he says, did not fall to his gun – and his various journeys on local leave took him into very remote places where, possibly, no other European had been before. This was part of the toughening-up process, and Speke was not unconscious of his own virtue in this matter. He was not like his brother officers in India, he wrote later, somewhat smugly. He never 'idled away his time or got into debt': he was away in the mountains collecting specimens and opening up the unexplored country; and the authorities approved of this.

Already in India, long before he met Burton, Speke had a great object in view; he had decided that as soon as his long leave fell due he would make a journey through unexplored Africa, travelling from the east coast to the headwaters of the Nile, and then sail downstream to Egypt. On the way he would gather specimens of rare birds and animals, and eventually he would build up a natural history museum in his father's country house in England. Of his three years' leave from the army, two were to be spent on the journey and the third year he was to recuperate at home. He saved his money, he planned, and when his ten years' service in India was up in 1854 he sailed for Aden, carrying with him £390 worth of beads and other barter goods with which he proposed to enlist the help of the natives when he crossed to the African mainland.

It was at this point – some two years before the outset of the present journey – that the two explorers met for the first time. Speke had been in Aden only a few days when Burton turned up with several other young officers on the outward journey of his Abyssinian expedition, and it was soon arranged that Speke should scrap his own plans and join forces with them.

From Burton's point of view this first African adventure had been a distinct personal success. With many manoeuvrings – it was the sort of cloak-and-dagger affair he loved so well – he had first got himself in and out of the fanatical Moslem stronghold of Harar, and had then made a rendezvous with the others on the Somaliland coast. For Speke, however, the expedition had been an unqualified disaster. His side of it had accomplished practically nothing. Soon after Burton had joined the coastal party at Berbera in April 1855 a concerted rush had been made on the camp by the local Somali tribesmen at midnight, and in the desperate struggle that had ensued one of the Englishmen had been killed, Burton had been wounded in the jaw, and Speke, having been repeatedly stabbed about the legs and arms, had been taken prisoner. There had been a sharp disagreement between Burton and Speke at the height of the fray. Speke said later that he ran back under the lee of the tent to get a better view of the attackers and Burton, mistaking this action, called out to him, 'Don't step back or they will think we are retiring.' Chagrined by this Speke rushed out against the attackers, and it was then that he was speared, stunned, tied up and carried away. He was badly wounded, and would certainly have been put to death, but he managed nevertheless to escape and rejoin Burton and another of the officers who had taken refuge aboard a friendly Arab vessel. They escaped eventually to Aden and there took ship for England. One other mortification awaited Speke while he was recovering from his wounds: Burton, as leader of the expedition, considered that he had full rights to the notes taken by his subordinates, and when his *First Footsteps in East Africa* was published it was found to contain an abridged version of Speke's diary tucked away ignominiously at the end of the book.

Burton wrote a curious note about Speke's frame of mind during these early days of their acquaintance, and although it hardly squares with what we know of this clear and resourceful man one is reluctant to disbelieve it. 'Before we set out,' Burton wrote, 'he [Speke] openly declared that, being tired of life, he had come to be killed in Africa.' This of course might have been nothing more than a young man's expression of a Byronic mood. Yet one sees here a glimpse of the solitary mountaineer dreaming visions in Tibet. Perhaps he had secretly a definite and compelling need to be a hero.

But still in 1855 there had been no real grievance between the two men, and certainly no lack of courage on either side. After their Somaliland adventure both had volunteered for the campaign in the Crimea, and when the war was over they had met again in London. Burton was now full of plans for the very kind of journey upon which Speke also had set his heart – an expedition to the sources of the Nile. When Burton asked Speke to join him, Speke immediately agreed.

And so now, at the end of 1856, the two men found themselves in Hamerton's house in Zanzibar preparing for their second adventure into the African wilderness. Since Burton had obtained a grant of £1,000 from the Foreign Office and the patronage of the Royal Geographical Society he was the official leader. So far as one can make out Speke accepted this state of affairs with very good grace, and was exhilarated by the adventure that lay before them. Burton, too, was very confident. He wrote from Zanzibar to the Secretary of the Royal Geographical Society in London: 'People here tell frightful stories about the dangers and difficulty of the journey [into the interior] and I don't believe a word of it.'

The explorers were in no particular hurry to get away from Zanzibar, and in this perhaps – in the calm and leisured use of time – one sees by how much we are divided from the nineteenth century. They debated at length about their plans with Hamerton, they called on the young Sultan Majid, they bartered for further men and supplies in the bazaar, and they set off on rather a haphazard preliminary trip along the coast in order to acclimatize themselves. They were away two months, calling at the neighbouring island of Pemba (which was supposed to be the burial-ground of Captain Kidd's treasure) and travelling a short distance inland through the country that lies south of what is now the border of Kenya and Tanganyika. After various adventures the two explorers finally got back to their boat near Pangani so ill with malaria that Burton had to be carried on board. It took them several weeks in Zanzibar to recover. Burton, however, declared that he welcomed this first experience of fever since he believed it would 'salt' them against further attacks; and here again he was wrong.

Finally on June 16, 1857, they set off in the Sultan's corvette *Artemise* for the mainland.

2

The Inspiration

──

Scarcely twenty miles divide Zanzibar from the African mainland, and on a clear day you can plainly see the island from the coast. A motor launch accomplishes the journey across the straits in an hour or two and by air it is a matter of ten or fifteen minutes. Yet there is an astonishing difference between the island and the mainland shore. In Zanzibar everything is soft and beguiling; it is as relaxing as a Turkish bath. There are no hills on the island, no harsh cliffs or torrents; the plantations spread away from the forest paths with the luxuriance of a hot-house, and everywhere there is a sense of established ease, of indolence declining into sleep.

It is no less hot on the mainland, but here the wildness of Central Africa, the sensation of vast primitive space, touches the traveller directly he steps ashore; and it is a little forbidding. He sees a dry hard scrub reaching away into the distance and the native huts are as uninspiring as chicken-coops – flat-roofed, oblong boxes made of crude wooden poles and plastered mud. The only really arresting sight in the landscape are the baobab trees, which here tend to grow in groups on the plain.

There is something gnomish about a baobab tree, a quality that might have appealed to the late Arthur Rackham; it stands like a round wooden tub with antlers for branches, and its colour is the colour of an elephant's hide. It is the sort of tree that a child might make in plasticine.

And so the country continues inland for ninety miles or so until you cross the maritime plain and the mountains break into view. Then one mounts up very quickly on to the great central plateau that stretches away for hundreds of miles into the heart of Africa. Now suddenly one realizes how the woolly air of the coast pressed against one's lungs. At three thousand feet – and that is the general level of the plateau – wide plains begin to appear, broken here and there with rough outcrops of rock, and there is never a moment when some distant mountain is not in sight. These are the real horizons of Central Africa. It is still not impossible to see here a troop of ostriches in the long grass, or a herd of antelopes on the run. In the remoter parts there is a deep silence in the bush, and if by chance an African appears he stands quite still for a moment and watches you with the alertness and wariness of an animal; and then he responds with a movement of his arm, sometimes a word of greeting.

For the most part the slave route from the coast led on from one watering place to another, and almost all the caravans headed for Kazeh (now called Tabora) in Central Tanganyika, some 500 miles inland from the sea. From Kazeh the paths of the caravans struck out in all directions, one directly north towards the southern shore of Lake Victoria, another round the western side of the lake towards the country known as Karagwe, another due westward to Ujiji on Lake Tanganyika, and still another southwards towards Lake Nyasa. Progress was extremely slow and possible only in dry weather.

There was, however, a moment of respite at the outset of these long journeys when travellers crossed from Zanzibar to the mainland coast at Bagamoyo. Bagamoyo means 'Lay down the burden of your heart', and it is a beautiful place, with a line of rustling coconut palms on the shore and beyond them, at the right season, one of the loveliest sights of Africa: the flamboyant trees that spread like chestnuts and blaze with the brightest shades of scarlet, flame and orange.

The Indian Ocean here has the texture, and no doubt the specific gravity, of warm, very salty soup and is infested with a thousand slimy things, broken fronds of sea-weed, livid jelly-fish, perhaps an empty coconut floating by. There is no harbour, but a coral reef breaks the force of the waves and the beach slopes very gently inland. At low tide the sea recedes for a quarter of a mile or more and all the debris of the shore lies stranded on a wet grey plain.

At Kaole, a little to the south of Bagamoyo, are the ruins of a coral mosque, and of graves and houses dating back to the thirteenth century, an incredible antiquity in this climate where every man-made thing seems destined to be overwhelmed by nature and forgotten. A plaque set up at Bagamoyo announces that it was from here that Burton and Speke started their journey inland in 1857.

There were of course the usual difficulties in setting out. Having come ashore from their corvette at Kaole they discovered that only a fraction of the porters they wanted were obtainable and consequently asses had to be bought instead. Great haggling took place in the bazaar before thirty-six men were eventually assembled, and it was decided in the end that the portable boat and other heavy baggage would have to be left behind. Hamerton had come over from Zanzibar with the two explorers to say good-bye and to help them get away, and it was an act of singular devotion, for he was dying. He was perfectly well aware that his strength had finally run out; he confided to Burton that he expected death and welcomed it and wished to be buried at sea. On June 26, 1857, he sailed away, and he survived only a few days after his return to Zanzibar. Eleven months were to elapse before Burton and Speke were to hear in the depths of the interior that he was dead.

Speke went ahead with some of the men on June 25 on the first stage of the journey, and on June 27 Burton followed him, mounted on a camel. They marched south-westward at first so as to avoid the country of the hostile Masai tribe to the north, and there was a pause at a place called Zungomero (since vanished from the map) while they regrouped. More porters were obtained, bringing up the numbers of the caravan to 132 in all, and early August found them climbing slowly up the escarpment to the central plateau. The expedition was launched at last.

There was no particular difficulty about the route: they followed beaten paths from one village to another, and from time to time they kept passing other caravans coming down to the coast with slaves and ivory. Yet it was a progress so slow, so tortuous and

Richard Burton aged 39, watercolour by Louis Desanges.

disordered that one marvels that it ever got ahead at all. The day began at 4 a.m. with the crowing of the cocks, while it was still dark and very cold. Then Burton and Speke had their coffee or tea and perhaps a plate of porridge, while the Arab guard turned to the east for morning prayers. By 5 a.m. the whole caravan was stirring round the camp-fires, and a long delay ensued while the cattle and the goats were rounded up and the porters quarrelled fiercely over their loads, the weaker men usually being left to take up the heavier burdens. The last act before the departure was to set fire to the grass huts that had been built the night before. The huts, of course, might have been useful for other travellers, but one left no gifts for strangers in this hostile world.

There was a rough and ready order in the long procession when it finally got under way. In the lead went the guide, wearing a ceremonial head-dress and carrying the red flag of the Sultan of Zanzibar, and behind him marched the drummer. The cloth and bead porters came next with their bolster-like bundles on their heads, then the men carrying the camp equipment, and their women, children and cattle. The armed guard was dispersed along the line, each man carrying a muzzle-loaded 'Tower-musket', a German cavalry sabre, a small leather box strapped to the waist and a huge cow-horn filled with ammunition. Many of them were accompanied by their women and personal slaves. Burton and Speke as a rule drew up the rear, either riding the camel and the asses or, if sick, being carried in hammocks. Almost every male member of the caravan had a weapon of some kind together with an assortment of pots and pans and a three-legged wooden stool strapped to the small of his back. A continuous and violent uproar of chanting, singing, whistling and shouting accompanied the march, for it was thought important to make as much noise as possible so as to impress the local tribes. If a hare chanced to run across the track all downed burdens at once to go in pursuit of the animal, which, if caught, was eaten raw.

The final halt for the day was made at any time from 8 a.m. onwards, but usually it was about 11 o'clock when the full fierceness of the midday heat was beginning, the caravan having then covered about ten miles. If they chanced to stop in a village a rush was made to occupy the best huts, and while a tent was erected for Burton and Speke the whole caravan was gathered inside a kraal of branches and thorns. Through the midday hours the two explorers sat in the shade, taking scientific observations, writing their diaries, making sketches and conducting the general business of the march. Cloth was issued to the porters at each halt so that they could purchase grain from the local inhabitants. At 4 p.m. the Goanese cooks served dinner, which consisted of some such dish as rice and goat's meat, unless Speke had gone out and bagged a partridge or a gazelle – a diversion that Burton did not encourage: 'Captain Burton,' Speke wrote later, 'being no sportsman, would not stop for shooting.'

At night, especially if the moon was shining, the dancing began, the women in one group, the men in another. 'They are such timists,' Burton wrote, 'a hundred pairs of heels sound like one.' But then as the excitement of the dance increased, bedlam broke out, confused rushings and screamings filled the camp, until at last, towards 8 o'clock, the dancers subsided exhausted around their fires and all was peace at last.

Such might have been a normal day in the caravan's progress, but then hardly any

John Hanning Speke, by J. Watney Wilson.

day was normal. At every stage the local chieftains demanded their *hongo* – a tax of so many yards of cloth, so many bags of beads – before they would allow the strangers to cross their territory. Hours, sometimes days, would go by before the haggling was over, and at last a drum was beaten in the chieftain's village to announce that the caravan was free to proceed. As they got further away from the coast many of the porters deserted and had to be replaced by new ones; the asses died one after another, and disease kept breaking out in the camp. Often they were hungry to the point of half-starvation, and both white men were constantly ill; Speke indeed seems to have been in a state of continually failing health all the way to Kazeh. Often too they were swamped by unseasonable rain. But still they struggled on.

'*Rumanika invited both Grant and myself to witness his New Moon levée . . . which takes place every month with a view of ascertaining how many of his subjects are loyal*.' (Speke) From a sketch by Grant.

In the late eighteen-fifties the Tanganyika tribes were probably not so disturbed and brutalized as they became later on when the slave trade grew worse. The traveller was given a relatively friendly reception, and although Burton and Speke passed huge slave caravans, some of them a thousand strong, and saw the tragic aftermath of their progress – the sick men, women and children dying beside the track – both of them made the point that the hardships of the journey were not quite so bad as they were made out to be. 'Justice,' Burton wrote, 'requires the confession that the horrors of slave-driving rarely met the eye in East Africa.' On the march, he says, the slaves were seldom chained, well fed and little worked. The porters, who were free and who made the long journey down to the coast for the hire of a few shillings, had much the worst of it. Then at Zanzibar and the coastal towns a much better life often awaited the slave than the one he had left behind in his squalid and diseased village in the interior.

For a man so immersed in the study of coloured races and so avid of travel among them, Burton throughout reveals an odd and contradictory contempt for the African. 'He seems to belong,' he writes, 'to one of those childish races which, never rising to man's estate, fall like worn-out links from the great chain of animated nature.'

The African's religion is nothing but 'a vague and nameless awe', his chief pre-occupation, drunkenness. Everywhere, Burton says, the drinking of *pombe*, the native beer, starts with the dawn and continues in the villages all through the day. These befuddled, ignorant, hopeless people have no code of morals: 'Marriage, which is an

Brewing pombe, *the native drink made from plantains. From a sketch by Grant.*

epoch amongst Christians, an event among the Moslems, is with these people an incident of frequent occurrence. Polygamy is unlimited, the chiefs pride themselves upon the number of their wives, varying from twelve to three hundred.'

Unfortunately, on its inland journey, the expedition by-passed places like the Olduvai Gorge in the Serengeti Plains, where there are evidences of the extreme antiquity of life in Africa, and Burton knew nothing of the overhanging rocks at Kondoa where one can see drawings of hunting scenes with match-like figures lunging at giraffes, and abstract designs that look like fish skeletons, whirls and sprays like falling stars, and weird circles filled with dots; and the Tanganyika wells with carved stone steps leading down to the water – the work of some vanished civiliza-tion – had not yet been discovered. Burton is one of the few explorers who would

OVERLEAF *African slaves being driven to Khartoum or Zanzibar by their Arab masters. 'Some few freed slaves take service in vessels . . . but most return to Africa to trade in slaves and ivory.' (Speke)*

have been deeply interested in these relics, but as things were he was merely oppressed by the apparent barrenness of the country's past.

Even when Burton is being amusing about Africans he cannot be kind. Since his and Speke's were the first white skins ever to be seen in these regions they were the victims of 'an ecstasy of curiosity'. Natives were constantly standing in a ring around them, pressing into their tent and reaching out their hands to touch them. Burton expostulated: 'At last my experience in staring enabled me to categorize the infliction as follows. Firstly is the stare furtive, when the starer would peep and peer under the tent, and its reverse, the open stare. Thirdly is the stare curious or intelligent, which generally was accompanied with irreverent laughter regarding our appearance. Fourthly is the stare stupid, which denoted the hebete incurious savage. The stare discreet is that of Sultans and great men; the stare indiscreet at unusual seasons is affected by women and children. Sixthly is the stare flattering – it was exceedingly rare, and equally so was the stare contemptuous. Eighthly is the stare greedy; it was denoted by the eyes restlessly bounding from one object to another, never tired, never satisfied. Ninthly is the stare peremptory and pertinacious, peculiar to crabbed age. The dozen concludes with the stare drunken, the stare fierce or pugnacious, and finally the stare cannibal, which apparently considered us as articles of diet.'

And so Burton's tirade against the Africans goes on, at times funny and at others vicious, and hardly for a moment does he pause to reflect that it was the foreign slavers in this country who were debauching and degrading these people quite as much as the *pombe* and the polygamy.

When at last, after nearly five months' journey, the party straggled into Kazeh on November 7, 1857, Burton went forward to meet the Arab traders there with joy. 'Striking indeed,' he cries, 'was the contrast between the open-handed hospitality and hearty goodwill of this truly noble race, and the niggardness of the savage and selfish African – it was heart of flesh after heart of stone.' He was back with his own kind again, grave, courteous, bearded men in turbans and long white robes, cultivated men with graceful manners, and never for a moment does it disturb him that the principal preoccupation of their lives was the herding of men, women and children down to the coast, and the sale of such as survived in the slave markets of Mombasa and Zanzibar.

There were about twenty-five Arab dealers living in Kazeh at this time, and they managed to keep up an outward show of civilization. Their houses, called *tembes*, were built of mud but were quite extensive buildings enclosing a central courtyard, with separate rooms for the domestic slaves and the harem. Fruit, vegetables and rice had been planted and in the bazaar most articles essential to East African trade were on sale, though at prices about five times higher than in Zanzibar. It was customary for the Arabs to eat at sunrise and again at midday, but only very light foods. Hardly any of them were healthy for two months together, and life, though bearable, can scarcely have been much more than a dreary round of petty bargaining and interminable waiting. They were delighted to see the two white men from the coast and were ready to help them in every way. And so a month went by at Kazeh, and Burton,

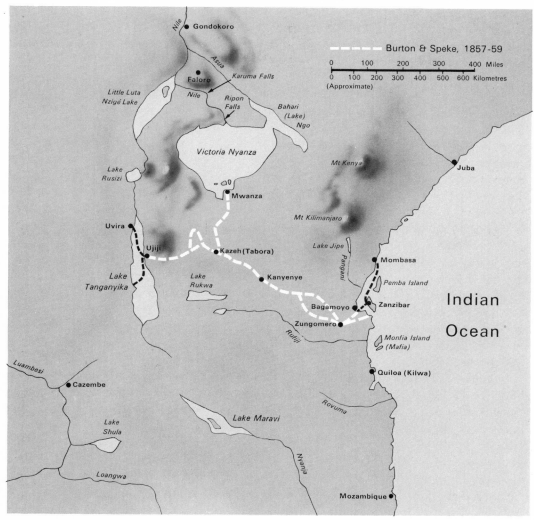

Map based on contemporary information showing the route taken by Burton and Speke, 1857–59.

at least, enjoyed himself, since he could engage in long profitable conversations with his hosts about the unknown country that lay before them to the west. Speke, one feels, being ill and unable to speak Arabic, was left a little in the cold.

Early in December, however, they set off again, and on February 13, 1858, reached Lake Tanganyika in the neighbourhood of the Arab slaving and ivory post at Ujiji. This was a moment of great triumph, a major discovery. Both men were seriously ill again – Speke, who had suffered since childhood from ophthalmia, was so blind he could barely see the lake, and Burton with an ulcerated jaw could take nothing but liquid food – but at least the expedition had accomplished the first of its great objects.

Speke, on recovering his eyesight, went off in search of a boat which would enable them to make a thorough exploration of the region, and although he returned empty-handed two native canoes were found at last, and in these both men set off towards the north. It was Burton's notion that they might find a river there which, flowing north, might well be the source of the Nile. But in this he was disappointed: the Rusizi flows southward into Lake Tanganyika, which in any case is only 2,535 feet above sea-level and therefore too low to be the origin of the Nile. 'I felt sick at heart,' Burton wrote. They turned back to Ujiji, and here at last a little good fortune came to them: their rearguard arrived with supplies from the coast, and after nearly a year they received letters giving them news of the outside world. Burton had the sardonic satisfaction of learning that he had been quite right about India: the mutiny had broken out. In June 1858 they were back at Kazeh again.

And here, in almost a haphazard way, there occurred the beginning of a chain of incidents which was to set this journey apart from all others in Central Africa and lead on through endless bitterness and tragedy to the solution of the problem of the Nile. Burton was anxious to pause awhile among his Arab friends in Kazeh so as to refit the caravan and compile his notes upon the discoveries they had already made. Speke wanted to go off and investigate the reports they had heard from the Arabs of the 'Nyanza', a lake larger than Tanganyika, which was said to lie some three weeks' journey to the north of Kazeh. Burton willingly let him go. With Bombay and a small party of porters and Baluchi guards Speke set off on July 9, 1858.

The traveller today will find that the region between Kazeh and Lake Victoria is, at first, anything but spectacular; the eternal scrub presses around one, mile after mile, monotonously repeating itself. But then one gradually passes into a landscape that is altogether different. The scrub thins out and wide refreshing plains begin to sweep away to the horizon. Here and there huge rounded granite boulders, dropped probably by the melting glaciers of some former ice-age, rise up grotesquely from the ground, and from the distance they often have the appearance of the walled hilltop towns of Southern Italy. One touch of rain on this countryside and it sprouts a lawn of grass. Myriads of storks and other birds alight on the swamps and water-holes, and there is a distinct element of change in the air, a feeling, as you move along, that you are approaching a frontier of some kind, a new experience. This feeling becomes steadily more pronounced as you approach the lake. The earth grows greener, the air more humid and soon you are surrounded by shady trees, palms, emerald-green mangoes and flamboyants. Finally, near Mwanza, the lake itself breaks into view. It is much more like a sea than a lake, a tropical sea with yellow sand beaches and wooded slopes coming down to the shore. To the north there is no visible end to the vast sheet of water. Occasionally it is ruffled up by tremendous storms with black clouds over-head, but on a normal day a light breeze blows and the white horses splash up casually on the shore. The lake takes on the colour of the sky so that it is blue in the sunshine, grey on a cloudy day and almost black in a storm. During the sunsets, and they can be astonishing at times, both sky and lake glow together in a magnificent explosion of theatrical light.

OPPOSITE *The Kenyan scrub.* OVERLEAF *The granite boulders known as the Bismarck Rocks on Lake Victoria.*

On the actual shore itself one often hears a continual crackling noise, especially where the papyrus grows, the slapping of the waves on the reeds, the whirring of countless insects, fire-flies and crickets, the slight but distinct sounds and cries made by the lily-trotters and the ibis; and the darter with his half-submerged, writhing neck looks like a snake coming through the water.

These scenes are very beautiful, and yet there is a mysterious and disturbing atmosphere about the lake. One feels here very strongly the primitiveness of Africa, its overwhelming multiplicity in emptiness. The lakeside Africans are mighty drinkers of *pombe*, and when they have drunk away the oppression of the boredom and idleness of their lives they give way very easily to infantile outbursts of passion and hysteria; and then the drums and the stamping dances have a quality that is uncouth, savage and sometimes menacing.

All these things – the surrounding plains, the peoples of the lakeside, and the immense mysterious reaches of the lake itself – were of course outside the range of civilized knowledge when Speke began his march. It is, then, hardly surprising that he should have been possessed by great excitement in the early morning of August 3, 1858, when he stood on the shore near Mwanza and saw the immense stretch of water for the first time. An inspiration seized him. 'I no longer felt any doubt,' he wrote later, 'that the lake at my feet gave birth to that interesting river, the source of which has been the subject of so much speculation, and the object of so many explorers. The Arabs' tale was proved to the letter. This is a far more extensive lake than the Tanganyika, so broad that you could not see across it, and so long that nobody knew its length.'

It was a reckless and astonishing conclusion to jump to, and it was quite impossible for Speke to back it up with any scientific proof. Yet he seems to have been genuinely convinced by this one short view of a tiny section of the southern shore – he stayed only three days on the lake – that he had discovered the source of the Nile. One wishes that he could have had any other companion than Burton to share his enthusiasm. Nevertheless, he hastened back and re-entered Kazeh only six weeks after he had left it on the outward journey. The party received a warm reception: 'the Baluchis and Bombay,' Speke says, 'could scarcely be seen under the hot embraces and sharp kisses of admiring damsels,' and Speke at once acquainted Burton with his discovery. It is not difficult to imagine the scene from Burton's description:

'We had scarcely breakfasted before he announced to me the startling fact that he had discovered the sources of the White Nile. It was an inspiration perhaps; the moment he had sighted the Nyanza, he felt at once no doubt but that "the Lake at his feet gave birth to that interesting river which has been the subject of so much speculation, and the object of so many explorers". The fortunate discoverer's conviction was strong; his reasons were weak . . .

'After a few days it became evident to me that not a word could be uttered on the subject of the Lake, the Nile, and his *trouvaille* generally without offence. By tacit agreement it was, therefore, avoided, and I should never have resumed it had my companion not stultified the results of the Expedition by putting forth a claim which

The Kaffirboom, Erythrina abyssinica, *growing in Tanganyika, described by Speke as 'a handsome scarlet flowering shrub with moulded stem and slightly bent down thorns.'*

no geographer can admit, and which is at the same time so weak and flimsy that no geographer has yet taken the trouble to contradict it.'

Speke's version of the matter is as follows:

'Captain Burton greeted me on arrival at the old house . . . I . . . expressed my regret that he did not accompany me as I felt quite certain in my mind I had discovered the source of the Nile. This he naturally objected to, even after hearing all my reasons for saying so, and therefore the subject was dropped. Nevertheless the Captain accepted all my geography leading from Kazeh to the lake, and wrote it down in his book – contracting only my distances, which he said he thought were exaggerated, and of course taking care to sever my lake from the Nile by *his* Mountains of the Moon.'

They had already fallen out over the Mountains of the Moon. Burton wanted to have them in one place on the map, Speke in another, and it was a vital point since these mountains, wherever they were, most probably provided the first drainage for the river. So now, like an old hand at chess, Burton neatly checkmated his opponent by dropping the mountains on to a point of the map where they stood fairly and squarely between the river and the lake.

Burton himself at this time had an idea that the real sources of the Nile lay further to the east in the general vicinity of Mt Kenya and Mt Kilimanjaro. At the same time he was not altogether satisfied that the Tanganyika basin should be disqualified. The most he would allow for Speke's new lake (which was now named Victoria in honour of the Queen) was that it might be a feeder to the Upper Nile; there was also the possibility that Lake Victoria was not one lake at all, but a series of lakes.

But Burton was not adamant about any of this. He simply wished to make it clear that Speke had no grounds whatever for his sweeping assertions; it was all guesswork. Therefore in Burton's opinion it was much better in their report to the Royal Geographical Society to stick to the ground they had thoroughly investigated together, namely the Tanganyika region, and to the reports they had heard from the more reliable Arabs; and in fact while Speke had been away Burton had obtained from the dealers in Kazeh some sound information about the district of Karagwe to the west of Lake Victoria, and even about Buganda and Bunyoro which lay off the map much further to the north.

And so from this time forward we find Burton concentrating more and more upon Lake Tanganyika and Speke upon Lake Victoria; each adopted his own lake and was determined to support it against all arguments. Their quarrel may seem futile, but one has to remember that the two men had now been closeted together in the most hazardous circumstances for well over a year, and had long since begun to get on one another's nerves. Also, this issue was almost their whole world at that moment, and it seemed to them to be of the most pressing importance.

'He [Burton]', Speke wrote later to the Secretary of the Royal Geographical Society, 'used to snub me so unpleasantly when talking about anything that I often kept my own counsel. B. is one of those men who never *can* be wrong, and will never acknowledge an error so that when only two are together talking becomes more of a bore than a pleasure.'

It cannot then have been a very congenial party that set off at the end of September 1858 on the long return journey to the coast. There were 152 in the caravan now, including slaves, women and children, and many of them, having already marched 1,500 miles or more since leaving Bagamoyo, were worn out. Burton and Speke collapsed almost at once and had to be carried. Speke appears to have been suffering from pleurisy and pneumonia, and soon it was impossible for him to continue. At the height of his delirium he raved and screamed at Burton, remembering every petty, pent-up grievance – even the incident of the skirmish in Somaliland when Burton, he believed, had accused him of cowardice. These spasms passed at length and the expedition dragged itself on slowly eastward, beset by sickness and desertions. Four months elapsed before they sighted the Indian Ocean at last just north of the present town of Dar-es-Salaam. It was now February 1859 and they had been away for 21 months, but Burton had undertaken to visit Kilwa further down the coast, and with a stubbornness which seems a little pointless he was determined to keep his word. He sent a message across to Zanzibar by dhow asking the British Consul to furnish him with a boat and when it arrived the two weary, antagonistic men sat sail for Kilwa. They accomplished nothing beyond their gesture; a cholera epidemic was sweeping along the East African coast and it had struck the slaving settlement at Kilwa with special force. Burton and Speke came away almost at once, and on March 4, 1859, finally reached Zanzibar.

Here everything was in turmoil; some ten thousand deaths through cholera had already occurred in the city, and the Sultan was preparing to resist an invasion which was about to be launched upon the island by his brother in Oman. The new British Consul, Captain Christopher Rigby, was an old rival of Burton's – both of them being remarkable linguists, they had competed against one another in interpreters' examinations in India – and Burton lost no time in falling out with him. The main contention between them seems to have concerned itself with Burton's failure to pay his porters all the money they expected, and when, later on, they complained at the Consulate both Rigby and Speke, to Burton's fury, supported them. He had another grievance against Rigby; he believed that he or someone connected with the Consulate had deliberately mislaid the manuscript of his book on Zanzibar since it contained criticisms of the white residents there.

For the moment, however, Burton was at the end of his tether. Those who saw him at this time describe him as wild-eyed and so gaunt and emaciated that the flesh hung in hollows on his cheeks; he himself says that the 'excitement of travel was succeeded by utter depression of mind and body'. He read French novels, avoided meeting people in Zanzibar and developed his hatred of Rigby. After barely three weeks on the island he embarked with Speke on the barque *Dragon of Salem* and they arrived at Aden twenty-five days later.

As yet there was no open breach between the two men: 'Still we were,' Burton says, 'to all appearances friends.' But Speke, the younger man, was recovering fast and was anxious to get home. It was agreed that while Burton continued his convalescence a little longer at Aden Speke should go ahead, and in mid-April he took passage in H.M.S. *Furious*. According to Burton, Speke's last word before he embarked was a promise that he would await his companion's arrival in London before revealing the results of the expedition. Upon that they parted for ever.

When Burton himself reached England on May 21 Speke had already been there for twelve days and had made good use of his time. One can explain his conduct only by remembering, as Professor Ingham of Makerere College, Uganda, suggests, 'the self-righteousness of his generation', which moved him to put 'justice before generosity'. He was filled with his conviction that he had solved the great secret of the Nile. Burton had derided his theory and washed his hands of it; therefore Speke had every right to regard his inspiration and his discovery as a personal matter, something quite apart from the official expedition.

Whether or not Speke himself used this justification is unknown, but the fact remains that, on disembarking, he went directly to Sir Roderick Murchison, the President of the Royal Geographical Society, and revealed to him the story of the expedition and his great conviction about the source of the Nile. Murchison, naturally, was intrigued, and Speke was asked to give an address to members of the Society at Burlington House; and here again he pressed his views. Within a week of his arrival word got around London that this intrepid and modest young man had made a discovery of extraordinary importance, and he was invited by the Society to go out to Africa again at the head of a new expedition. A sum of £2,500 was quickly raised to finance it, and Speke was soon at work on his plans; he proposed to strike inland again from Zanzibar along the same route as before and then work his way up the western side of the new inland sea he had discovered. On its northern coast he hoped to find its outlet which would be the source of the Nile, and then he would follow this stream northwards wherever it might lead him until he emerged at last in Egypt.

There was much enthusiasm in London for the new expedition since, in effect, Speke proposed to march straight through the blank space on the map in Central Africa, and at one stroke settle the immemorial problems of the inland lakes, the Mountains of the Moon and the fountains of the Nile.

Burton meanwhile, a lean and haggard figure, landed in England to find that he had been almost forgotten. The public was only mildly interested in his careful and scientific report on Lake Tanganyika, and he was not invited to take part in the new expedition; he was replaced by another Indian Army officer, Captain James Augustus Grant. Five years were to elapse before he was to have his full and terrible revenge.

3

The Vales of Paradise

───

There are no written records of Uganda – the territory that Speke now proposed to enter – before the middle of the nineteenth century. Sir John Gray describes its history as being like 'a crime to which there have been no eye-witnesses'. It seems certain, however, that at some point in the unrecorded past a superior race of cattle-owning men came south from the Ethiopian highlands, and these people set themselves up as a ruling aristocracy among the negroes on the northern and western borders of Lake Victoria. By 1860 three separate kingdoms were established, Bunyoro in the north, Buganda in the centre and Karagwe to the south, on the western shore of the lake. Many other tribal formations existed as well, but these three little states had a certain coherency in the midst of a wilderness of utter barbarity; they formed, as it were, a tiny capsule of semi-civilization in the centre of the continent, and the outside world knew hardly anything at all about them.

A single Arab trader named Ahmed bin Ibrahim had penetrated into Buganda in the eighteen-forties, and a few others had reached Karagwe, but that was all: no white man had ever been there, no notion of other worlds and other ways of life disturbed the inhabitants. They could scarcely have been more isolated had they been living on the surface of the moon.

Normally in Central Africa it was the fate of such people to remain in a state of arrested development. In a mysterious way the light of human ambition was extinguished, the villages stayed chained to the Stone Age, and from century to century life revolved in an endless ant-like cycle of crude customs and traditions. There was no curiosity to explore, no desire for change or improvement. Every new generation gave way to the same passive fatalistic acceptance of things as they were, and reason was suffocated by habit and superstition.

But with these three puppet kingdoms it was not like this at all; they advanced marvellously. Without any precedent to guide them or any outside help they had achieved by the middle of the nineteenth century a native culture which was well in advance of any other south of the Sahara. And yet the extraordinary thing about these people is not that they should have got so far but that their progress should have been so irregular. They did well in one direction only to fail completely in another, they left enormous gaps behind them, and the most barbarous customs survived in the midst of an exceptional sophistication.

Their houses, for example, had nothing in common with the dull coffin-shaped contraptions of Tanganyika; they were large, beautifully made conical structures of tightly woven canes and reeds that often soared fifty feet into the air. These dwellings were dry and comfortable in the rain and cool in the hot seasons, and they were infinitely more attractive than any building that has been erected in Uganda in the twentieth century. The musical instruments of the tribesmen – their drums, harps and trumpets – were equally remarkable, and they travelled on the lake in immense canoes, some of them 70 feet in length.

'The king [Mutesa] sent his royal musicians to give us a tune. The men composing the band played on reed instruments made telescope fashion, marking time by hand drums.' (Speke) From a sketch by Grant.

Their basketware was so finely woven it would hold water, and they had discovered the art of making a soft and durable cloth from the bark of trees. No man attended the court of his king unclothed: in fact, in Buganda it was a criminal offence to do so; he wore sandals on his feet, his body was completely covered by a long and graceful toga, and sometimes this was surmounted by a cape of antelope skins which had been pieced together with the skill of a Parisian seamstress.

Neither men nor women disfigured their bodies with scars or tattoos like the other Central African tribes, and when they sat down to eat they washed their hands, either by squeezing a wet napkin or by pouring water over them from a jug. Domestic slaves, who were treated as part of the household like Russian serfs, served the meal, and the food was distinctly civilized: a kind of gruel made from coarse bananas, fish and meat stews, chickens, sweet potatoes, maize and wild sugarcane. Coffee beans were chewed as a digestive and they brewed their beer from bananas. Both men and women smoked.

ABOVE 'I had constantly wondered, ever since I first came here and saw the brutal manner in which the Turks treated the natives that these Madi people could submit to their "Egyptian taskmasters" and therefore was not surprised now to find them pull down their huts and march off with materials to a distant site.' (Speke) From a sketch by Grant.

BELOW A collection of small villages in Northern Uganda: game was abundant here but the area is now heavily over-grazed.

In Buganda especially, the richest and most progressive of the three states, the power of the king was absolute, but he was advised by a group of counsellors who formed a kind of cabinet in which each man had some special duty. Thus there was the vizier or prime minister, the treasurer, the commander-in-chief of the army and the admiral of the fleet of war-canoes on the lake, the chief executioner, and others with more picturesque titles such as the chief brewer and the keeper of the drums. These men, together with the provincial chiefs, formed a hierarchy of nobles, and they were obliged to be in constant attendance on the king in his court. Here the etiquette was elaborate. No man could sit down in the king's presence, be incorrectly dressed, or speak without permission. Whenever the king appeared it was customary for the courtiers to abase themselves on the ground before him, since he was considered to be almost divine, or at all events the personification of the spirit of the race.

And yet, with all this sophistication and refinement, these people had no method of writing or counting, no means of measuring the passage of time by weeks or months or years, no mechanical contrivances even as simple as the plough or the wheel, no religion that amounted to more than the most primitive kind of superstition and witchcraft. They gave way to their passions and their appetites like spoiled and delinquent children and they were unbelievably cruel. From time to time they seem to have been seized with a wild and frantic hysteria, and it was common practice for both men and women to drink themselves into a drunken stupor.

There were strong differences between the three kingdoms, and perhaps these differences were conditioned by the geographical nature of the country. Bunyoro, to the north, is drier and harsher than the land around the shores of Lake Victoria. For months at a time no rain falls and one travels for miles through a dry hard scrub which is not unlike Central Tanganyika. The people here have a reputation for toughness and resilience; they are less sophisticated than the lakeside inhabitants, but more warlike and aggressive. These qualities were certainly reflected in their King, Kamrasi. He was a man who was both harsh and suspicious, a chieftain with the instincts of a pirate, and the absorbing hatred of his life was directed partly against Buganda in the south, and partly against a rebellious brother called Rionga, who lived on an island in the Nile.

Karagwe, on the western side of the lake, is more open country, much of it five thousand feet above sea-level, and there is a remarkable freshness and clarity in the landscape. A century ago large herds of cattle grazed across the sweeping grassy plains, and along the shores of the lake itself there are scenes that remind one of the downs in southern England: high, sharp cliffs fall sheer into the water, and except for the heat, the emptiness of land and the tropical islands off-shore this might be Folkestone or Dover. At one time this was fine country for wild animals: thousands of elephants, giraffes, buffaloes, antelopes and rhinoceroses roamed about, and even now, by night, one can watch the hippopotamuses come ashore from the lake to browse like dark lumbering ghosts on the water's edge.

Here, at a place called Bweranyange, Rumanika, the King of Karagwe, kept his little provincial court. He was a large and friendly man who had the reputation of

Among the more spectacular creatures still to be found is the crested crane, Balearica pavonina. *'The black velvet head of this crane, surrounded by a golden crest, was a favourite ornament of the Lakookas, and they were immediately arranged as crests for their helmets.' (Baker)*

being hospitable to strangers. Being by some way the weakest of the three kings, Rumanika took care to remain on good terms with the rulers of Bunyoro and Buganda. He sent them gifts from time to time and even acknowledged himself to be a vassal or at any rate a dependant of Buganda. Yet Rumanika had his eccentricities. He kept an extraordinary harem of wives who were so fat they could not stand upright, and instead grovelled like seals about the floors of their huts. Their diet was an uninterrupted flow of milk that was sucked from a gourd through a straw, and if the young girls resisted this treatment they were force-fed like the *pâté de foie gras* ducks of Strasbourg: a man stood over them with a whip.

Buganda, on the northern shore of the lake, has neither the dryness of Bunyoro nor the horizons of Karagwe; it is a region of jungles and broken hills and it is as lush and exuberant as Zanzibar. The climate is hot, changeable and damp, and all things spring from the earth in a blaze of exotic colour. The earth itself is red, the plantations of bananas make avenues that are filled with a warm greenish-yellowish light and the surrounding jungle is a vast aviary filled with tropical birds and flowering shrubs. These conditions create an impression of intimacy, of quickness and liveliness and of a kind of luxurious excitement, and that is the nature of the Baganda.

In 1860 Mutesa, the young king of Buganda, had only recently got his grip upon the throne and had established his capital a few miles inland from the lake on a hilltop which is not far from the modern city of Kampala. The traveller came into the town on a broad earthen road cut through the jungle and saw, scattered about the hillsides, a settlement of gracefully proportioned round huts with crowds of people moving about between them. The women for the most part went naked or wore a short cloth around their waists, but the men in their togas reminded one, Harry Johnston says, of saints – they 'recalled irresistibly the conventional pictures of evangelical piety which represented the Blessed walking in the vales of Paradise'.

Mutesa's court was a compound of especially spacious huts in the centre of the town, and here he held his daily levées, sitting upon a platform of grass covered with a red blanket, and surrounded by his nobles, his pages and his wives, who numbered a couple of hundred or so. At this time he was a slim, well-built young man in his early twenties with beautiful teeth and liquid, but rather striking eyes. His tonsured hair was built up like a cockscomb on his head, his toga was neatly knotted over one shoulder, and on his arms and legs he wore broad bands of coloured beads. At his feet were his symbols of royalty, a spear, a shield and a white dog. When he went walking the whole court followed, and he affected an extraordinary stiff-legged strut which was meant to imitate the gait of a lion. In the manner of Queen Victoria he did not look round when he chose to sit down; a chair was automatically placed in readiness for him, except that in his case it was a page crouching on his hands and knees. When he chose to speak the courtiers listened in a strained and respectful silence and then, in a body, threw themselves on the ground, uttering over and over again a curious cry that sounded like 'n'yanzig', and was meant to indicate both gratitude and the deepest humility. Mutesa, in short, was a very impressive figure, even at this early stage of his long career, and there might even have been a certain dignity about

ABOVE *'The gruff hippopotamus is as widespread as any, being found wherever there is a water to float him.' (Speke)* BELOW *Baker records an incident: 'The black soldiers, armed with swords and bill hooks, immediately attacked the crocodile, who . . . had not exactly fallen into the hands of the Royal Humane Society. He was quickly despatched, and that evening his flesh gladdened the cooking pots of the Soudani regiment.'*

him had it not been for the fact that he was very far from being a saint in the vales of Paradise; he was a savage and bloodthirsty monster.

Hardly a day went by without some victim being executed at his command, and this was done wilfully, casually, almost as a kind of game. A girl would commit some breach of etiquette by talking too loudly, a page would neglect to close or open a door, and at once, at a sign from Mutesa, they would be taken away, screaming, to have their heads lopped off. A roll of drums obliterated the cries of the death-throes. Nothing that W. S. Gilbert was about to invent with his Lord High Executioner in *The Mikado*, nothing in the behaviour of the raving Red Queen in *Alice's Adventures in Wonderland*, was more fantastic than the scenes that occurred whenever Mutesa held a court, the only difference being that here these scenes were hideously and monstrously real. Torture by burning alive, the mutilation of victims by cutting off their hands, ears and feet, the burial of living wives with their dead husbands – all these things were taken as a matter of course. This was more than a simple blood-lust: Mutesa crushed out life in the same way as a child will step on an insect, never for an instant thinking of the consequences, or experiencing a moment's pity for the pain he was inflicting. He felt no pain, except his own. He, and all the people about him at his court, give the impression of playing at life, of living with an air of mad make-believe.

'Incredible as it may . . . be I have seen one, two or three palace women, tied by the hand, and dragged along by one of the body-guard crying out as she went to premature death.' (Speke) From a sketch by Grant.

OPPOSITE *Mutesa. 'The king's gait in retiring was intended to be very majestic, but did not succeed in conveying to me that impression . . . founded on the step of the lion; . . . the outward sweep of the legs . . . appeared to me only to realise a very ludicrous kind of waddle.' (Speke) From a sketch by Grant.*

To be fair, it has to be recorded that it was not Mutesa himself who had invented these practices; all his ancestors (and there is known to have been a line of at least a score of kings behind him) behaved in exactly the same way, and a similar law of the jungle prevailed in all the minor tribal groups. Unless the ruler surrounded himself with an atmosphere of dread and superstitious awe he did not stay very long on his throne. Mutesa, on becoming king, had instantly put to death some sixty of his brothers by burning them alive, and this was apparently regarded as a perfectly normal precaution against rebellion. He had other attributes besides this inherited bloodthirstiness. He was very far from being stupid: in this savage world he had the appearance and the manner of royalty, and an instinctive knowledge of politics.

This, then, was the strange little island of native civilization that had been left undisturbed to work out its own destiny in the heart of Central Africa a hundred years ago. It would naturally be absurd to suggest that there was any real enlightenment here; the three puppet kingdoms were still bound to a primeval way of life, and fear was the dominant factor in every man's mind. On the other hand, these people were still insulated from the abuses of civilization: there was no syphilis or smallpox, no rinderpest to kill their cattle. Mutesa's cruelties did not touch the general run of the people; they had plenty to eat and drink, and it seems not impossible that they believed themselves to be happy. Only the barest echoes of other things reached them from the outside world – of the slavers coming up the Nile from Egypt and the Arab caravans from Zanzibar. Perhaps it really was a Garden of Eden of a kind, savage but fatalistic; at all events, it was still intact when Speke and his new companion, Grant, marched into Karagwe at the end of 1861, and with this the capsule was destined to burst at last.

The two explorers had taken over a year to get inland from Zanzibar, and most of the experiences of the previous expedition had been faithfully repeated; all their men save a few like Bombay and Mabruki had deserted, the local chieftains on the way had ferociously demanded their *hongo*, their goats and cattle had been stolen, and Grant had gone down with malaria. They had even failed as yet to catch a glimpse of Lake Victoria. Burton, who was now leading a separate expedition in the Cameroons on the other side of Africa, must have smiled had he heard the news. But now at last in November 1861 Speke and Grant extricated themselves from the local tribal wars to the north of Tabora and marched on into the terra incognita of Karagwe.

In Grant Speke had found an ideal companion. The two men were of the same age and had been friends in India, where they had often gone on shooting excursions together. But Grant had another quality: he was the perfect lieutenant. He must surely be rated as the most modest and self-effacing man who ever entered the turmoil of African exploration; he never puts himself forward, he never complains, never questions any order of his leader. Burton would have found him a paragon. Grant's devotion, however, was entirely fixed upon Speke, and it was almost doglike in its completeness. 'Not a shade of jealousy or distrust or even ill-temper,' he says, 'ever came between us.' Speke he describes as 'above every littleness'. General Gordon, whose judgments about people were often rash, thought that Grant himself was something of a bore, and possibly he was a little dull as a conversationalist. Yet it would be foolish to regard Grant as a colourless nonentity. He was a cool and very steady man, a soldier and a sportsman well out of the ordinary, and in his own private and modest way he was a competent artist and a genuine amateur of botany. He had fought in a number of engagements that led up to the Mutiny in India, and had taken part in the relief of Lucknow.

James Augustus Grant 'in Dress worn in Africa.'

Rumanika was delighted to meet the two white men, the first he had ever seen. He shook hands warmly, addressed them in good Swahili, and established them in his best huts with an abundant supply of provisions. Speke had a pleasant month at Bweranyange. He exchanged presents with Rumanika, drank his *pombe*, and with a tape measure ascertained the dimensions of his fat wives. He did great execution among the rhinoceroses with his gun, and made notes about even more formidable animals which, he was told, inhabited the jungles further to the west: 'monsters who could not converse with men and never showed themselves unless they saw women pass by; then, in voluptuous excitement, they squeezed them to death.' If this was meant to be a description of a gorilla, one of the most timid and gentle of animals, it is not accurate. But then hardly any of the things they were seeing and hearing in this new land were very credible. Rumanika, for example, warned Speke that he must not proceed into Buganda until Mutesa sent for him, and that it would be impossible for him to appear at Mutesa's court wearing his unmentionables (Speke in his account uses this Victorian word for trousers); he would have to obtain a gown. And so messengers were sent off to warn Mutesa of the expedition's approach and while they waited the month of December slipped by.

Grant meanwhile was having a very bad time. He was assailed by a dreadful sore

Map based on contemporary information showing the route taken by Speke and Grant, 1860–63.

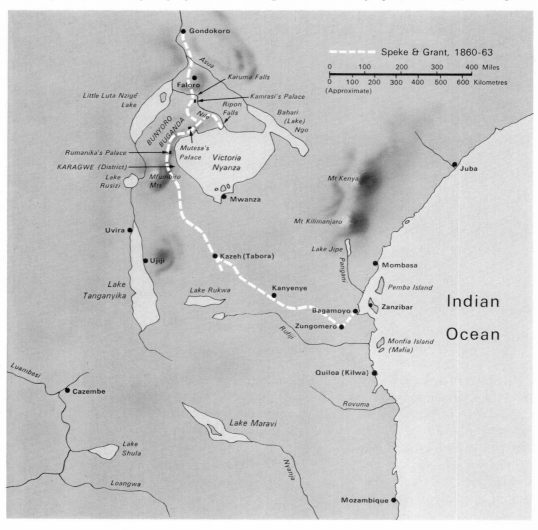

'The next day, when I called on Rumanika, the spoils were brought into court, and in utter astonishment he said: "Well, this must have been done with something more potent than powder, for neither the Arabs nor the Nnanaji could have accomplished such a great feat as this. It is no wonder the English are the greatest men in the world".' (Speke)

in his leg, and presently the infection became so agonizingly painful he was unable to stir from his hut. Certainly he was in no condition to walk or even to be carried when, on January 8, 1862, a troop of messengers arrived from Mutesa bearing with them an invitation for the expedition to proceed. It was therefore decided that he should remain behind in Rumanika's care while Speke went forward alone. For the next three months Grant remained a prisoner in his hut, unable to go out, often in agony and without news of any kind.

It took Speke six weeks to walk to Mutesa's court, and in the course of the journey he at last came within sight of Lake Victoria opposite the Sesse Islands. More than ever now he felt that his original conjecture had been correct: the lake was a vast inland sea and somewhere on its northern shore he would find its outlet to the north – the fountains of the Nile. For the moment, however, he was forced to put his geographical work aside and prepare himself for his reception by Mutesa.

He tells us that on his arrival he unpacked his best suit, dressed his men in red blankets, and with a handsome collection of gifts got ready to present himself at the palace. But rain fell and in the best manner of royal garden parties the reception was put off until the following day. On February 20, 1862, he set forth again flanked by his red-blanketed bodyguard, with the Union Jack leading the way, only to find himself out-faced by a rival delegation which was given precedence; Speke was told to wait in the hot sun outside the palace. He stood it for five minutes and then in a fury turned round and walked back to his own hut a mile away. The courtiers who were conducting him to the King watched his retirement with consternation –

evidently such a thing had never happened before – and presently they came running to say that it was all a mistake; the King would see him at once and he would be allowed to bring his own chair to sit on, an unheard-of privilege.

When Speke got back to the palace all was ready for his reception. A band playing five-stringed harps and trumpets ushered him through the outer courts where small pages were rushing around gathering their cloaks about them so as not to show their legs; and finally he came into the presence of the monarch himself. Speke set up his chair in front of the throne, erected his umbrella and awaited events. Nothing happened. For an hour the two men sat gazing at one another, Mutesa occasionally

'We came in sight of the king's palace. It was a magnificent sight. A whole hill was covered with gigantic huts, such as I had never seen in Africa before.' (Speke) From a sketch by Grant.

turning to his courtiers to pass a remark on the umbrella, on the bodyguard or on Speke himself. From time to time a draught of beer was handed to him. Speke simply sat and waited.

At length a man approached with a message: had he seen the King?

'Yes,' Speke answered, 'for full one hour.'

When this was translated to Mutesa he rose and walked away into the interior of his palace on the tips of his toes in his imitation of a lion. There now ensued a long wait while the King ate his dinner: as an act of courtesy, it was explained to Speke, Mutesa had refrained from eating until the meeting had taken place. Finally, at the end of the day, when they met again by the light of torches, Speke offered his presents; several rifles and guns together with ammunition, a gold watch, a telescope, an iron chair, beads, silk cloths and knives, spoons and forks. Mutesa in return sent him a gift of cattle, goats, fish, fowls, porcupines and rats, all of which apparently were regarded as suitable items of diet.

It was at a further interview that the notorious shooting incident took place. Speke was invited to display the magic of his pistols by taking a pot-shot at four cows, a feat he accomplished a little awkwardly: one of the cows, charging upon him, required a second bullet before it was dispatched.

'. . . we proceeded to Court but found it scantily attended, and after a first sitting retired to another court and saw the women . . . the King entered into conversation at first about the ever-engrossing subject of stimulants, till we changed it by asking him how he liked the gun.' (Speke) Zwecker, from a sketch by Grant.

'The king,' Speke says, 'now loaded one of the carbines I had given him with his own hands, and giving it full-cock to a page, told him to go out and shoot a man in the outer court: which was no sooner accomplished than the little urchin returned to announce his success, with a look of glee such as one would see in the face of a boy who had robbed a bird's-nest, caught a trout, or done any other boyish trick. The king said to him, "And did you do it well?" "Oh yes, capitally." He spoke the truth, no doubt, for he dared not have trifled with the king: but the affair created hardly any interest. I never heard, and there appeared no curiosity to know, what individual human being the urchin had deprived of life.'

Nothing would keep Mutesa away from his new toys after this. On fine days he would march round his capital, gun in hand, his wives, pages and courtiers following behind and the band playing; and if by luck he managed to hit a vulture on a tree he would be thunderstruck by his own magical powers, and would run forward to the fallen victim crying out 'woh, woh, woh' in infantile excitement. The court, grovelling and n'yanzigging, would fall upon the ground around him.

The women who followed Mutesa about in hordes wherever he went appeared to occupy a privileged position, but it was slavery nonetheless. 'Young virgins . . .' Speke wrote, 'stark naked, and smeared with grease, but holding for decency's sake a small square of *mbugu* (bark cloth) at the upper corners in both hands before them, are presented by their fathers in propitiation for some offence and to fill the harem.' From time to time one of these girls would be sent to Speke as a gift, and he parcelled them out as wives among his followers.

The Queen-Mother, however, whom Speke describes as 'fair, fat and forty-five', was a figure of some power in the state and kept her separate court at a little distance from Mutesa's palace. She was not often sober. Drinking, smoking and dancing to the music of her personal band were the usual occupations of the Queen-Mother's hut, and it was not surprising that she complained to Speke that she was suffering from bad dreams and illness of the stomach. He dosed her from his medicine chest and advised her to give up drinking. But she was not a good patient. Returning to her hut one day Speke found himself involved in an orgy which ended in the Queen-Mother and her attendants drinking like swine on all fours from a trough of beer.

After Speke had been for three months in these bizarre surroundings Grant finally arrived. He was still limping from the effects of the sore in his leg but otherwise restored to health, and now both men were eager to push on towards their goal. On their separate journeys from Karagwe they had crossed a considerable river, the Kagera, but since it flowed into Lake Victoria and not out of it they dismissed it as a possible source of the Nile. At Mutesa's court, however, they heard very definite reports of another stream that emerged from the lake only a short distance to the east. The lake was said to pour itself out in a wide fall of water towards the north. Speke, who had never been permitted to leave Mutesa's capital in all his three months' stay, was now determined to make his way to this spot and then follow the river downstream wherever it might lead.

Mutesa was much opposed to their going. It amused him to have the two white men at his court and he was not altogether sure that he had extracted every possible gift from them. For another six weeks he prevaricated and delayed, and then at last on July 7, 1862, he let them go. The two explorers with Bombay and their caravan and a Buganda bodyguard marched out to the east. They were on the eve of the climax of their tremendous journey.

And now occurred one of the strangest incidents of the whole adventure. Their guide had led them somewhat north of the lake, and in order to reach the Nile and trace it to its source it was necessary for the caravan to turn sharply south. A conference was held, and as a result it was decided that the expedition should split once more: Speke alone was to go to the source while Grant turned north and opened up the way to Kamrasi's court in Bunyoro. One can only take the two men's word for it that they were entirely agreed upon this arrangement. From Grant we have no hint of reproach or disappointment. He had staked his life on getting to this goal, and now at the last minute, when it was within his reach, he quietly turned away from it in order to please his companion. Grant merely says that he was invited by Speke to make a flying march to the source and was forced to decline since his bad leg made it quite impossible to manage 20 miles a day. Just why it was necessary for Speke to

Captain Grant leaving Karagwe. Many years later, in 1877, Gordon wrote to Burton, '. . . that old creature Grant, who for seventeen or eighteen years has traded on his wonderful walk.'

dash off at the rate of 20 miles a day is not explained; but then there is so much between these two that cannot be understood unless one constantly remembers Grant's utter devotion to his leader. As with a marriage, a veil falls down between this partnership and the outside world, and no one can presume to know the intricacies of their relationship. Speke, of course, was a man with an *idée fixe*; his whole being was centred upon proving that his theory of the Nile was the right one, and no doubt he was now in a state of intense impatience to get to his objective. To have hung about waiting for Grant to keep up with him – and this at a time when some accident or mischance could still wreck the expedition – was intolerable. Grant presumably felt this strongly, and with an almost feminine resignation gave way; better to stand in the reflection of Speke's glory then to strain their friendship too much.

At all events, Speke went off with his flying column and reached the Nile on July 21, 1862, at a place called Urondogani about forty miles downstream from the lake: 'Here at last I stood on the brink of the Nile; most beautiful was the scene, nothing could surpass it!' The crocodiles, the high grassy banks, the hippopotamuses, the herds of hartebeest – it was everything they had imagined, and Speke in his exaltation told his men that 'they ought to shave their heads and bathe in the holy river, the cradle of Moses . . .' Bombay soberly replied that, being Mohammedans, 'we don't look on these things in the same fanciful manner as you do: we are contented with the commonplaces of life. . . .'

They were keen enough, however, when they marched upstream and came within sight of their goal at last on July 28; all forgot their fatigue and rushed forward along the river bank. A hill blocked their view of the lake but there, at their feet, the great stream poured itself like a breaking tidal wave over a waterfall. 'It was a sight that attracted one for hours,' Speke says, '– the roar of the waters, the thousands of passenger-fish leaping at the falls with all their might; the Wasoga and Waganda fishermen coming out in boats and taking post on all the rocks with rod and hook, hippopotami and crocodiles lying sleepily on the water. . . .'

He named the place the Ripon Falls 'after the nobleman who presided over the Royal Geographical Society when my expedition was got up'.

It now remained for the explorers to keep themselves alive until they could get back to civilization to tell the story, and there was still no guarantee whatever that they would succeed. A month went by before Speke and Grant rejoined their forces (now reduced to some seventy men and four women), and together they marched into Bunyoro, where King Kamrasi received them somewhat sourly; he filched Speke's fifty-guinea gold chronometer from him before he would allow the expedition to proceed.

While they were in Bunyoro the explorers heard reports of another large lake a short distance to the west, the Lŭta Nzigé, and it seemed possible that this might be a second source of the Nile. But it was now November 1862, and they were worn out and bereft of nearly all their possessions; to have made a further detour might have settled their last chance of survival. And so they pushed on slowly to the north. They had at least one bright hope to lead them on; before leaving London Speke had arranged with the Royal Geographical Society for an expedition to be sent south from Gondokoro in the Sudan to meet them with fresh supplies and porters. It was, of necessity, a loose sort of arrangement, since it was impossible to fix a definite point of rendezvous in that unmapped country, and Speke and Grant were already a year late in keeping the appointment. But John Petherick, the British Vice-Consul at Khartoum and the leader of the relief column, was an experienced and reliable man, and the Society had provided him with a sum of a thousand pounds with which to buy boats and supplies. These were to be sent up the river from Khartoum and stationed at Gondokoro or some other suitable place to await Speke's and Grant's arrival. It was with the prospect of meeting Petherick that the two explorers now pushed on towards the north.

The journey was increasingly wearisome. On November 19, 1862, they reached the Karuma Falls in Central Uganda, and at the end of the month they were still toiling slowly onwards through depressing scrub. As they advanced northward they found that the tribes grew increasingly more primitive; they were back in a region of naked, painted men who carried bows and arrows and who knew nothing of the arts and crafts of Buganda.

Sunset on December 3 was the moment that hope revived again. Welcoming rifle shots were heard in the distance, and presently there advanced to meet them a column of Egyptian and Nubian soldiers dressed in Turkish uniforms. A drum and fife band was playing and red flags waved overhead; it was almost the first sign of civilization Speke and Grant had seen since they had left Bagamoyo on the Zanzibar coast over two years before.

This garrison, named Faloro, was the southernmost trading post of the Egyptians on the Upper Nile, and its black commander, Mohammed Wad-el-Mek, came forward to embrace the travellers. He declared that he was the agent of Petherick and of a Maltese trader named de Bono, and that he had orders to convey them to the Egyptian stronghold at Gondokoro. Soon they were sitting down to a meal of bread, honey and mutton eaten off plates of crockery. That night they slept on genuine bedsteads; but they found soap to be the greatest luxury of all.

They were, however, not quite out of the wood as yet. Mohammed Wad-el-Mek, though friendly, was also a dyed-in-the-wool slave-driver, and was by no means ready to move north until he had plundered the district of the last available slave and tusk of ivory. It was not until January 10, 1863, that the cavalcade set out, the leaders riding cows and donkeys, the porters carrying tusks, and a disorderly mob of slaves, women, children, goats and cattle following on behind. By the time they entered the Bari country the party was a thousand strong, and the helpless tribesmen could do little more than make hostile demonstrations against them.

On February 13, 1863, nearly two years and five months after the outset of their journey, Speke and Grant marched into Gondokoro. There was no sign of Petherick, but they saw the red brick house and sheds of the Austrian Mission and a number of boats on the river; and presently a wholly unexpected figure came out to meet them. 'We saw hurrying towards us,' Speke says, 'the form of an Englishman . . . my old friend Baker, famed for his sports in Ceylon, seized me by the hand. [They had first met aboard ship when Speke was travelling from India to Aden in 1854.] A little boy of his establishment had reported our arrival, and he in an instant came out to welcome us. What joy this was I can hardly tell. We could not talk fast enough, so overwhelmed were we both to meet again.'

The sportsman Samuel Baker and his wife had come up the Nile to look for them, and there had been others as well who had arrived at Gondokoro on the same mission, three Dutch ladies, the Baroness van Capellan and Mrs and Miss Tinne, but they had been forced to return to Khartoum through sickness. Soon, too, three Austrian priests arrived. The two explorers could relax at last.

'Speke', Baker says, 'appeared the more worn of the two: he was excessively lean, but in reality he was in good tough condition; he had walked the whole way from Zanzibar, never having once ridden during that wearying march. Grant was in honourable rags; his bare knees projecting through the remnants of trousers that were an exhibition of rough industry in tailor's work. He was looking tired and

OVERLEAF *The Ripon Falls: '. . . the most interesting sight that I had seen in Africa . . . the roar of the waters, the thousands of passenger-fish, leaping . . . with all their might.' (Speke) From a drawing by Speke.*

feverish, but both men had a fire in the eye, that showed the spirit that had led them through.'

There was much news to give – the death of the Prince Consort in England, the outbreak of the Civil War in America – but for the moment Speke's and Grant's immediate interest was Petherick. Where was he? Why had he not come to meet them? Baker assured them that he was not far away, travelling in the West Nile district, and in fact Petherick and his wife arrived a few days later. Outwardly the little white community appeared to be an extremely friendly group and they dined together. But Speke was furious with Petherick. It was the kind of pettiness which can sometimes overtake a man who has been under a great strain, and nothing would convince him that Petherick, having taken £1,000 from the Royal Geographical Society, had not forgotten all about the expedition and instead had gone off trading for ivory in another direction. In point of fact, Petherick and his wife had spent a dreadful year struggling overland to Gondokoro and had very nearly died. But Speke would not be appeased. When Mrs Petherick came and begged him to accept the trade goods and the boat they had brought to Gondokoro for his use Speke replied acidly that he 'did not wish to recognize the succour dodge'; his good friend Baker had supplied him with all his needs and he preferred to go down to Khartoum in Baker's boat. When Speke and Grant sailed north from Gondokoro at the end of February it was plain that they intended to speak their minds about Petherick when they got back to England; and indeed, they attacked him harshly in their reports to the Royal Geographical Society and in the books they wrote. Petherick was removed from his post as British Vice-Consul at Khartoum and was all but financially ruined when he was accused of being involved in the slave-trade. Some years elapsed before he could get a hearing for his side of the case, and his reputation is not perhaps re-established even yet.

With his own men Speke was much more generous. Of the original members of the expedition, one had died and 143 porters had deserted, hardly a bad casualty list in the circumstances. At Cairo, where Speke and Grant stayed at Shepheard's Hotel, a camp was made in a public park for the remaining 22 survivors – 18 men and 4 women – and they were fêted at a round of public concerts and *tableaux vivants*. Three years' pay was given to each man, and a passage was arranged for them all to Zanzibar, where a further bonus was awaiting them.

On his way down the Nile Speke had triumphantly cabled to London: 'Inform Sir Roderick Murchison that all is well, that we are in latitude 14° 30′ upon the Nile, and that the Nile is settled'; and he had been awarded the Royal Geographical Society's Founders' Medal. Both men could look forward to a warm reception when they reached London.

But the Nile was not settled. Speke had left too many rivals and enemies in the field for anything to be settled just yet.

Watercolours by Speke: Wasegava Hills and Kisanga – a view of the blue mountain. 'I took the opportunity to ask for my paint-box which he [Mutesa] had borrowed for a day and kept in his possession for months ... [he] at last sent the paint-box with some birds of his own shooting which he wished painted.' (Speke)

Wasegara Hills alias Kobeho Chain Laying N 10° E

The Kiwa 1st Dec 1856 (J.H.S.)

Kisanga View of the Blue Mountain S 26° E

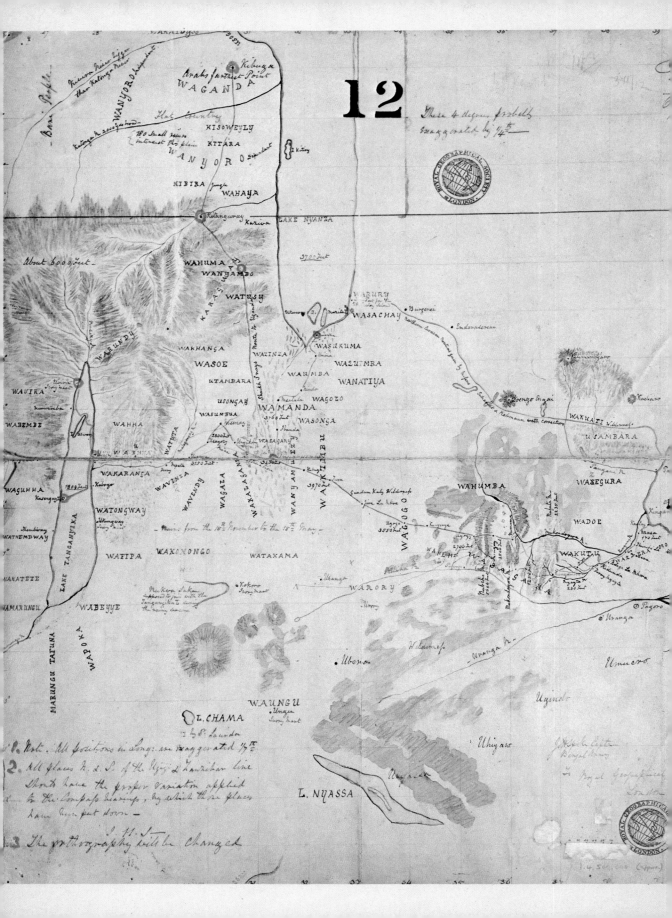

4

The Coy Fountains

In the Victorian age explorers' books exerted an extraordinary power over people's minds: they supplied the drama and the entertainment that now very largely belongs to the documentary cinema and television, and although such magazines as *Blackwood's* were widely circulated, there was as yet no illustrated press of any consequence to compete with them; they had the quality of science fiction. Few publications have captured people's imagination or influenced political policy like Livingstone's three works on South and Central Africa, or Stanley's accounts of his Congo travels, or Gordon's Journals which, for a time, focused the attention of all England upon Khartoum and the Sudan.

These books tended to be intensely personal and were propaganda of a kind. The author pleaded his special cause, often with a note of religious and passionate conviction; he reached out, as it were, to his reader, stirring up his sympathy and indignation. And since these appeals were interlarded with themes of bravery and high adventure the response was enormous. If he was attacked by jealous rivals people sprang to his defence; and in the speculative and highly charged arena of African exploration there was a great deal of jealousy. Anyone with practical knowledge of archaeological expeditions at the present time will recognize the atmosphere at once. It was as patriotic and as partisan as war.

In the 'sixties the great outpouring of these African publications began. Burton's *Lake Regions of Central Africa* appeared in 1860, and in 1863 Speke's *Journal of the Discovery of the Source of the Nile* was shortly followed by his *What Led to the Discovery of the Source of the Nile*. In 1864 Grant published *A Walk Across Africa* (a title suggested to him by Palmerston's remark, 'You have had a long walk, Captain Grant'), and Burton collaborated with the geographer James M'Queen in *The Nile Basin*. Then followed the Pethericks' *Travels in Central Africa*, Baker's *Albert N'yanza* and Burton's *Zanzibar*.

Burton, who was first in the field with his *Lake Regions* (his account of his journey with Speke to Lake Tanganyika), said in later years that he rather regretted some of the things he wrote, but he had been exasperated by two articles which Speke had contributed to *Blackwood's Magazine* on his return to England in 1859. In these articles Speke first put forward his idea that Lake Victoria was the source of the Nile, and this seemed to Burton to make nonsense of the whole expedition. So now, at the opening of his *Lake Regions*, Burton set about putting things to rights in his own drastic fashion:

The map drawn by Speke for the Royal Geographical Society in 1858.

'I have spoken out my feelings concerning Captain Speke, my companion in the expedition which forms the subject of these pages. The history of our companionship is simply this: – As he suffered with me in purse and person at Berberah, in 1855, I thought it but just to offer him the opportunity of renewing an attempt to penetrate into Africa. During the exploration he acted in a subordinate capacity; and as may be imagined amongst a party of Arabs, Baloch [Baluchis] and Africans, whose languages he ignored, he was unfit for any other but a subordinate capacity. Can I then feel otherwise than indignant when I find that, after preceding me from Aden to England, with a spontaneous offer on his part of not appearing before the Society that originated the Expedition until my return, he had lost no time in taking measures to secure for himself the right of working the field which I had opened, and that from that day he has placed himself *en évidence* as the *primum mobile* of an Expedition in which he signed himself "Surveyor" . . . ?'

Speke, he makes out, completely misconstrued the real nature of the expedition. They were not looking for the 'coy fountains' of the Nile at all. Their instructions from the Royal Geographical Society merely required them to investigate reports of the 'Ujiji lake' and to inquire generally into the geography and ethnography of the region. Speke's hallucinations about the 'Victoria Nyanza' were his own affair and were not to be confused with the practical achievements of the expedition.

This was the first broadside. When it was delivered in 1860 Burton, of course, was smarting from the acclaim which had been given to Speke by the Society and its relative coolness towards himself. And now here was Speke in 1863, just back from his new expedition with Grant, and more in the limelight than ever. When the two men landed at Southampton in June the town authorities were there to receive them, together with a group of enthusiastic supporters and friends, including Burton's old rival, Consul Rigby of Zanzibar. On June 22, 1863, the Royal Geographical Society gave Speke an ovation at a special meeting; so great indeed was the crowd which had come to hear the explorer lecture that several windows of the building were broken. And what had Speke got to say? 'The Nile is settled.'

To Burton, who had returned to England from West Africa about this time, it was the same old folly, the same reckless guesswork. What, in fact, had Captain Speke done? He had had a glimpse of a large sheet of water when he had visited Mwanza on the Tanganyika expedition in 1858. He had had another glimpse of another large sheet of water, 200 miles to the north, when he had visited King Mutesa with Grant in 1862. And at once he had jumped to the conclusion that the vast area between these two points – an area of some thirty thousand square miles, an area almost as large as England – was one immense lake. Had he circumnavigated this so-called lake? Not at all; he had not even bothered to visit its western shore when he was staying with Rumanika. He was entirely unable to say what rivers flowed into it or out of it.

It was quite true that he had found one outlet when he visited a waterfall (the so-called Ripon Falls), and a northward-flowing stream to the east of Mutesa's palace; but what possible excuse had he for declaring with such authority that this was the Nile? Had he followed the river downstream from the lake to Gondokoro?

Speke and Grant at the Royal Geographical Society's reception for them, Saturday, July 4, 1863.

By no means. He had marched overland most of the way to Gondokoro, and when by chance on the journey he had caught sight of a river – any river – he had airily concluded that it was the same stream that he had seen issuing from the lake. It was much more likely that he had seen not one stream but several, not one lake but the edges of a series of lakes. Rivers, in any case, did not arise in lakes but in highlands. Speke had invested the Nile Basin 'with an amount of fable unknown to the days of Ptolemy'. His *Discovery of the Source of the Nile* and his *What Led to the Discovery of the Source of the Nile* (which was largely a reprint of his *Blackwood's* articles) both contained 'an extreme looseness of geography'.

There was quite enough logic here to convince other geographers besides Burton that Speke had left far too many questions unanswered, and that much more scientific exploration would have to be undertaken before the matter of the Nile was settled. Presently various members began to dispute Speke's conclusions at meetings of the Royal Geographical Society, and this dispute soon spread to the press.

David Livingstone in 1864.

It was now evident that two rival camps were forming: Grant of course was solidly on his leader's side, and so were others like Rigby who were fired by the young man's zeal and determination. But there were others again who had fallen out with Speke or who considered themselves as rivals; and so for personal as well as scientific reasons they came down on Burton's side of the fence. The row with Petherick dragged on. Speke in a speech at Taunton implied that Petherick in addition to failing to keep his word had been engaged in the slave-trade. The two explorers had now made an enemy who was every bit as implacable and bitter as Burton.

But soon a much more formidable opponent appeared, the great Dr Livingstone himself. Livingstone, like Burton, was convinced that the true solution of the origin of the Nile was to be found well south of Lake Victoria and of the Equator. 'Poor Speke,' he wrote, 'has turned his back upon the real sources of the Nile . . . his river at Ripon Falls was not large enough for the Nile.'

Livingstone, as ever, had been firm but polite, but there were other members of the Royal Geographical Society who felt very strongly that the Speke cult had gone too far. They were out for blood. James M'Queen, in a series of reviews of *The Discovery of the Source of the Nile* published in the *Morning Advertiser*, launched an overwhelming attack. Burton was delighted, and subsequently reprinted the reviews in *The Nile Basin*. Never, Burton thought, in all M'Queen's fifty years as an African geographer, had he shown 'greater acumen or higher spirit – to say nothing of his incomparable dryness of style – than in these compositions, put forth at a time when the English world was bowing down before their latest idol'.

What Burton thought of as 'dryness of style' might seem to us today more like scurrilous and libellous abuse. M'Queen was a talented and scholarly geographer. It was perhaps unfortunate, however, that he had practised his geography in England and had no real idea of what it was like to travel in Africa; and it was just as easy to jump to conclusions in London as it was on the shores of Lake Victoria.

M'Queen began by denouncing Speke's ungenerosity and unfairness towards Petherick, and then proceeded to demolish Speke's character. He was especially enraged by Speke's account of his dealings with the Chief Rumanika's fat wife: 'Speke was to obtain a good view of her naked, and then to measure her, upon a like reciprocity on his part. After getting her "to sidle and wriggle into the midst of the hut, I did as I promised". With bare limbs and shirt sleeves well tucked up, Speke began his measuring and, as he called it, "engineering" process, thus: – Round the arm, 1 ft. 11 in.; chest, 4 ft. 4 in.; thickest part of the thigh, 2 ft. 7 in.; calf, 1 ft. 8 in.; height, 5 ft. 8 in. The height, we are told, is not quite certain, because he could not get her laid upon the floor . . .

'We believe none of our readers ever met with or ever heard of such a piece of "engineering" as this, and we dare say will never wish to meet with such another.'

Speke, M'Queen goes on, writes with admiration of Mutesa and his court. But what went on there? 'Every day saw one, two or three poor females dragged from the harem to a cruel execution and death. In one day and at one time no fewer than four were thus dragged forth.'

As for Speke complaining of being lonely during his sojourn at Mutesa's palace, this was manifestly untrue; he was constantly accepting presents of girls and rejecting all but the prettiest. They kept him so busy he did not even have time to go and look at his famous lake. 'It is almost incredible that any man who had come one thousand miles to see the position of the outlet of the Nile, supposed it to be in that spot, should remain five months within eight miles of it, without hearing or seeing something certain about the great object of his research, or have found some means to see it.'

Turning next to the geography of Speke's journey M'Queen reproduces most of Burton's arguments, and with some skill manages, by using Speke's own figures, to prove that the explorer makes the Nile flow uphill. What had Speke really gained and brought back? – 'The sacrifice and ruin of zealous associates – a mass of intelligence, if such it can be called, so muddled and confused in everything that we really believe he himself cannot find his way in it.'

Since his return to England Speke had made a speech in which he declared that he planned to open up Central Africa by returning there and traversing the continent along the Equator from east to west. His object was, he said, 'nothing less than to regenerate Africa'.

But Speke was the last man to send back to Africa. On hearing of the project even the Prime Minister of the King of Buganda might properly exclaim, 'Woh, woh, woh, what will happen next?' Grant might be the man to go. He at least was a gentleman and was modest: 'we never find him engaged in drinking *pombe*, flirting or coquetting, and collecting harems.'

M'Queen's review naturally attracted great attention. It was all very Victorian, very malicious, very hypocritical, and might not have mattered tuppence had not the underlying issues been so serious. Indeed the whole quarrel might be regarded as trivial and absurd, but it was fundamental to the history of the Nile, and in the years ahead its echoes were to continue with an astonishing persistence.

It would have been extraordinary, of course, had it all been plain sailing for Speke. He had a fantastic story to tell, and he had been both impulsive and a little over-bearing in presenting it. After all, the problem of the Nile had engrossed the most distinguished minds for thousands of years, and it was hardly likely that a young Indian Army officer of no particular qualifications had lighted on the truth where all others had failed. Moreover there was a strong tradition of scepticism in England. Speke had rushed straight into print, and a public controversy had been stirred up. Clearly it was now only a matter of time before the two principal antagonists were brought face to face to have the matter out.

Eventually, in September 1864, just over a year after Speke's and Grant's return to England, a meeting was arranged at Bath of the British Association for the Advancement of Science, and both Burton and Speke promised to attend it. They were to meet on the platform on September 16 before an audience of several hundred geographers and scientists and present their rival points of view. Dr Livingstone (who, incidentally, respected Speke but had not much time for Burton) was also to be there.

One does not know much about Speke's state of mind prior to the meeting. He was a man given to keeping his own counsel and he was not at his best in public debate. He must have been aware that Burton was a formidable rival with a command of language and a grasp of logic that he himself certainly did not possess. Burton was an intellectual, Speke was not; and there were some very damaging errors in Speke's *Journal* which as yet he had made no attempt to explain. He had not even brought a libel action against M'Queen and the *Morning Advertiser*, and some of M'Queen's statements were definitely libellous. At one point of the controversy M'Queen had actually accused Speke of condoning the slave-trade. Just possibly this might have been said about Burton, but Speke's record in the matter was absolutely clear; he was very sympathetic towards the Africans. But he had let all this pass by, and even Burton's worst sneers had gone unanswered. Yet Speke was a tenacious and self-confident man; so far as we know it was not in his nature to give way without a fight. He came down to the Bath meeting apparently determined to defend himself, and he stayed with his uncle John Fuller at Neston Park, near Box in Wiltshire.

Of Burton's attitude towards the meeting we know somewhat more, partly through the loving eyes of his wife Isabel, and partly through his own subsequent writings. As usual he had prepared his notes with care, and now he was not only ready to demolish Speke's theory; he was going to advance a brand new theory of his own. This, in effect, was a violent swing back to his original idea that Lake Tanganyika and its feeder streams were the true headwaters of the Nile. He had prepared a sketch map which showed the Rusizi River flowing northward *out* of Lake Tanganyika and entering the Lŭta Nzigé – that other large lake to the west of Lake Victoria which Speke and Grant had heard about when they were travelling towards Gondokoro. Speke's Lake Victoria he all but banished from his map, merely describing it as the 'supposed site' of a lake.

Now, as we know, Burton and Speke together had been to the northern end of Lake Tanganyika in 1858, and although they had not actually seen the Rusizi River, they had satisfied themselves from the reports of the local Africans that it flowed *into* the lake and thus could not possibly be the Nile. Burton had felt 'sick at heart' at the time. But now, upon the basis of further reflection, he felt much better. He simply reversed his previous decision and made the Rusizi flow the other way. The local Africans had misinformed them about the river: that was all there was to it. He and Speke, in any case, he declared, had been in no condition to verify matters when they were on the lake in 1858 since 'Speke was deaf and almost blind, I was paralytic, and we were both helpless'.

Before the meeting took place Isabel Burton tried unsuccessfully to bring about a reconciliation between the two men. 'It is interesting *now*,' she wrote (in 1892), 'to mark in their letters how they descend from "Dear Jack" and "Dear Dick" to "Dear Burton" and "Dear Speke", until they become "Sir".' And she records that before the meeting a friend 'conveyed to Richard that Speke had said that if Burton appeared on the platform at Bath (which was, as it were, Speke's native town) he would kick him. I remember Richard's answer – "Well, *that* settles it! By God he *shall* kick me" – and so to Bath we went.'

Yet Burton was nervous as well as pugnacious about the coming encounter; he was anxious to get it over and done with. He came down to Bath with Isabel, she being elaborately dressed and almost the only woman at the conference, and they went off to attend a preliminary session in Section E (Geography and Ethnography) on the morning of September 15 – the day prior to the great debate. There they saw Speke. The two men cut one another dead. It seemed to Burton that his rival looked ill and his eyesight and his hearing appeared to be troubling him again. Presently, about 1.30 p.m., Burton saw someone beckon to Speke from the bottom of the hall. Speke at once got up, and ejaculating, 'I can't stand this any longer,' left the room.

On the following morning, September 16, Burton, Isabel, Sir Roderick Murchison and several hundred other gentlemen assembled once more in the hall for the opening of the debate. 'All the distinguished people,' Isabel says, 'were with the Council. Richard *alone was excluded*, and stood on the platform – *we two alone*, he with his notes in his hand.'

One can perhaps best follow what happened next from Burton's own description: 'Early in the forenoon fixed for what silly tongues called the "Nile Duel" I found a

*Isabel Burton, by Louis Desanges. A companion piece to
the colour plate of her husband on page 35.*

large assembly in the rooms of Section E. A note was handed round in silence. Presently my friend Mr Findlay broke the tidings to me. Captain Speke had lost his life on the yesterday, at 4 p.m., whilst shooting over a cousin's grounds. He had been missed in the field and his kinsman found him lying upon the earth, shot through the body close to the heart. He lived only a few minutes and his last words were a request not to be moved.'

Mr Seton Deardon, in his study of Burton, says that 'Burton staggered visibly on the platform, then sank into a chair with his face working. "By God, he's killed himself!" he exclaimed. When he got home he wept bitter tears, repeating over and over again the name "Jack", "Jack".' Isabel also has recorded that 'when we got home he wept long and bitterly, and I was for many a day trying to comfort him'.

Burton, however, did manage to recover himself at the meeting. After Sir Roderick Murchison had delivered a moving address of condolence to Speke's relatives, Burton filled the gap in the morning's proceedings by reading a paper on 'The Ethnology of Dahomey'.

What had actually happened on the previous day was this: directly he left the hall Speke drove to Neston Park, which was six or seven miles from Bath, and there at 2.30 p.m., with his cousin George Fuller and a gamekeeper, Daniel Davis, he had gone out after partridges. In the course of the next hour he was heard by the others to fire off both barrels of his gun, which was a Lancaster breech-loader with no safety catch. About 4 p.m. Fuller, who was 60 yards away, heard a third very loud report from Speke's gun, and looking up he saw Speke himself standing on a two-foot stone wall. Then Speke fell. Fuller rushed up to discover his cousin lying on the ground with a terrible wound in his chest. One barrel of his gun had been discharged, the other was at half-cock, and it appeared that in getting over the wall Speke had drawn up the gun after him. It had gone off while he was holding its muzzle very close to his chest.

Speke was still conscious, but was bleeding profusely and it was impossible to move him – he himself said feebly, 'Don't move me.' Leaving the gamekeeper to look after the wounded man Fuller ran for help, but by the time he got back with a Mr. Snow, a surgeon of Box, Speke was already dead. He had lived only fifteen minutes and had said no more.

The body was taken to the house of Speke's brother at Corsham, and there an inquest was held on September 16. The jury returned a unanimous verdict: the deceased had died from the accidental discharge of his own gun after living for a quarter of an hour.

On Monday, September 19, 1864, *The Times* devoted a leading article to Speke. The newspaper took the view that Speke had actually succeeded in discovering the source of the Nile – 'the blue riband of the Geographers' – but at the same time it compared the exploit rather unfavourably with the discoveries which had recently been made by the explorers Stuart, Burke and Wills in Australia:

'A gallant soldier, who had borne himself bravely in some of the bloodiest battles in our Indian wars, and a sagacious and enterprising traveller, who had by sheer pluck and endurance solved a problem which has vexed the curiosity of mankind since the dawn of history, has in the full vigour of manhood fallen lifeless in a moment, the victim of a paltry, commonplace accident . . . We will not claim for Speke a precedence over the genius of Stuart or Burke or Wills; but it was a brilliant exploit, and we were still proud of the bold adventurer.'

The Times had decided views on how the accident had occurred: 'His gun was found with one barrel discharged, and the other with the hammer at half-cock. It is evident therefore that he had laid his gun down at half-cock while he mounted the wall, and that he had then taken it by the barrel and drawn it up towards him with the barrels pointed at his body.

'One of the hammers must have struck against a stone or hitched in a bough, and

IN MEMORY OF
OBᵗ SEPᵗ 15ᵗʰ 1864 ÆT 37

JOHN HANNING SPEKE
PRESENTED BY HIS UNCLE JOHN LEE LEE

LEFT *A letter from Speke's cousin George Fuller to* The Times *in 1921 throws a curious light on Speke's death, which does not accord with the evidence given at the inquest.* RIGHT *The memorial obelisk to Speke.*

the blow just lifted the hammer, and then allowed it to fall back upon the pin of the cartridge.'

The article concluded: 'This unfortunate accident will put an end to the controversy which was to have amused the Geographers at Bath.'

The burial took place at Dowlish Wake church close to Speke's family home, and it was attended by Murchison, Livingstone and Grant. A window and a monument were erected at the church to his memory, and later a granite obelisk was put up in Kensington Gardens in London. The inscription on this obelisk reads quite simply, 'In memory of Speke, Victoria Nyanza and the Nile, 1864' – as though we all should know the man and remember him with admiration.

Speke was unmarried and just 37 when he died, and a strange and persistent anonymity surrounds his memory. Where other, lesser explorers are revered, he is neglected; while their characters and their achievements can often seem very real to us, Speke is hardly more than a name; and it is not even a name that is instantly and indelibly associated with the Nile as Burton's is with Arabia and Livingstone's with Africa. Burton and Livingstone have their biographers in nearly every generation; no book of any consequence has ever been written about Speke. No phrase he uttered, not even 'The Nile is settled', no idiosyncrasy of manner or oddity of behaviour has fixed him in the public mind. He remains a virtuous shade, a self-centred, pertinacious man, a keeper of the best traditions of English enterprise – but one would rather be with Burton.

Speke's very death remains obscure, since there are many who still think that he preferred suicide to facing Burton, though there is no evidence to prove it. Indeed

The Speke memorial window in Dowlish Wake church.

everything we know about Speke must dispose us to think that if he contemplated suicide at all it would have been after his fight with his antagonist, not before. And yet the doubt remains.

There was no great remorse in England at the time of Speke's death; rather a feeling of embarrassment. *The Times*, however, was wrong in saying that the controversy was finished; Speke's opponents gained strength from his death and lost little time in still further diminishing the importance of his last tremendous journey. Grant lived on until 1892 and was eventually made a Companion of the Bath, but not for his exploit on the Nile; the distinction was awarded for some inconspicuous service he rendered in Abyssinia. Speke, of course, had had the Royal Geographical Society's medal, but some time elapsed before Queen Victoria was moved to observe that he had died 'before he had received any mark of our Royal favour'. The omission was then rectified: Speke's father was advised that he was permitted to add a crocodile and a hippopotamus to his coat of arms.

Later again a plaque was placed at the Ripon Falls.

The plaque at Ripon Falls.

'This source', one notes: not *the* source. But it hardly matters. The Ripon Falls have now been submerged beneath a hydro-electric dam, and somewhere in the green depths of the great river the place where Speke's plaque used to stand has been obliterated for ever.

5

Baker of the Nile

Obviously the problem of the Nile was never going to be cleared up by learned speculation in London. The answer could be found only in Africa itself, and now the chief
hopes of the geographers were fixed upon Samuel Baker and his wife, who in March
1863, following their meeting with Speke and Grant, had set off southwards from
Gondokoro. It was known that Speke had confided to them the general position of the
Lŭta Nzigé, which was the possible second source of the Nile, and that they had
decided to go in search of it.

Baker is a kind of fulcrum in African exploration. He stands in the centre of all
theories, emotions and moral attitudes, never deviating too far one way or the other.
Without being in the least dull he is a practical, down-to-earth man, who knows
precisely what he wants and where he is going to go. One feels with him that the fates
are fighting an unequal battle; however outrageous the odds against him, things will
calm down in the end and everyone will come round to his sober and sensible way of
thinking. In some ways he is almost a caricature of the professional Victorian, the
solid, whiskered clubman-figure who is absolutely fixed in his habits and his loyalties,
but equally determined to enjoy himself. Yet he is a difficult man to define; having
attached one label to him you find that you must quickly add another. Thus you
might describe him as a splendid specimen of Thackeray's hunting-and-shooting
Anglo-Indian nabobs, but then he writes extremely good books and is a very fair
linguist; he is a prosperous member of the trading middle-class, but then he himself
does not engage in business, he travels abroad on the most hazardous and daring
journeys; he rears a large Victorian family and then, on the death of his wife, he
marries a blonde and beautiful Hungarian girl, Florence Ninian von Sass, some
fifteen years his junior; he is pompous, conservative, sentimental and stubborn, and
at other times none of those things; and yet, in the midst of all this, he is not a chame-
leon. He is as steady as the captain of a ship.

Baker was born in 1821 (the same year as Burton), and he came from a line of naval
captains and planters in the colonies. His father was a wealthy shipowner and the
director of a bank and a railway. He was a fair, blue-eyed boy, passionately fond of
shooting and the out-of-doors, and he grew up to be a broad-shouldered man of
medium height, very tough and very solid; his fair hair sprouted from his chin
in a massive beard. He completed his education in Germany, and then married the
daughter of an English clergyman, and was off to the outposts of the world, hardly
ever to return to England for very long until the end of his life. At one time Baker

founded an agricultural settlement in Ceylon, and at another he was the construction manager of a railway along the Danube; but it was his obsession with big game shooting that led him on. He shot elephants in Ceylon, tigers in India, bears in the Balkans, and in the early eighteen-sixties he went over to Africa with his lovely young second wife (his four surviving children by the first marriage being safely disposed with relatives in England) to see what was offering for his gun in the wilds of the Sudan. He had, too, a second object in view; he thought he would combine a little exploring with the sport. Why not a journey up the Nile, perhaps even an expedition that would take him to the very source of the river?

As with all else in Baker's life, he prepared for this excursion with great thoroughness. He decided that first of all he would spend a year in the Sudan following up the Nile tributaries to the Abyssinian border and learning Arabic as he went along; then he would assemble his expedition in Khartoum and tackle the White Nile itself. Baker did himself well: delicacies from Fortnum and Mason's, a battery of guns made to his own specifications by the leading gunsmiths in London, the best of camping equipment and scientific instruments. In a sense he was a new kind of explorer: since he was wealthy, he was a private traveller having no connection with the government, the Church or the scientific societies, and he was under no instructions from anybody; he was simply out to please himself. Yet a more professional explorer never set foot in Africa. The first part of his programme was followed out to the letter. Just over a year after the outset of his journey from Cairo he arrived at Khartoum, having by then a very fair command of Arabic, and having shot a large number of wild animals on the upper reaches of the Atbara River. He had been corresponding with Petherick, and at Petherick's invitation he and his wife put up at the empty British Consulate at Khartoum.

Khartoum in the eighteen-sixties had been in existence for more than forty years, and was, in its own way, as strange and as wild as Zanzibar; indeed, these two towns between them drained off the great bulk of the slave and ivory trade of East Africa, all the caravans south of the Equator going out south-eastwards to the Indian Ocean and those to the north descending the Nile to Khartoum. In a rough and haphazard fashion the Egyptians ruled the Sudan from Khartoum; but perhaps pillaged is a better word than ruled. Practically every official from the Governor-General, Musa Pasha, downwards was involved in some way in the slave-trade, and the garrison of fifteen thousand Egyptian and Nubian troops lived on the land as an army of occupation might live, except that it was far more ruthless and disorderly. Its main business was gathering taxes, and these were extorted in kind from the natives either by the use of the whip, or by armed raids on the cattle and the grain stores in the villages.

Baker and his wife loathed Khartoum on sight: 'A more miserable, filthy and unhealthy place,' he says, 'can hardly be imagined.' Beyond the river, nothing but an appalling desert; within the town itself some thirty thousand people densely crowded into huts of burnt brick that were occasionally flooded by the Nile. Dead animals lay rotting in the undrained streets and the only supply of water was a muddy fluid brought up from the river by Persian wheels with hanging earthen jars that were

Lady Baker. Samuel Baker met Florence in Hungary and according to his letters they went through a form of marriage together there and subsequently remarried five years later on their return to London.

worked by circling oxen. There was, of course, a tax on every water-wheel. Nothing in the town could be done except by bribery; torture and flogging took place as a matter of course in the prisons; and Musa Pasha himself combined 'the worst of Oriental failings with the brutality of a wild animal'. Throughout most of the year the heat was overwhelming, and when the *haboob* blew up the sand-filled sky was black as night.

Baker describes one of these storms. 'I saw,' he says, 'approaching from the S.W. apparently, a solid range of immense brown mountains, high in the air. So rapid was the approach of this extraordinary phenomenon, that in a few minutes we were in actual pitchy darkness. At first there was no wind, and the peculiar calm gave an oppressive character to the event. . . . We tried to distinguish our hands placed close before our eyes – not even an outline could be seen. This lasted for upwards of twenty minutes; it then rapidly passed away and the sun shone as before.'

And yet, at this time, Khartoum was a fascinating place: 'the air was full of wonderment'. This was almost the last point of civilization on the edge of an immense wilderness which had hardly as yet begun to yield up the endless treasures and monstrosities it contained. Every caravan that set out was an exploration; every boat that returned down the Nile brought with it something that was phenomenal and strange: animals and birds that had not been classified as yet; wild tribesmen with outlandish ornaments stuck through their lips, ears and noses; plants and flowers that produced new drugs and perfumes; stones that might prove to contain silver or gold. The ivory trade alone was worth £40,000 a year.

Apart from the Africans, the population of Khartoum was made up chiefly of Syrians, Greeks, Copts, Armenians, Turks, Arabs and Egyptians, and many of these had taken Galla girls from Abyssinia – 'the Venuses of that country' – as their wives or concubines. About thirty Europeans were living in the town, and life for them was not intolerable. They had somewhat better and cooler houses than the general run, a monthly camel post kept them in touch with the outside world, and many luxuries such as wines, Bass's pale ale, French biscuits, soaps and perfumes were brought to them over the desert. The local Turkish and Egyptian grandees liked to entertain at long and elaborate banquets which usually wound up with a performance by African dancing girls.

But it was the slave-trade that kept Khartoum going. Any penniless adventurer could become a trader provided he was willing to borrow money at anything up to eighty per cent interest. On a normal expedition such a trader would sail south from Khartoum in December with two or three hundred armed men, and at some convenient spot would land and form an alliance with a native chieftain. Then together the tribesmen and the Khartoum slavers would fall upon some neighbouring village in the night, firing the huts just before dawn and shooting into the flames. It was the women that the slavers chiefly wanted, and these were secured by placing a heavy forked pole known as a *sheba* on their shoulders. The head was locked in by a crossbar, the hands were tied to the pole in front, and the children were bound to their mothers by a chain passed round their necks. Everything the village contained would

Samuel and Florence Baker – detail from one of Samuel's watercolours.

be looted – cattle, ivory, grain, even the crude jewellery that was cut off the dead victims – and then the whole cavalcade would be marched back to the river to await shipment to Khartoum. With the stolen cattle the trader would buy ivory, and sometimes for ivory he would be willing to ransom a slave. Sometimes too the trader would turn upon his native ally and despoil him in the same way as the others; but more often these alliances were kept on from year to year, the native chieftain building up a fresh store of slaves and ivory while the trader was disposing of the last consignment at Khartoum. Every trader had his own territory and by mutual agreement the country was parcelled out all the way from Khartoum to Gondokoro and beyond.

In a good season a slaver in a small way could reckon on obtaining 20,000 lb. of ivory worth £4,000 in Khartoum, plus 400 or 500 slaves worth £5 or £6 each – a total of perhaps £6,500. With this capital he paid off his debts, mounted a fresh expedition and year by year expanded his business.

Officially the trade was illegal, but the only effect of this was that the slaves were not sold openly in Khartoum; they were disposed of at established points of rendezvous in the desert outside the town, and thence marched off along the caravan routes to the Red Sea for shipment to Arabia or Persia or sent directly down the Nile to Cairo.

Probably nothing more monstrous or cruel than this traffic had happened in history, for it was more highly organized than the slaving in Tanganyika. Baker records the terrible facts with a juridical calm which is very effective; and yet, like Burton, and unlike Speke, he did not really take to Africans and he was no blind believer in immediate emancipation. 'However we may condemn the horrible system of slavery,' he wrote, 'the results of emancipation have proved that the negro does not appreciate the blessings of freedom, nor does he show the slightest feelings of gratitude to the hand that broke the rivets of his fetters.'

Elsewhere he attacks the Africans for the savagery and brutality of their tribal customs. 'Charming people, these poor blacks, as they are termed by English sympathizers,' he exclaims when a Nuer chief 'exhibited his wife's back and arms covered with jagged scars . . . he was quite proud of having clawed his wife like a wild beast.' And again: 'Polygamy is, of course, the general custom; the number of a man's wives depending entirely upon his wealth, precisely as would the number of his horses in England. There is no such thing as *love* in these countries . . . everything is practical, without a particle of romance. Women are so far appreciated as they are valuable animals . . . I am afraid this practical state of affairs will be a strong barrier to missionary enterprise.'

Later on Baker was to be strongly criticized in England for these views, and for his harsh treatment of the tribes. But for the moment the slave-trade had great personal importance for him – it had so savaged and antagonized the tribes south of Khartoum that the whole country was in an uproar. This made it hazardous for any private traveller to proceed without a large armed escort. There was another difficulty which was even more serious: the Egyptian officials at Khartoum were by no means eager to have a stray white man roaming about in the slaving areas to report on their activities to the outside world. Musa Pasha therefore did all he could to prevent the Bakers

Papyrus. 'Sailed at 3 p.m. Masses of beautiful but gloomy papyrus rush, growing in dense thickets about eighteen feet above water. I measured the diameter of one head, or crown, four feet one inch.' (Baker)

from getting on. He denied them boats. He contrived to prevent their engaging an escort. He smiled and smiled and told them to come back another day.

But it would have needed a great deal more determination than Musa Pasha possessed to thwart the Bakers. On their arrival in Khartoum in June 1862 they found that they had an additional and urgent reason for continuing into the interior. A report had come in that Petherick and his wife, who had gone south some months earlier, were dead, and the Royal Geographical Society now asked Baker if he would

Slaves being marched to Egypt. 'Avarice, however, that fatal enemy to the negro chiefs, made them overreach themselves by exorbitant demands of taxes. . . . Had they only sense to see, and patience to wait, the whole trade of the interior would inevitably pass through their country . . . They require a government like ours in India; and without it, the slave-trade will wipe them off the face of the earth.' (Speke)

take Petherick's place in the search for Speke and Grant. The two explorers had already been missing for over a year. Baker accepted this charge at once and privately decided that if Speke and Grant had also perished or had failed to reach their objective he himself would go on and find the source of the Nile.

After six months' persistent effort in Khartoum he acquired three sailing boats, 96 men, some of whom he armed and dressed in uniform, provisions for four months, 21 donkeys, 4 camels and 4 horses. He was also joined by a German traveller, Johann Schmidt, whom he had picked up in the Sudan. On December 18, 1862, they set sail for Gondokoro.

The Nile south of Khartoum is a complicated stream. For five hundred miles it proceeds through the desert on a broad and fairly regular course, with trees and occasional low, bare hills or *jebels* on either bank. But at the point where the Sobat comes in from the Abyssinian mountains, a short distance above the present town of Malakal, the river turns west, the air grows more humid, the banks more green, and this is the first warning of the great obstacle of the Sudd that lies ahead. There is no more formidable swamp in the world than the Sudd. The Nile loses itself in a vast sea

Arrival at the stoppage: 'We only made about two miles yesterday and today, being stopped by vegetation...'
Balaeniceps rex : 'a curiosity of the rarest kind, known amongst the sailors as the Abu-Markoob (or slipper shape) a name derived from the peculiar form of its beak. Its scientific name is due to the disproportionate magnitude of its head. Before 1850 no skins of this bird had been conveyed to Europe.' (Baker)

of papyrus ferns and rotting vegetation, and in that foetid heat there is a spawning tropical life that can hardly have altered very much since the beginning of the world; it is as primitive and as hostile to man as the Sargasso Sea. Crocodiles and hippopotamuses flop about in the muddy water, mosquitoes and other insects choke the air and the *Balaeniceps rex* and other weird water-birds keep watch along the banks — except that here there are no ordinary banks, merely chance pools in the forest of apple-green reeds that stretches away in a feathery mass to the horizon. This region is neither land nor water. Year by year the current keeps bringing down more floating vegetation, and packs it into solid chunks perhaps twenty feet thick and strong enough for an elephant to walk on. But then this debris breaks away in islands and forms again in another place, and this is repeated in a thousand indistinguishable patterns and goes on forever.

Baker remarks that on the Upper Nile there are no ruins or relics of past civilizations, 'no ancient histories to charm the present with memories of the past; all is wild and brutal, hard and unfeeling . . .' These effects were redoubled in the Sudd. Here there was not even a present, let alone a past; except on occasional islands of hard ground no men ever had lived or ever could live in this desolation of drifting reeds and ooze, even the most savage of men. The lower forms of life flourished here in a mad abundance, but for black and white men alike the Sudd contained nothing but the threat of starvation, disease and death. In the wet season it covered an area as large as England.

There were three main waterways through the Sudd, and all or any of them might be blocked at any time; some sixty miles beyond Malakal the Bahr-el-Zeraf, the River of the Giraffes, split off to the south; then, another fifty miles further on, there was a sheet of fairly open water known as Lake No and here the stream divided, one section, the Bahr-el-Ghazal, the River of the Antelopes, striking off in a general south-westerly direction, while the other, the Bahr-el-Jebel, continued directly south. This last, the Bahr-el-Jebel, was the main channel used by the traders. About 500 miles south of Lake No they got free of the Sudd and arrived at Gondokoro. With luck, which meant a fair wind and the ability to cut their way through the matted vegetation, they hoped to complete the journey from Khartoum in about a month and a half.

Beyond Gondokoro they could proceed no further by water; the Nile there broke up into cataracts that continued intermittently for about eighty miles. Thus Gondokoro had become the main entrepot in the interior, even though it was nothing more than a miserable collection of huts 25 feet above the river on the east bank. Already in the 'sixties it had been in existence for some twenty years, and an Austrian Roman Catholic Mission had been established there as early as 1851. But all had come to grief: fifteen out of the twenty missionaries who had been sent there had died and not a single convert had been made.

Very few of the slave and ivory traders had managed to get far beyond Gondokoro, since they despoiled their line of march and the opposition of the tribes rose up before them; in general the area beyond Nimule and the further course of the river were unknown. This region Baker now proposed to penetrate in search of Speke and Grant.

The Sudd that year was fairly clear, and Baker's little flotilla accomplished the 1,000-mile voyage from Khartoum to Gondokoro in 40 days. On the way Johann Schmidt died, others fell ill, and the whole party, both animals and men, suffered terribly from mosquitoes. Gondokoro, says Baker, 'was a perfect hell', a sort of Yukon gold-rush camp in the tropics, with six hundred traders and their men forever drinking, quarrelling and insanely shooting off their guns into the air. However, there was a moment of respite. The Bakers had been only a fortnight in Gondokoro when, as we have seen, Speke and Grant arrived from Bunyoro. In his account of the

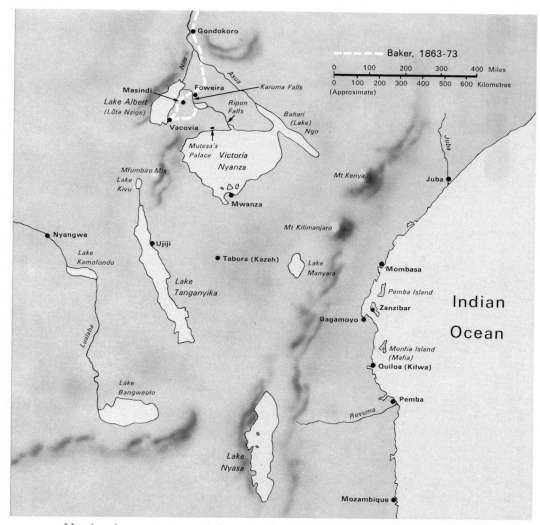

Map based on contemporary information showing the route taken by Baker, 1863–73.

meeting Baker very handsomely covers up his disappointment at hearing that they had already reached the source of the Nile: 'At the first blush of meeting them,' he says, 'I had considered my expedition as terminated . . . but . . . Speke and Grant with characteristic candour and generosity gave me a map of their route, showing that they had been unable to complete the actual exploration of the Nile, and that a most important portion still remained to be determined . . . a large lake called the Lǔta Nzigé.'

Soon after Speke and Grant had gone north to Khartoum the Bakers set out for the lake.

The Albert N'yanza, Great Basin of the Nile, Baker's account of his next two years' wanderings, is the most readable of explorers' books. It contains indeed the ingredients of almost all African adventure stories that have been written from that day to this. Here is Allan Quartermain in his broad-brimmed hat setting forth into the jungles with a young and lovely girl at his side, and they face every hazard with marvellous determination. When wild beasts charge, Baker with his deadly aim stops them in their tracks. At the outset of the journey he quells a mutiny among his own men by striking down the ringleader with his fist. Then, as they advance, all their baggage animals die and they are forced to ride oxen, their food supplies fail and they are reduced to eating grass, fever lays them prostrate for days and weeks on end, deceitful guides mislead them, hippopotamuses overturn their boats, the slave-traders cheat them, the tribes attack with poisoned arrows, and they are never for long out of sight and hearing of the war drums and savage dancing. Through it all Mrs Baker never flinches. 'She was not a *screamer*,' her husband says. When she hears stealthy foot-steps approaching their hut at night she quietly touches him on the sleeve and he reaches for his revolver to deal with the intruder. When heavy dew drenches her Victorian skirts and they bring her to the ground she has no compunction about getting into men's clothing.

For nine months they wandered aimlessly, unable to get forward because of the lack of porters. Their immediate objective was to reach the headquarters of Kamrasi, the King of Bunyoro, whom Speke and Grant had met on their journey north, but Kamrasi was still at war with his brother Rionga and he kept putting them off. And so all this time they continued in the wilderness, barely a fortnight's journey from the Lŭta Nzigé but quite unable to make any move to reach it.

By now both were suffering terribly from malaria and there were days when Mrs Baker had to be carried on a litter. At last, on January 22, 1864, in the company of an Arab slaver named Ibrahim they reached the Nile near the Karuma Falls where the river turns sharply to the west. Here they were on the borders of Bunyoro, and Kamrasi's tribesmen hailed them from the opposite bank. Baker's interpreter explained that he was 'Speke's brother', and had come with rich presents for Kamrasi, but the tribesmen feared that this was just another slaving raid, and although they came close to the shore in a canoe they would not land. Baker describes the scene:

'"Let us look at him!" cried the headman in the boat; having prepared for the introduction by changing my clothes in a grove of plantains for my dressing-room, and altering my costume to a tweed suit, something similar to that worn by Speke, I climbed up a high and almost perpendicular rock that formed a natural pinnacle on the face of the cliff, and waving my cap to the crowd on the opposite side I looked almost as imposing as Nelson in Trafalgar Square. . . . Upon landing through the high reeds, they immediately recognized the similarity of my beard and general complexion to that of Speke; and their welcome was at once displayed by the most extravagant dancing and gesticulating with lances and shields, as though intending to attack, rushing at me with the points of their lances thrust close to my face, and shouting and singing in great excitement.'

Finally Baker's party – 110 of them in all – was allowed to cross the river. Mrs

Baker caused a great sensation. She chose this moment to wash her hair, and the tribesmen and their families gathered round in amazement at the sight of the long golden tresses reaching to her waist. There followed then a wearisome palaver before the local chiefs agreed to lead the party to Kamrasi's headquarters, ten days' march to the south at Mrooli, at the head of Lake Kyoga. By the time they reached their destination Baker was so ill and weak that he had to be carried into the King's presence on a stretcher and laid like a trophy at his feet. Kamrasi, surrounded by his subordinate chiefs, sat on a copper stool that had been placed on a carpet of leopard skins, and he surveyed his helpless guest with equanimity. He explained that he had greatly feared that Baker was an ally of his enemy Rionga, and had come to plunder his country. But now it was evident that he was Speke's brother, merely another impoverished traveller: he was too weak to be bad. Thus reassured, the King set about the customary business of demanding presents — shotguns, beads, carpets, lengths of cloth, everything he could lay hands on. He also insisted that Baker should repair the fifty-guinea gold chronometer Speke had given him in 1862 — it had 'gone dead' after he had poked at the works with a needle to discover where the ticking came from.

It was a miserable time for the Bakers. The rain poured down. Regularly each day Baker was seized by a violent attack of malaria, and all his quinine was exhausted. Again and again he asked Kamrasi to supply him with porters and a guide, so that he could proceed to the mysterious lake to the west, but he was invariably met with a demand for more presents. 'We shall be nailed for another year in this abominable

'My Examination by the Chiefs on entering Bunyoro. Resolved, that I am "Speke's brother".' (Baker)
Speke and Baker had first met aboard ship when Speke was travelling from India to Aden in 1854.

'Altogether I never saw a more unearthly set of creatures, they were perfect illustrations of my childish ideas of devils – horns, tails, and all, excepting the hoofs; they were our escort! furnished by Kamrasi to accompany us to the lake.' (Baker)

country,' Baker wrote in his diary, 'ill with fever, and without medicine, clothes or supplies.'

The crisis came in February 1864. Kamrasi announced that Baker should go to the lake, but Mrs Baker must remain behind: he would provide Baker with a good-looking Bunyoro virgin in exchange for her. Baker drew his pistol and pointing it at Kamrasi's chest told him he was about to shoot him dead. Mrs Baker, meanwhile, rising from her sick-bed, rushed at the King and withered him with an outburst of furious indignation; and at this Kamrasi gave way.

On the following day porters and an escort were produced, and the travellers set off for the goal of their great adventure. They were held up almost at once by the swamp and the matted vegetation on the Kafu River to the south-west of Mrooli. 'It was equally impossible,' Baker wrote later, 'to ride or to be carried over this treacherous surface; thus I led the way and begged Mrs Baker to follow me on foot as quickly as possible, precisely in my track. The river was about eighty yards wide, and I had scarcely completed a fourth of the distance and looked back to see if my wife followed close to me, when I was horrified to see her standing in one spot, and sinking gradually through the weeds, while her face was distorted and perfectly purple. Almost as soon as I perceived her, she fell, as though shot dead. In an instant I was by her side; and with the assistance of eight or ten of my men, who were fortunately close to me, I dragged her like a corpse through the yielding vegetation, and up to our waists we scrambled across to the other side, just keeping her head above the water: to have carried her would have been impossible, as we should all have sunk together through the reeds. I had her under a tree, and bathed her head and face with water, as for the moment I thought she had fainted; but she lay perfectly insensible, as though dead, with teeth and hands firmly clenched, and her eyes open, but fixed. It was a *coup de soleil*.'

Since there was no food to be had on the river Baker struggled forward for two more days, his unconscious wife lying on a stretcher, and on the third morning she woke demented. For a week then Baker sat with her through the day and night while she raved deliriously in a waking trance. He managed to obtain a little wild honey and a guinea-fowl or two, but they were by now half starved and still the rain poured down. At the end of a week Baker himself collapsed, but when he woke many hours later he found that his wife's brain had cleared at last, and that she was able to recognize him. After two further days to recuperate they pushed on again, following the general direction of the Kafu River to the south-west. By March 13 they had reached the 31st degree of longitude, about 25 miles north of the Equator, and their guide announced that they should come within sight of the lake on the following day.

'That night,' Baker says, 'I hardly slept. For years I had striven to reach the "sources of the Nile". In my nightly dreams during the arduous voyage I had always failed, but after so much hard work and perseverance the cup was at my very lips, and I was to *drink* at the mysterious fountain before another sun should set – at that great reservoir of Nature that ever since creation had baffled all discovery.

'*The 14th March.* – The sun had not risen when I was spurring my ox after the guide, who, having been promised a double handful of beads on arrival at the lake, had caught the enthusiasm of the moment. The day broke beautifully clear, and having crossed a deep valley between the hills, we toiled up the opposite slope. I hurried to the summit. The glory of our prize burst suddenly upon me! There, like a sea of quicksilver, lay far beneath the grand expanse of water – a boundless sea horizon on the south and south-west, glittering in the noon-day sun; and on the west, at fifty or sixty miles' distance, blue mountains rose from the bosom of the lake to a height of about 7,000 feet above its level.'

Baker had long since planned to give three cheers when he reached his goal, but now he found himself overcome with emotion. He and his wife dismounted from their oxen and in a fever of excitement began to drag themselves down the steep cliff towards the water's edge.

'I led the way, grasping a stout bamboo. My wife in extreme weakness tottered down the pass, supporting herself upon my shoulder, and stopping to rest every twenty paces. After a toilsome descent of about two hours, weak with years of fever, but for the moment strengthened by success, we gained the level plain below the cliff. A walk of about a mile through flat sandy meadows of fine turf interspersed with trees and bush, brought us to the water's edge. The waves were rolling upon a white pebbly beach: I rushed into the lake, and thirsty with heat and fatigue, with a heart full of gratitude, I drank deeply from the Sources of the Nile.'

Well, perhaps it was not *the* source of the Nile, he explains, but at any rate it was *a* source, and for the moment it was marvellous. With solemnity he named it Lake Albert in honour of Queen Victoria's husband, who had so recently died.

'It was with extreme emotion,' he goes on, 'that I enjoyed this glorious scene. My wife, who had followed me so devotedly, stood by my side pale and exhausted – a wreck upon the shores of the great Albert lake that we had so long striven to reach. No European foot had ever trod upon its sand, nor had the eyes of a white man ever

The storm on Lake Albert. 'My men looked rather green at the ominous black clouds and the increasing swell, but exclaimed, "Inshallah, there will be no wind." With due deference to their faith in predestination I insisted on their working the spare paddles, as our safety depended on reaching the shore before the approaching storm. . . .' (Baker)

scanned its vast expanse of water. We were the first and this was the key to the great secret that even Julius Caesar yearned to unravel, but in vain. Here was the great basin of the Nile that received *every drop of water* even from the passing shower to the roaring mountain torrent that drained from Central Africa towards the north. This was the great reservoir of the Nile.'

And now they faced the inevitable problem that besets all explorers – how to get home? From fishermen on the lakeshore they managed to obtain crude canoes made of hollowed-out tree trunks, and in those they paddled northwards for the next two weeks, through fearful storms, until they reached the point where the Nile entered the topmost corner of the lake. Here there was another reward awaiting them: continuing a short distance up the river to the east, through what is now a national park for wild animals, they came upon a spectacular waterfall. The Murchison Falls (so named by Baker in honour of the President of the Royal Geographical Society) are only 20 feet across and some 130 feet high, but Mr Rennie Bere has very well described them as 'the most exciting single incident in the Nile's long journey to the sea'. The whole pent-up volume of the river dashes out of a ravine like a burst water-main; it is really more of an explosion of water than a fall, and it can exert a curious mesmerism in the mind if one stands there and watches for a while. The pattern of thundering water is endlessly repeated yet never for two seconds quite the same.

The Bakers did not have much leisure to enjoy their discovery – it was here that the hippopotamus bull charged them and lifted their boat half out of the river. The scene of the accident is still a favourite haunt of crocodiles and they were lucky to be swept by whirlpools on to the bank.

They now abandoned their boat and took refuge above the falls on the island of Patooan and there once more they collapsed. Civil war was now raging throughout Bunyoro, and two more months went by before the Bakers, on the point of starvation, were able to get back to Kamrasi's headquarters. Here it was revealed to Baker that the man whom they had previously seen before starting out for the lake was not the King at all, but a younger brother named M'Gambi whom Kamrasi had prudently sent in his place in case the Bakers should prove to be dangerous. M'Gambi or Kamrasi, it hardly mattered very much to the two desperate fugitives – but Baker thought it advisable to put on a show for his meeting with the real King: he got out a kilt, a sporran, and a Glengarry bonnet from his kit and in these presented himself at the palace. Kamrasi was sufficiently impressed to offer food to his guests and then, in the usual way, doggedly set about relieving them of their last possessions.

And now six months went by and nothing happened. Regularly in the afternoon Baker went down with malaria, and it was not until he devised a means of distilling alcohol from sweet potatoes that he rallied a little. There was no ending to the wars – Mutesa was now attacking Bunyoro with an army from the south – and the hostilities made it impossible for unescorted travellers to get about. When Kamrasi was forced to flee to the north from the invading army, the Bakers had no choice but to go with him. By September 1864 they had all but resigned themselves to dying in Central Africa when an Arab slave caravan came in from Gondokoro bringing with it not only stores for the Bakers but mail as well. From Speke (who had died in Wiltshire just a few days before) they received a copy of *The Illustrated London News* containing his own and Grant's portraits, and also a copy of *Punch* with a cartoon on the discovery of the source of the Nile.

The Bakers now had cloth with which to obtain both food and porters, and they joined forces with the Arab caravan on its return to the north. It was a slow progress, delayed at every step by the inevitable cattle and slave raids on the villages, but finally in February 1865, after two years' absence, they reached Gondokoro. The party made a ceremonial entry, Baker and his wife mounted on oxen, guns firing, and the Union Jack flying, and they were met by a bitter anti-climax: no Europeans were there to welcome them and, worse still, there was no mail. The Bakers had long since been presumed dead.

Tragedy and misery were to pursue the explorers to the very end. Baker managed to hire a boat for the return to Khartoum for £40, but the Sudd blocked them for many weeks, and while they waited for a favourable wind, plague broke out. A number of the men, including the boy Saat who had followed them throughout, went mad and died.

They had a warm welcome from the European community when they reached Khartoum (where they heard for the first time of Speke's death), but even the normally uneventful onward passage to Cairo was hindered by near shipwreck in the cataracts and a skirmish with the Arabs. At last in October 1865, nearly five years after they had first set foot in Africa, they reached Suez, and Baker was able to indulge in a luxury which for a long time had been haunting his imagination – a tankard of iced Allsopp's pale ale. A job was found in Shepheard's Hotel in Cairo for Richarn, their last surviving follower, and they set sail for home. 'Had I really come from the Nile sources?' Baker asked himself. 'It was no dream. A witness sat before me; a face still young, but bronzed like an Arab by years of exposure to a burning sun; haggard and worn with toil and sickness, and shaded with cares, happily now past; the devoted companion of my pilgrimage, to whom I owed success and life – my wife.'

There was enough here for half a dozen film scenarios and the British public

Speke and Grant in The Illustrated London News, *July 4, 1863.*

SUPPLEMENT, JULY 4, 1863.   THE ILLUSTRATED LONDON NEWS   17

DISCOVERY   OF   THE   SOURCE   OF   THE   NILE.

loved it. Speke and Grant in their accounts of their journeys had been a little too bizarre and at the same time pedestrian; Burton's treatises had been too sharp and too esoteric except for the sophisticated few; and Dr Livingstone belonged to a high moral plane that was sometimes beyond the average reach. But Baker's book *The Albert N'yanza* was just right; he and his wife had the sort of reactions that everyone could enjoy and understand. One suffered and lived vicariously with this couple in the terrible African jungle just as one lived with the characters in a novel. And how brave she was. How gallant and determined he had been. They deserved their success.

There was another quality about Baker that people liked; he was not forever, like Speke, pushing on impatiently to reach the journey's end; while he was in Africa he lived there, he made a home of it. Whenever he came to a cul-de-sac he accepted the fact for the time being, and like Robinson Crusoe at once set about making himself comfortable in the wilderness. Being an extremely practical man he would with equal facility make a boat, an alcoholic still or a suit of clothes from wild animal skins. He and his wife gathered a little group of personal retainers round them, and these were taught to cook, serve at the table and make beds like any other domestic servants. They had their pet monkeys and their pet birds who travelled with them and

Shepheard's Hotel, Cairo.

even their riding oxen were properly broken in and trained. Baker's observations of native life are full of interest: he notes that the tribal drums are sometimes made from an elephant's ear, that the goods the natives brought to market were packed in fresh reeds, and that the beer gourds were covered with a lid and their contents drained through a straw. He describes just how the bark of trees was beaten into a cloth, and how the tribesmen made needles and sewed squares of goatskin into mantles 'as expertly as a French glover'. He supplies details of the vast Nile perch: one half of a fish they caught in Lake Albert (the other half having been eaten by a crocodile) weighed 150 lb.

Baker, in other words, had a pleasant intimacy with the things he found in Africa, and when he described them he wrote as Defoe might have written.

Before ever he got to England he was awarded the gold medal of the Royal Geographical Society, and his knighthood soon followed. The press was delighted with Sir Samuel and Lady Baker (now no longer a wreck but dressed in the height of fashion), and so was society in London. Presently they had the pleasure of seeing *The Albert N'yanza* run into three editions, and it was to be reprinted frequently in the years ahead. His *Nile Tributaries*, the account of his first year's shooting safari in the Sudan, soon followed and was equally successful. In 1868 Baker tried his hand at fiction, and his adventure story, *Cast Up by the Sea*, pleased the public just as well. But it was with the Nile that his name was associated in the public mind. From now on he was Baker of the Nile.

It would be unfair, of course, even facetious, to leave Baker and his reputation here. His books were much more than adventure stories and his journeys had an importance that went far beyond their popular interest. He had imported something quite new into the Central African scene; he had made it comprehensive. He formed a kind of bridge between the original myths and legends and the reality of what was actually to be found in the country. Central Africa now was no longer a fantasy or a blank space on the map: it was an undeveloped but quite habitable region, with perfectly recognizable people living in it, and it was being exploited with the utmost savagery and brutality by the Mohammedans. The Nile, in short, had now become more than a geographical interest: it had a political, humanitarian and commercial importance as well, and Baker drove home the point that, unless England stepped in, this promising wilderness would be utterly despoiled by the slavers and lost forever to Christianity.

And yet until the mystery of the physical nature of the region and its great river was cleared up it was difficult to know precisely how to act. Despite all the careful scientific data Baker had brought back it had to be admitted that he had not really accomplished very much on the Upper Nile. Compared with the journeys of the other explorers his wanderings had taken him an astonishingly short distance (at the present time one could easily traverse in a car his whole route south from Gondokoro within the space of a couple of days), and his discovery of Lake Albert had by no means resolved the mystery of the Nile; in fact, it was soon to become apparent that he had only confused the issue still further. Like Speke he had seen a large body of

Samuel Baker, 1865. By 1874 he was described on the title-page of Ismailia: *'Sir Samuel W. Baker, Pacha, M.A., F.R.S., F.R.G.S. Major-General of the Ottoman Empire, Member of the Orders of the Osmanié and the Medjidié, Late Governor-General of the Equatorial Nile Basin, Gold Medallist of the Royal Geographical Society, Grande Médaille d'Or de la Société de Géographie de Paris . . . Author of "The Albert N'yanza Great Basin of the Nile" . . . "The Rifle and Hound in Ceylon", etc., etc.'*

water and had concluded that it ran on indefinitely, perhaps for hundreds of miles, to the south. But he had no means of proving this; he had not circumnavigated the lake. All he could really assert was that the stream which Speke had seen pouring westward at Karuma Falls in Central Uganda did in fact flow into his newly discovered Lake Albert and then out of it again towards the north. But whether or not this was the Nile he could not say with any authority, for he had not followed the stream northwards from Lake Albert to Gondokoro.

Another question remained, and it was vital: suppose this *was* the Nile, which lake was the true source, Speke's Victoria or Baker's Albert? If Baker's Albert stretched as far south as he thought it did, then surely it had the better claim. Baker himself left the matter in the air: Lake Albert, he said, was at least the *western* source of the river and a considerable, if not its principal, reservoir. The *full* Nile, he claimed, began only when the stream issued from it. Geographers in London saw his point but still it was not conclusive.

Speke's detractors naturally lost no time in exploiting the possibilities of Lake Albert. Surely it could be argued, they said, that this new lake might be fed by a river still further south, and if so then Speke's claims about Lake Victoria (if that lake really did exist) were nonsense. Even before the Bakers returned to England Sir Roderick Murchison felt bound to acknowledge the force of this reasoning. On May 22, 1865, he delivered a eulogy of Speke to the Royal Geographical Society, but he wound up his address by announcing that he proposed to send Livingstone out to Africa once more. His mission was to endeavour to settle once and for all the problem of the watersheds of Central Africa, and he was to pay particular attention to the area south of Lake Tanganyika. Livingstone, as all his intimates knew, believed that it was there he would come upon the true source. He was further charged with proceeding to Lake Tanganyika itself, so as to determine whether Burton's Rusizi River flowed into or out of the lake. The implication was that Burton's second thoughts about the Rusizi would probably turn out to be correct; it was expected that the river would be found to flow north and join Baker's Lake Albert; and thus Lake Victoria would be excluded from the pattern of the Nile. 'Speke,' as Professor Ingham says, 'was still on trial.'

The Murchison Falls.

THE LIFE & EXPLORATIONS
OF
DR. LIVINGSTONE

BORN AT BLANTYRE, MARCH 19, 1813   DIED IN CENTRAL AFRICA, MAY 4, 1873

6

Kudos and Baraka

We tend to think of Livingstone as an old man, but he was only fifty-two when he set out upon his last journey in 1865, and now, more than ever, he had that quality which the Arabs describe as *baraka*. In the most improbable circumstances he had the power of enhancing life and making it appear better than it was before. His mere presence seems to have conferred a blessing on everyone who met him; even the Arab slavers felt it and helped him when they could.

It was perfectly true that his Zambezi expedition, when he ascended the Zambezi River to the Victoria Falls and discovered Lake Nyasa, had been a disaster for his companions; even those who had survived had been pushed beyond all reasonable limits and had often found him self-willed and impatient of any weakness. Livingstone was never at his best when he was travelling with other white men, since he forced his own incredibly high standards upon them. But in 1865 he was on his own again, and no one had to suffer but himself. Moreover that extraordinary concentration upon Africa had not diminished in the least. The others who went there might lose faith and become confused in quarrels amongst themselves, he never. Africa by now had become an essential part of his existence, he lived for Africa, and it is only when this is understood that one can find some purpose in the apparent aimlessness of his wanderings – the 'sublime obstinacy' with which he kept on and on when there appeared to be no point in his continuing any more. The other explorers proceed, as it were, in a straight line on their African journeys, and when they have accomplished their missions their one desire is to return home. But Livingstone's mission begins and ends in Africa. He travels in circles. He dwells with the Africans themselves, eating their food, sleeping in their huts, and, without losing his own identity, he makes their life his own. No one understands the African negroes and the fearful hardships to which they were submitted better than he did. Only he could have written: 'The strangest disease I have seen in this country seems really to be broken-heartedness, and it attacks free men who have been captured and made slaves.' In those few words he came to the root of the matter and they may have been just as effective as all the evidence of the atrocities and all the humanitarian outpourings that were then being broadcast from the pulpit, the House of Commons and the Anti-Slavery Society in England.

One might perhaps find some parallel between this man's life and the career of Dr Schweitzer in Lambaréné, except that Livingstone was a traveller and a nomad: he had to keep on – and how clearly one sees that calm and rugged figure, with the flapped

David Livingstone. The frontispiece to The Life and Explorations of Livingstone.

cap on his head, his walking stick in his hand, marching through the bush – because he was one of those people who cannot bear not to look over the other side of the next hill. Then too, one must remember how complete and steady men's convictions were in Victorian times. The doubts and uncertainties that have overtaken life in the twentieth century through two world wars and a plethora of political and scientific inventions were unthinkable then. Livingstone's faith in God was absolute, and since he felt instinctively that his true approach to God was in Africa, it seems possible that he went to meet his death there rather more gladly, more spiritually content, than he would have done in any other place.

And so we can hardly think that he was serious when he said in 1865 that he did not really wish to return to Africa and would have preferred to remain on at home. Even if Murchison had not asked him to make one more effort to clear up the question of the Nile, even if the slave-trade had not existed, his twenty-two years in Africa must have drawn him back. There was so much work there still to be done. Through the years of his great journeys Livingstone had developed more and more from the medical missionary into the explorer. He had come to believe that his real work in Africa was not so much in the saving of individual human souls as in the suppression of the slave-trade and in the opening up of the country so that Christianity and civilization could follow in his wake.

In 1865 there were no really urgent duties to hold him in Britain; he had no home or parish there, he had left the London Missionary Society (though he remained on the best of terms with it), and his wife had died three years before in Africa. Robert, his eldest son, was also dead; he had been impressed at Boston into the Northern forces in the American Civil War and had succumbed to wounds at the age of 18 in a prisoners' camp at Salisbury, North Carolina. As for the other children, they were being well cared for by their trustees in England.

Livingstone's books had made him the most famous of all African explorers, but he cared nothing for fame or the life of a public personality in England. His royalties had brought him in enough money to be as independent as he wished to be on his own spartan scale of living; and now there was this stimulating invitation from the Royal Geographical Society which would allow him to travel in the best of circumstances and to carry on with the work to which he had given his life; to strike one more blow against slavery and to resolve finally the great enigma of the lake and river system in the centre of the continent.

Like Burton before him Livingstone was coming round to the view that the true solution of the Nile had already been propounded by Herodotus and the ancient geographers, if not by the Old Testament itself. He was fascinated by Herodotus's description of the Nile springing from fountains of bottomless depth at the foot of high mountains somewhere in the centre of Africa. In reality this last journey of Livingstone's was a half-mystical attempt to re-discover those fountains, to find a unity with the past, a divine pattern in the geography of the river. This was to be the final achievement of his life. Of course he had to go.

Physically he appears to have been strong enough to undertake the journey. His health had not been seriously impaired by his previous work in Africa, and in any case he had been rested by a year in England. His shoulder, which had been crushed by a lion some twenty years before and had never properly set, still troubled him from time to time, but this was not a grave impediment. It may be worth while here, however, to recount in Livingstone's own words the circumstances of this accident, since it was of so much importance at the end of his life:

'. . . I heard a shout. Starting, and looking half round, I saw the lion just in the act of springing upon me. I was upon a little height; he caught my shoulder as he sprang, and we both came to the ground below together. Growling horribly close to my ear, he shook me as a terrier does a rat. The shock produced a stupor similar to that which seems to be felt by a mouse after the first shake of the cat. It caused a sort of dreaminess in which there was no sense of pain nor feeling of terror, though quite conscious of all that was happening. It was like what patients partially under the influence of chloroform describe, who see all the operation, but feel not the knife. This singular condition was not the result of any mental process. The shake annihilated fear, and allowed no sense of horror in looking round at the beast. This peculiar state is probably produced in all animals killed by the carnivora; and if so, is a merciful provision by our benevolent creator for lessening the pain of death.'

The words have almost a valedictory sound.

But in 1865 there was no such shadow over the years ahead. All was confidence and hope in the new journey that was about to start. Everyone wished him well. Murchison had written: 'As to *your future* I am anxious to know what *your own wish* is as respects a renewal of African exploration . . .' Did he wish to proceed by way of the Rovuma River and round the south end of Lake Tanganyika and perhaps reach the sources of the White Nile? Such a journey would enable him to settle 'all the great disputes now pending'. But there was no obligation for Livingstone to go; another man could be found to lead the expedition, perhaps John Kirk who had been with him on the Zambezi?

Livingstone replied that he himself had been contemplating a new expedition of the very kind that Murchison suggested. '. . . If I can get a few hearty companions,' he wrote, 'I shall enjoy myself, and feel that I am doing my duty.'

He invited Kirk to accompany him but Kirk was about to marry, and no doubt he felt that for the moment he had had enough of Livingstone's formidable campaigning. Livingstone bore him no grudge at all, and instead busied himself in getting Kirk the desirable post of Surgeon and Vice-Consul at the British Agency at Zanzibar. And so it was resolved that Livingstone should go alone.

The Foreign Office came forward with the not overwhelmingly generous gift of £500 for the expedition (though later they provided an additional £1,000), the Society produced another £500, and Livingstone and his friends found the rest. The explorer was appointed 'Consul for Central Africa' without salary, and in August 1865 he sailed from Folkestone. He travelled via Paris (where he dropped off his daughter Agnes at school), Cairo and Bombay, and at the end of January 1866 he arrived at Zanzibar.

Not a great deal had happened in Zanzibar since Burton's time. The Sultan, Seyyid Majid bin Said, had survived a revolt led by his brother Barghash and the island was being gradually drawn into the network of Western commerce and politics. Now there were half a dozen foreign consulates on the seafront, and many of the Arab and Indian merchants were growing rich. It was no longer a great event when the town drum was beaten to announce the approach of an ocean-going ship (one beat for a ship from the north and two for a ship from the south); the island was constantly visited by merchantmen and men-of-war from almost all the European powers. The traffic in slaves had grown if anything still heavier; it was now estimated that between 80,000 and 100,000 were brought down from the interior every year, and although none were supposed to go beyond the Sultan's dominions there was no real check on the dhows that sailed back to Arabia and the East in June when the south-west monsoon began to blow.

'It is the old, old way of living,' Livingstone wrote, 'eating, drinking, sleeping; sleeping, drinking, eating, slave-dhows coming and slave-dhows going away; bad smells . . . it might be called Stinkibar rather than Zanzibar. . . . On visiting the slave market I found about 300 slaves exposed for sale. . . . All who have grown up seem ashamed at being hawked about for sale. The teeth are examined, the cloth lifted to examine the lower limbs, and a stick thrown for a slave to bring, and thus exhibit his paces. Some are dragged through the crowd by hand, and the price called out incessantly; most of the purchasers were Northern Arabs and Persians.'

However the Sultan, upon whom Livingstone called, was both amiable and helpful: he gave him a *firman* to the sheikhs in the interior and loaned him a large square house that still stands on the sea wall on the outskirts of the town. It was conveniently placed for dropping stores directly down into boats in the harbour below. Kirk had also arrived to take up his new job at the Agency, and was very ready to assist in organizing the expedition.

There was a complex relationship between these two. Although Kirk was so much younger than Livingstone their backgrounds were very similar; Kirk too had come from a religious household in Scotland, he too had taken his degree in medicine and had come abroad to satisfy a craving for adventure, at first in the Crimea and then in Africa. Livingstone had taken him on the Zambezi expedition in 1858 as physician and naturalist and they had established the kind of intimacy that can develop only through a long series of shared experiences on a dangerous journey. There had been differences of course. Kirk had been too close to Livingstone to hero-worship him blindly. He had written to a friend, 'He [Livingstone] must have saved a good deal of money, not that I think that he sets much value on that. He would give all for a C.B. or better a K.C.B., and there will be a push made in some quarters to get it him.' This was unfriendly and yet it was probably true (even though Livingstone in the end never received any honour from the government); and there were other failings – Livingstone's whitewashing of his own brother's far from heroic behaviour on the Zambezi, for example, about which Kirk had written home very tartly at the time.

But all this was over and done with, and in any case there was no doubt whatever that Kirk's fundamental loyalty to his old leader was quite unshakable. So now they were together again for a few weeks in Zanzibar while Livingstone was assembling his caravan, and it was arranged that Kirk should act as the expedition's representative in the island; at a later stage he was to send on porters and supplies to await Livingstone's arrival at Ujiji on Lake Tanganyika.

John Kirk.

This was a modest expedition compared with the usual thing, but Livingstone thought it lavish; he had brought a number of sepoys with him from Bombay and he now recruited others in Zanzibar, including three boys who had marched with Speke and Grant, bringing the total number in the caravan to sixty. In addition there was a small train of camels, buffaloes, mules and donkeys which were to serve as baggage animals.

Livingstone's plan was to keep well south of the usual caravan routes and to strike directly inland towards the unexplored country south of Lake Tanganyika; and with that object in view he landed in March 1866 at the mouth of the Rovuma River, which now divides Tanganyika from Portuguese East Africa. There then began that incredible series of wanderings which were to continue for seven years and to end in a failure which was also the triumph of a man's unconquerable mind.

Dhow used for transport of Dr Livingstone's camels. 'Dr Livingstone, though no artist, had acquired a practice of making rude sketches of scenes and objects which have furnished material for the engravers.'

Never can there have been a journey which was founded upon so many mis-assumptions as this one. It was a search for the source of a river in a region where it did not exist; it was an anti-slavery expedition that had no power whatever to put down slavery; it was the march of a man who believed that he alone, unarmed and unsupported, could pass through Africa, and that was almost impossible. But none of this made any difference. Through a series of paradoxes all comes right in the end; the march goes on – but only because the Arab slavers take care of the sick and lonely man in the wilderness. Slavery is dealt a blow from which it never recovers – not because Livingstone was able to raise a hand against it, but because he was the helpless witness of a massacre. Even the mystery of the Nile is resolved – not by

Livingstone himself but because he inspired another man to go off in another direction. And to Livingstone no doubt all this was as it should have been: it was the will of God.

It is astonishing that he did not die much sooner. Quite early in his march he lost nearly all his men and animals, and, what was just as disastrous, he lost his medicine chest as well. At the end of a year he struggled up to the southern end of Lake Tanganyika, where the Arab slavers took care of him, though at the same time they made it almost impossible for him to go on; here, as in the Sudan, they had aroused bitter

Chitapanga receiving Dr Livingstone. 'We passed on to an enormous hut, where sat Chitapanga, with three drummers and ten or more men, with two rattles in their hands. I declined to sit on the ground, and an enormous tusk was brought for me. The chief saluted courteously. He has a fat, jolly face, and legs loaded with brass and copper leglets.' (Livingstone)

hatred among the tribes, and porters were unobtainable. Yet he did manage to go on, striking out west to the Lualaba River, then south to Lake Bangweolo which no white man had ever seen before, then north again to Lake Tanganyika. In March 1869, three years after leaving the coast, he arrived at Ujiji, almost toothless and half dead with malaria and other illnesses, 'a ruckle of bones', only to find that the stores that Kirk had sent had been looted on the route up-country and hardly anything of use remained. There was no quinine and, what was almost worse, no mail. The absence of news from the outside world seems to have afflicted the explorers almost more than any other hardship. In the hope of finding mail at some outlandish spot they would rouse themselves from their illnesses and march on for weeks or even months on end; and here the deprivation was even worse since the Arab traders refused to carry Livingstone's own letters down to the coast. He had written forty-two of them, and the Arabs knew all too well that the package contained a full account of the atrocities they were committing in the interior.

So then there was nothing to be done but go on again without medicine and without supplies. Once more he headed west for the Lualaba, for he had begun to believe that it was the Nile. Now the Lualaba is nothing to do with the Nile; it is, in fact, the upper Congo River that flows north in a great westward-bending arc to the Atlantic Ocean – but Livingstone had no means of discovering this. His outward journey came to a fearful halt one morning at Nyangwe when he saw the Arab traders there open up with their rifles at point-blank range on the natives in the village.

Livingstone had enjoyed this place; he liked to watch the people coming into market, sometimes as many as three thousand of them, to barter their chickens and fruit, and the broad river flowing by into the jungle. His description of what happened on the morning of July 15, 1871, reveals, as no other incident ever has, the depths of the tragedy that occurred to the Central African negroes when the outside world burst in upon them hardly as much as three generations ago. The Dugumbe referred to was one of the better established and therefore more restrained traders – but a slaver nonetheless – and Tagamoio who appears in the last paragraph more nearly represents the Arabs and their terrorist methods in Central Africa at the time.

'It was,' Livingstone says, 'a hot, sultry day, and when I went into the market I saw Adie and Manilla, and three of the men who had lately come with Dugumbe. I was surprised to see the three with their guns, and felt inclined to reprove them, as one of my men did, for bringing weapons into the market, but I attributed it to their ignorance, and, it being very hot, I was walking away to go out of the market, when I saw one of the fellows haggling about a fowl, and seizing hold of it. Before I got thirty yards out, the discharge of two guns in the middle of the crowd told me that slaughter had begun; the crowds dashed off from the place, and threw down their wares in confusion, and ran. At the same time that the three opened fire on the mass of people near the upper end of the market-place volleys were discharged from a party down near the creek on the panic-stricken women, who dashed at the canoes. These, some fifty or more, were jammed in the creek and the men forgot their paddles in the terror that seized all. The canoes were not to be got out, for the creek was too small for so many: men and women, wounded by balls, poured into them, and leaped and scrambled into the water shrieking. A long line of heads in the river showed that great numbers struck out for an island a full mile off: in going towards it they had to put the left shoulder to a current of about two miles an hour: if they had struck away diagonally to the opposite bank, the current would have aided them, and, though nearly three miles off, some would have gained land: as it was, the heads above water showed the long lines of those that would inevitably perish.

'Shot after shot continued to be fired on the helpless and perishing. Some of the long line of heads disappeared quietly: whilst other poor creatures threw their arms high, as if appealing to the great Father above, and sank.

'By-and-by all the heads disappeared; some had turned downstream towards the bank, and escaped. Dugumbe put people into one of the deserted vessels to save those in the water and saved twenty-one, but one woman refused to be taken on board from thinking that she was to be made a slave of; she preferred the chance of life by swimming, to the lot of a slave; the Bagenya women are expert in the water, as they are accustomed to dive for oysters, and those who went downstream may have escaped, but the Arabs themselves estimated the loss of life at between 330 and 400 souls. The shooting-party near the canoe were so reckless, they killed two of their own people; and a Banyamwezi follower, who got into a deserted canoe to plunder, fell into the water, went down, then came up again, and down to rise no more.

'My impulse was to pistol the murderers, but Dugumbe protested against my getting into a blood-feud, and I was thankful afterwards that I took his advice. Two wretched Moslems asserted "that the firing was done by the people of the English"; I asked one of them why he lied so, and he could utter no excuse: no other falsehood came to his aid as he stood abashed before me, and so telling him not to tell palpable falsehoods, I left him gaping.

'After the horrible affair in the water, the party of Tagamoio, who was the chief perpetrator, continued to fire on the people there and fire their villages. As I write I hear the loud wails on the left bank over those who are slain, ignorant of their many friends who are now in the depths of the Lualaba. Oh, let Thy kingdom come! No one will ever know the exact loss on this bright sultry summer morning. It gave me the impression of being in Hell.'

After this there was no hope of obtaining boats or men to follow the course of the river.

Sickened by what he had seen and now seriously broken in health Livingstone struggled back to Ujiji unable for the moment to accomplish any more. He had read the Bible four times on this second journey to the Lualaba. Now on his return after an absence of two years, he was practically reduced to begging from the Arabs in order to keep alive: and thus it was that Stanley found him when he came marching into Ujiji on November 10, 1871.

'. . . When my spirits were at their lowest ebb,' Livingstone wrote, 'the good Samaritan was close at hand, for one morning Susi came running at the top of his speed and gasped out, "An Englishman! I see him!" and off he darted to meet him. The American flag at the head of the caravan told of the nationality of the stranger. Bales of goods, baths of tin, huge kettles, cooking-pots, tents, etc., made me think, "This must be a luxurious traveller, and not one at his wits' end like me."'

Stanley's famous description of the meeting is more lively:

'Selim said to me, "I see the Doctor, sir. Oh, what an old man! He has got a white beard!" And I – what would I not have given for a bit of friendly wilderness, where, unseen, I might vent my joy in some mad freak, such as idiotically biting my hand, turning a somersault, or slashing at trees, in order to allay those exciting feelings that were well-nigh uncontrollable. My heart beats fast, but I must not let my face betray my emotions, lest it shall detract from the dignity of a white man appearing under such extraordinary circumstances.

OVERLEAF *'Dr Livingstone, I presume?'* *Florence Nightingale described* How I Found Livingstone *as the worst possible book on the best possible subject.*

'So I did that which I thought was most dignified. I pushed back the crowds, and, passing from the rear, walked down a living avenue of people, until I came in front of the semicircle of Arabs, before which stood "the white man with the grey beard". As I advanced slowly towards him I noticed he was pale, looked wearied, had grey whiskers and moustache, wore a bluish cap with a faded gold band around it, had on a red-sleeved waistcoat, and a pair of grey tweed trousers. I would have run to him, only I was a coward in the presence of such a mob – would have embraced him, but that I did not know how he would receive me. So I did what moral cowardice and false pride suggested was the best thing – walked deliberately up to him, took off my hat, and said, "Dr Livingstone, I presume?" "Yes," he said, with a kind smile, lifting his cap slightly.

'I replaced my hat on my head, and he replaced his cap, and we both grasped hands, and then I said aloud: "I thank God, Doctor, I have been permitted to see you."

'He answered, "I feel thankful that I am here to welcome you." '

This then is the story of an incident which has been more frequently recalled than any other single event in African exploration. And yet a strange air of unreality remains. One is bound to wonder why it should have taken so long for help to arrive. For nearly five years now Livingstone's whereabouts had been a perennial mystery. At one time, as far back as 1868, he had been thought dead: the porters who had deserted him announced on their return to the coast that he had been killed on the shores of Lake Nyasa (which was a convenient way of explaining their desertion), and Murchison had published this news in a letter to *The Times*. But Murchison himself had not entirely believed it, and the Royal Geographical Society had sent out an expedition to discover the truth. This expedition had scarcely got under way when word reached the coast that the explorer was still alive, and soon afterwards letters were received in Zanzibar from Livingstone himself. Upon this the expedition had turned back. Thereafter a strange apathy about the explorer appears to have overtaken both officials and public alike.

From time to time vague inquiries are made, Kirk sends up his supplies from Zanzibar but without any real assurance they will ever reach their destination; Baker keeps a general lookout from Bunyoro far away in the north; and in the Royal Geographical Society in London there are speculative discussions as to just what direction the explorer might have taken in the last twelve months or so. But for a long time no one actually makes a move to go to the assistance of the lost man. Burton, no great admirer of missionaries, affected a sardonic indifference. He wrote to a friend, when at last the hunt for Livingstone began, 'rather *infra dig.* to discover a mish'. In the twentieth century, of course, radio and aircraft have entirely altered the nature of exploration, and it requires a slight effort to remember that only fifty years ago it was nothing unusual for a ship at sea or a traveller in a distant land to be lost sight of for many months at a time; but even so it is strange that Livingstone's silence was received with so much complacency. And stranger still that it was a man like Stanley who should have come to the rescue. Even Stanley had not precisely hurried to Ujiji. Long before – actually in 1869 – his employer James Gordon Bennett

Two plaques marking Livingstone's parting from Stanley on March 14, 1872, and the site of Livingstone's home after his meeting with Stanley until August 25, 1872, on which date he set off on what was to be his last journey.

of the *New York Herald* had summoned him to an interview at the Grand Hotel in Paris and had said: 'I want you to attend the opening of the Suez Canal and then proceed up the Nile. Send us detailed descriptions of everything likely to interest American tourists. Then go to Jerusalem, Constantinople, the Crimea, the Caspian Sea, through Persia as far as India. After that you can start looking round for Livingstone. If he is dead bring back every possible proof of his death.'

Stanley, the most assiduous foreign correspondent who ever lived, had accomplished this programme in fourteen months. Having attended the Canal opening he had gone up the Nile and interviewed Baker's engineer, Higginbotham; he had inspected the battlefields of the Crimea and visited Persepolis in Persia, where he carved his name on the ruins; he had described the awful poverty of India and now he had arrived at Ujiji.

And who was Stanley? He was full of surprises. He was a man whose real name was not Stanley at all, but Rowlands, a Welshman who was an American, a soldier who was a sailor, and now a journalist who was leading a successful expedition into the centre of Africa. Soon the world was to know all about his picaresque background: the awful Dickensian childhood in a workhouse in Wales, his arrival as a cabin-boy at New Orleans where he took the name and nationality of a kindly American who adopted him as a son, his soldiering in the Civil War, at first for the South and then for the North, his rejection by his squalid mother on his return to England, his adventures in the American navy and in General Hancock's campaign against the Red Indians, and latterly as a journalist in the British campaign against the Emperor in Abyssinia. This was the career of a man of iron, an adventurer who was every bit as hard and ruthless as the world in which he had lived. Professor Coupland remarks pungently: 'No other famous man of his time got so high from a start so low. No one who can understand him forgets that. He never forgot it himself.'

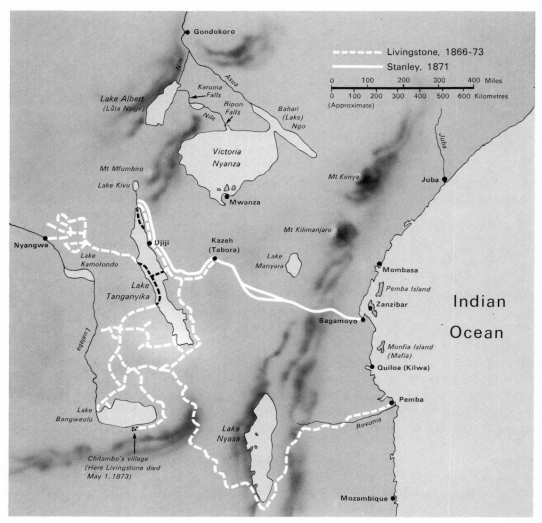

*Map based on contemporary information showing the route taken by Livingstone, 1866–73, and the route
taken by Stanley, 1871.*

At Ujiji he was only thirty years of age and still on the threshold of his success; it
was the hardness, the quickness and the egocentricity in him that were uppermost.
He most distinctly lacked *baraka*. In all the world no two men could have differed so
much from one another as Livingstone and Stanley, nor could there have been two
men, who, for the moment, were so beholden to one another. Livingstone needed
medicine, supplies and news of the outside world, and his young visitor had them all.
Stanley needed fame – the 'kudos' (it was a word he was fond of using) of having found
this celebrated man, and in fact he received a great deal more. His brief companionship with Livingstone was, Professor Coupland says, 'the supreme experience of his

life. He had come close to moral greatness, and he was startled, captivated, subjected by it.'

At the outset of his journey Livingstone had been for Stanley another 'assignment', another 'story', which, if successfully reported, would help him on with his journalistic career. At Zanzibar he had behaved very much as a newspaperman in search of a scoop. He had scented at once the opposition of the African professionals amongst the European officials, especially in the English colony, which he regarded as stiff and effete, and especially Kirk. When Stanley asked casually one day if Livingstone would receive him should he chance to cross the explorer's path in the interior, Kirk answered briefly that he thought Livingstone would not like it at all; he had an aversion to publicity. This little exchange possibly explains Stanley's cautiousness with Livingstone when he first arrived at Ujiji. But at Zanzibar he had not been deterred by it in the least, and he had gone about his plans very methodically. He had engaged Bombay as his factotum, and since he had plenty of money to spend he had bought the best of stores and had hired the best of porters at the highest rates. His eight months' march from the coast to Ujiji was no bad achievement at all, considering that he had gone down with malaria on the way, had encountered a war between the Arab dealers and the African tribes at Tabora and had actually taken part in the fighting himself. Two white assistants he had engaged, Farquhar and Shaw, had both died. And now at the journey's end there was this comforting reception from Livingstone, this revelation of a charitable and fascinating mind. During the long conversation that now began between the two men Stanley stored up every grain of wisdom and information that Livingstone let fall, and while Livingstone's health rapidly improved, the two fell into a leader-and-follower relationship which was very agreeable to them both. Soon it seemed an excellent plan that they should make a journey together, and what better than to go up to the head of Lake Tanganyika and settle the question of the Rusizi River? They were away three weeks on this trip, and when Livingstone discovered that Burton was wrong – the Rusizi flowed into and not out of the lake – he returned more strongly than ever to his theory that the Lualaba was the Nile. To go back to the Lualaba, however, meant that he had to have further stores and porters, and these, he believed, could be obtained only in Tabora, some 300 miles away. The two men walked there from Ujiji at the end of 1871.

At Tabora few stores and no porters were to be found and Stanley promised to make good the deficiency himself. It never seems to have occurred to Livingstone for an instant that he might return to Zanzibar and civilization – he said he would not come until his work was finished – and at the end of a month Stanley set off for the coast alone. He left behind all he could spare from his own supplies, and it was arranged that Livingstone should stay on in Tabora until Stanley could get a gang of porters up to him from the coast. In the remarkably quick time of 54 days Stanley reached Zanzibar carrying with him more treasure than any slave and ivory trader had ever yet been able to get out of Africa: all Livingstone's journals, his own notes, which shortly were to blossom forth in his dispatches to the *New York Herald* and his first African book, *How I Found Livingstone*, and in addition to all this, a letter which

Livingstone had specially written for his paper. It was in this letter that Livingstone wrote *à propos* the massacre at Nyangwe: 'If my disclosures regarding the terrible Ujijian slavery should lead to the suppression of the East Coast slave-trade, I shall regard that as a greater matter by far than the discovery of all the Nile sources together.' In this at least he was to have his wish.

Stanley had been just in time. On his way down to Bagamoyo he met a new expedition which the Royal Geographical Society had at last sent out from England to find news of the lost man, and he was able to assure them that their help was no longer needed: and so it was Stanley who, in May 1872, caused a sensation throughout the world with his description of the Ujiji meeting and of all that had since followed. He went on to a tremendous reception in England – a letter and diamond-studded snuff-box from the Queen, a medal from the Royal Geographical Society, and a round of banquets and public meetings. On the surface all this was very gratifying, but it was soon evident that the British were anything but pleased with Stanley's exploit. They did not like the idea of their greatest explorer being rescued by what was regarded as a journalistic stunt, they did not like the fact that Stanley was an American citizen, and they did not much care for Stanley himself. This, at any rate, was Stanley's appreciation of the situation, and he bitterly resented it. Indeed, he had genuine grounds for complaint here – some of the rival newspapers were even referring to his journey as a hoax – and no doubt the criticism would have died down had he not, unwisely and unnecessarily, attacked Kirk. He declared that Kirk had 'let Livingstone down' by not bestirring himself more in sending up reinforcements from the coast as he had promised to do; Kirk, as an official, could not reply, but he had friends who were very ready to defend him against this journalistic outsider; and if Kirk never entirely cleared his name in this matter, Stanley also was much harmed. Kirk's own reactions in Zanzibar were indignant, but private. He wrote to his friends giving the facts as he saw them, and he said to Oswell Livingstone who had come out on a Royal Geographical Society expedition: 'Stanley will make his fortune out of your father.' When Livingstone came to hear of this he made the comment, 'He [Stanley] is heartily welcome, for it is a great deal more than I could ever make out of myself.' At the same time he wrote to Kirk and soon the misunderstanding between them was explained and privately, if not publicly, forgotten.

Livingstone meanwhile was filling out the lonely months in Tabora. He was not short of stores; with the addition of those that Stanley had left him he had enough to carry on for four years. But now only Susi and Chuma and one or two other boys who had followed him from the beginning remained in his service, and they were quite inadequate for the porterage of a long journey. Thus he had to wait until the men Stanley had promised him came up from the coast. He waited five months in all, and in that time hardly an echo reached him of the acclaim that was gathering round his name in the outside world. He held his small Bible classes under the mango trees, he read Baker's *Albert N'yanza*, he prayed, he went for walks, he wrote his journal, he thought, he waited. The *tembe* in which he lived was a lonely spot, somewhat on the outskirts of the Arab settlement, and even now there is a feeling of solitude and

H. M. Stanley, by R. Gibb, 1885.

claustrophobia about the place. It was the usual sort of Arab trader's house, a flat earthen roof that was never absolutely proof against the rain, a 'reception room', a room for sleeping and eating, an inner courtyard where the cattle and other livestock were herded at night, and quarters for the Africans. The floors were of earth tramped down by the bare feet of the household servants passing in and out.

These were the last remotely civilized surroundings that Livingstone was to know. He was now 59, and though he had rallied somewhat in Stanley's company his health was undermined beyond all real hope of recovery. Yet if he felt that he was nearing death there is little in his journals to show it: he was filled with hope about his theory of the Nile and perhaps by now in his loneliness the river had begun to assume for him a religious significance. However shaken he was by fever – and there must have been days when he was delirious and unable to move from his bed – there was at least no weakening in the extraordinary steadiness of his mind. The notes and letters he sent down to the coast from time to time were written in a firm and flowing hand. Often they dealt with very practical details. If, he writes, a chronometer can be lent him by the Navy without detriment to the service it will be of very signal benefit to his exploration. He signs himself, 'David Livingstone, H.M. Consul, Inner Africa'.

At the same time he kept dreaming of the day when he would return home: he wrote to a friend asking him to look out for rooms on Regent's Park in London which he could share with his daughter Agnes.

In August 1872 the fifty-seven porters sent by Stanley finally arrived, and within a few days Livingstone led his caravan out into the bush. He was very clear about his direction, for by now he had made up his mind that the source of the Nile would prove to be a stream running into Lake Bangweolo, which he had discovered four years before; and so he marched slightly south of west, and, having reached the shores of Lake Tanganyika about its centre, he turned directly south. By the end of April 1873, eight months after leaving Tabora, he was working round the south of Lake Bangweolo, still hoping to come on some feeder stream which would flow on through the lake into the Lualaba and perhaps join Baker's Albert Nyanza far away to the north in Uganda. He had some uneasy doubts that just possibly the Lualaba might turn out to be the Congo and not the Nile; but he hated that idea and turned away from it. He had fixed his heart upon the Nile.

It was dreadful country. The little column waded about through an interminable swamp and close to the village of a chieftain named Chitambo Livingstone became so weak he had to be carried in a litter. In the early hours of May 1, 1873, his boys came into his hut and found him dead. He was kneeling across his bed in prayer.

However often the story is told of Susi's and Chuma's journey to the coast with Livingstone's body it remains incredible, and perhaps it was a miracle of a kind, since such devotion among primitive and uneducated men can hardly have been inspired by any ordinary emotion. They cut out the heart and viscera, and dried the body in the sun for a fortnight. It was then wrapped in calico and placed in a cylinder of bark taken from a tree, and this in turn was sewn into a sheet of sailcloth and lashed to a pole so that it could be carried by two men. In the middle of May, Susi, Chuma

Livingstone's house at Zanzibar. 'The Sultan had a toothache and gumboil, and could not receive us; he however placed one of his houses at my disposal.' (Livingstone)

LEFT *Livingstone's own* Last Journals *were 'continued by a narrative of his last moments and sufferings obtained from his faithful servants, Chuma and Susi'.*

and sixty odd men who had remained faithful to the end, set out for Zanzibar. Well over a thousand miles divided them from the Indian Ocean, and it was not really feasible that such a strange burden could be carried over that distance in the heart of Africa where so many tribes were out to despoil every wayfarer who came by. Nevertheless the journey was accomplished in eleven months. During that time two more expeditions set out from England in search of Livingstone, one of them intending to strike inland from the west coast of Africa, and the other from the east coast. Susi and Chuma met the east coast party led by the naval officer, Lovett Cameron, when they reached Tabora in October 1873. Cameron then continued on to Ujiji (where he salvaged a quantity of Livingstone's papers) and eventually emerged on the Atlantic

Evening Ilala, April 29, 1873. 'It would seem that his strength was here at its very lowest ebb. So great were the pangs of his disease during this day that he could make no attempt to stand. Still wending their way on, it seemed as if they would not complete their task, for again at a clearing the sick man entreated them to place him on the ground, and to let him stay where he was.' (Horace Waller)

coast two years later. Susi and Chuma meanwhile went on to the Indian Ocean, and when they walked into Bagamoyo on February 15, 1874, H.M.S. *Vulture* was waiting to take the body across to Zanzibar. Here for a time it was placed in Hamerton's old house on the seafront, which was still the British Consulate, awaiting trans-shipment to England. There could be no doubt about the dead man's identity; when a surgeon came to open the improvised coffin the mark of the old lion wound on the shoulder was plainly visible.

A special train was sent to Southampton to take Livingstone on his last journey to

Westminster Abbey on April 18, 1874, and on that day England went into mourning.

In London the body had remained overnight in the Map Room of the Royal Geographical Society in Savile Row, and when the cortège set out in the morning the streets were lined with silent crowds. Admission to the Abbey could be obtained only by ticket and the building was crammed. Stanley, Grant and Kirk were among the pallbearers who carried the body to the grave.

Today if one enters the Abbey by the main door and continues down the nave one comes first upon the tomb of the Unknown Soldier and then, a little beyond it, Livingstone's grave, with its epitaph inscribed in brass lettering on the grey stone. It reads, 'Brought by faithful hands over land and sea here rests David Livingstone, missionary, traveller, philanthropist, born March 19, 1813 at Blantyre, Lanarkshire, died May 1, 1873 at Chitambo's village, Ulala.

'For 30 years his life was spent in an unwearied effort to evangelize the native races, to explore the undiscovered secrets, to abolish the desolating slave trade, of Central Africa, where with his last words he wrote: "All I can add in my solitude is may Heaven's rich blessing come down on everyone, American, English or Turk, who will help to heal this open sore of the world."'

Even before he wrote those words Livingstone's great power over men's minds had reached out from Central Africa. The sources of the Nile eluded him at the end, but his description of the massacre at Nyangwe had raised a storm of indignation which had forced the Sultan of Zanzibar to close the slave market on the island forever.

Statue of Livingstone at the Victoria Falls.

7

Le Briseur d'Obstacles

———

A curious combination of hatred and love drew the explorers back to Africa. They were like men who make a life at sea; having once committed themselves to its hazards they feel impelled to go back again and again even if Africa kills them. At one time or another most of them rail against the country and its inhabitants, declaring them to be ugly, brutal, scheming, debauched and finally hopeless. It is extraordinary in the accounts of their journeys how seldom they are touched by the beauty or the grandeur of the landscape, the tremendous plains of the central plateau with the blue mountains in the distance and the herds of wild animals roaming there; to the explorers it is all basically hostile, incomplete, not to be regarded with an aesthetic eye until it is reformed and reduced to order by civilization and Christianity.

Dr Schweinfurth, one of the calmest and most self-sufficient of explorers on the Upper Nile, remarks, 'The first sight of a throng of savages, suddenly presenting themselves in their naked nudity, is one from which no amount of familiarity can remove the strange impression; it takes abiding hold upon the memory, and makes the traveller recall anew the civilization he has left behind.'

Recoiling from the savagery of Africa, Schweinfurth returned to Europe. But he found he could not remain there; within a year or two Africa called him back. It was the same with all the others, whether they were missionaries like Livingstone, scholars like Burton, soldiers and collectors like Speke, or sportsmen like Baker.

All of them in their books claim that they are in Africa because they have a mission there; they want to resolve the geographical problems and they want to reform the country, to convert the untilled land into useful farms, to open up commerce and to lift the natives out of their animism and savagery into a higher way of life. And yet one cannot help feeling that there is still another reason for their journeys: a fundamental restlessness, a simple absorbing curiosity in everything that is strange and new. To satisfy that curiosity they are prepared to put up with anything, even the prospect of death itself.

Now Stanley does not fit into this scheme of things at all easily. He is a new kind of man in Africa, a modern man who at the same time has many attributes of a *condottiere* in Renaissance Italy. You might call him a businessman-explorer, not in the sense of his wanting to trade in Africa, but in the extremely logical, sensible and efficient way in which he went about the problem of setting up an expedition and getting it to the journey's end. It may have been ruthless but it was also expert, and one must never lose sight of the fact that he was very determined and very brave.

H. M. Stanley, Briseur d'Obstacles.

Perhaps he resembles Speke more than any of the others, but not even Speke was as concentrated as Stanley was. Stanley was not in Africa to reform the people nor to build an empire, and he was not impelled by any real interest in such matters as anthropology, botany or geology. To put it bluntly, he was out to make a name for himself, and it must be judged as the supreme irony of African exploration that in the end he should turn out to be the greatest empire-builder and explorer of them all. He was even able to open up the field for the missionaries and the scientists rather more effectively than anyone who had gone before. A recent study of the explorer by Jean-Jacques Laufer has been well entitled *Stanley, Briseur d'Obstacles*.

Naturally this brusque and philistine irruption into Africa was not very endearing to an educated public in England who had been following the exploits of its own favourite explorers for years past; here was a man, it was felt, who would take on any adventure for the sake of publicity and under any patronage, an interloper who had changed his nationality once and might do so again (as in point of fact Stanley did; he reverted later to his British citizenship).

But then Stanley was a man who attracted prejudice almost as strongly as Livingstone attracted love. His only course was to baffle his enemies with his achievements and this he resolutely proceeded to do. Fortunately he had no need of friends to put his case for him. He was the most readable of authors; his books have a pace and an excitement which not even the purple passages and the occasional pomposities can subdue, and the facts he had to give were incontrovertible facts based upon his own close and hard-won observation.

So now in 1874 he set about the arrangements for a new journey, which in many ways was his greatest, with a dispatch and far-sightedness that even Baker could hardly have equalled. He set himself three objectives: he planned to circumnavigate Lake Victoria and thus establish whether or not it was one great lake and whether or not the stream pouring out at Ripon Falls was its only outlet. Next he proposed to put Burton's theories to the ultimate test by sailing around Lake Tanganyika in the same way. Finally he planned to take up Livingstone's unfinished work on the Lualaba: he was resolved to get a boat on the river and follow it downstream wherever it led until he reached the mouth. In short, he was going to make a last settlement, not only of the Nile, but of the whole pattern of lakes and rivers in Central Africa.

As a first step towards this extraordinarily bold design he managed to get the *New York Herald* to combine with the London *Daily Telegraph* in financing him (a thing which they did handsomely) and then in England he settled down to reading every scrap of information about East and Central Africa he could find; he purchased, he says, 130 books. The companions he chose to take with him on the journey were distinctly unusual, in fact they were not companions at all, but rather hired assistants who came from working-class families and who knew nothing whatever about Africa. There were two young sons of a Kentish fisherman, Francis John Pocock and Edward Pocock, and a clerk named Frederick Barker who had happened to catch Stanley's eye at the Langham Hotel in London. All three were much younger than

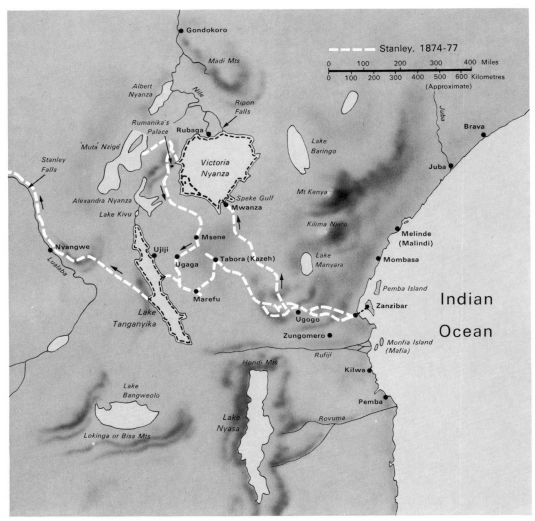

Map based on contemporary information showing the route taken by Stanley 1874–77.

Stanley and were chosen, one fancies, for their toughness and sense of discipline – the sort of qualities that make a good sergeant in the army. None of them was in the least likely to come home and write books about his adventures or to dispute Stanley's views in the Royal Geographical Society. When five dogs had been purchased the little party was complete and it sailed for East Africa in August 1874.

The expedition that set out from Zanzibar early in the following November was the largest and best equipped explorer's caravan that had ever been seen in East Africa. They had with them a forty-foot wooden boat, the *Lady Alice*, which had been built in sections for porterage, eight tons of stores and 356 men. It was an unwieldy procession that stretched out for half a mile along the forest paths and by the time Stanley got it on to the shores of Lake Victoria three and a half months later, Edward Pocock was dead of typhus and a hundred men had been lost through desertion, sickness and skirmishes with the local tribes. Such was to be the pattern of all Stanley's marches: the quick advance, the shooting down of any African tribes that opposed him, the heavy loss of life among his own men and the final attainment of the objective. For anyone to accompany Stanley on an expedition in Africa was rather like being in the *corps d'élite* of a successful general – you triumphed and you died. Anything less like Livingstone's journeys cannot be imagined.

They reached the south shore of Lake Victoria at a little Arab village slightly to the west of Mwanza where Speke sixteen years before had first seen the great stretch of water and had indulged in his guess that it was the source of the Nile. Stanley was not a guesser. He was here to find facts and he at once assembled the *Lady Alice* on the shore. Leaving the two surviving Englishmen and the bulk of his expedition behind him, he set sail with a picked band of eleven Africans on March 8, 1875. They

The Lady Alice *with its eleven Africans.*

travelled up the eastern shore, and in three weeks' hard sailing and paddling arrived at Speke's Ripon Falls. Presently a dignitary in a red robe came forward to meet them with gifts of bullocks and other presents; and on April 5, 1875, Stanley was conducted into Mutesa's presence.

Great changes had taken place in Buganda since Speke's day. Its population had risen to something like three millions, and the little kingdom stretched for about 150 miles along the north-western shore of the lake. Mutesa was now in his early forties,

Rubaga, Mutesa's new capital: '. . . situated in the centre of an amphitheatre formed by seven high walls or palisades through which entrance is had by opposing gates to which cow bells are attached.' (Chaillé-Long) From a sketch by Chaillé-Long.

and Stanley describes him as 'a tall, clean-faced, large-eyed, nervous-looking thin man', clad in a tarbush, a black robe and a white shirt belted with gold. He seemed to be completely at ease. He shook hands warmly with his visitor, addressed him in fluent Swahili, and invited him to take a seat on an iron stool. The capital, now moved to a different site nearby called Rubaga, was a considerable settlement that covered the hills for several miles around, and there were splendid huts for visiting caravans. Guns had become a commonplace in Buganda, and Mutesa could now deploy a force of 150,000 warriors in addition to his fleet of war canoes on the lake. His personal retinue had grown larger than ever – Stanley estimated the horde of wives at 200 or more – and all manner of manufactured objects were to be seen about the palace, bales of cotton cloths, wooden stools to sit on, steel knives and other tools and ornaments of Venetian beads. There was no longer any evidence of murders and other atrocities taking place about the court.

Stanley was enchanted. It was quite impossible, he declared later, to reconcile Speke's description of Mutesa and his brutalities with this intelligent and affable man. Mutesa had been taking an interest in Mohammedanism, and Stanley resolved at once to change all this; he declared that the king must be converted to Christianity,

'*I was surprised to see Wat-el-Mek with ten of his men, with difficulty dragging something that seemed to me the body of a tree. To my astonishment it proved to be a huge boa-constrictor they had just killed behind my hut, and which they had brought to me as a surprise.*' *(Chaillé-Long)*

and he actually began a series of Bible-readings at the court. Mutesa listened very willingly.

Now in fact no radical change had taken place in Mutesa's nature, but his nineteen years on the throne had done a great deal to polish his natural talents as a politician. He had long since realized that there were other powerful states outside his own little world in Central Africa, and that there was every advantage to be had in befriending them; they could supply him with the guns and ammunition with which to fight off Kamrasi in Bunyoro and his other enemies. Their inventions and their ideas could be very useful in Buganda. As far back as 1869 he had received a caravan with a present of eight bullocks from the Sultan of Zanzibar, and had replied by sending to the

coast a gift of 150 tusks and a baby elephant. Since then a further gift had arrived
from Zanzibar of a quantity of gunpowder, guns, soap, brandy and gin. Within the
past year he had also had a visitor from the north: a white man named Chaillé-Long
had arrived on horseback from the Sudan, declaring that he was the emissary of a
'Gordoom Pasha', who had taken the place of Baker there. Mutesa had welcomed him
to Rubaga and had slaughtered thirty human beings in his honour (an incident he
was wise enough not to mention to Stanley), and now Gordoom Pasha was sending
him another envoy who was expected any day.

And so, for the moment, all was peace and friendship at the court. The King and
the explorer had their daily meetings in an atmosphere that was increasingly cordial,
and presently Colonel Gordon's new envoy turned up. This was a likeable and
courageous young Frenchman named Linant de Bellefonds, who, like the American,
Chaillé-Long, had taken service under Gordon with the Khedive of Egypt, and was
reconnoitring the land south from the Sudan with a view to its future annexation. He
was very willing to promote Stanley's plan for the Christianization of Buganda, and
offered to take back with him a dispatch of Stanley's to the London *Daily Telegraph*
urging that missionaries should be sent out from England. Upon this the two men
parted: de Bellefonds to report to Gordon at Gondokoro, and Stanley to continue his
voyage round the lake.

On May 6, 1875, Stanley was back at his starting-point at Mwanza after a voyage
of 1,000 miles and 57 days, and the first of his great objectives was accomplished: it
was now proved beyond all doubt that the Victoria Nyanza was a single lake. Speke
had been right and his detractors hopelessly wrong. Moreover, this voyage had
established that the lake had only one major outlet – at the Ripon Falls – and only one
major intake – the Kagera River that flowed in on the west coast to the north of
Karagwe.

'. . . Speke,' Stanley wrote, 'has now the full glory of having discovered the largest
inland sea on the continent of Africa, also its principal affluent as well as its outlet.
I must also give him credit for having understood the geography of the countries we
travelled through better than any of those who so persistently opposed his
hypothesis. . . .'

One observes that Stanley is not yet quite ready to concede that Speke's Nile is the
true Nile; still, he is beginning to approach that conclusion and soon he was to go the
whole way towards it.

There now lay before him the second objective: to explore the Tanganyika Lake
thoroughly and to discover just what connection it had, if any, with Baker's Albert
Nyanza and any other lakes that might lie in the unexplored country on the Equator.
In July 1875 he put the whole of his expedition into canoes on Lake Victoria, and
with the *Lady Alice* in the van, sailed north again to Buganda. His force was much
depleted – Frederick Barker, the clerk from the Langham Hotel, had died at Mwanza,
and others had deserted or fallen ill – but Mutesa had promised to supply him with
reinforcements.

First, however, he had a score to settle with the natives on the island of Bumbire, which lies off the western shore of the lake, somewhat south of the present town of Bukoba. On his journey south from Buganda in the *Lady Alice* he had been roughly handled by these natives, and now, coming into sight of the island again, he had his revenge. He was fortunate to be joined just at this moment by a fleet of Mutesa's war canoes which had come south looking for him. Between 2,000 and 3,000 Bumbire

Colonel C. Chaillé-Long. 'Central Africa, with all its seductive fields of allurement to the adventurous, could not but be regarded as a bourne from which but few travellers returned, a path of glory that led to the grave.' (Chaillé-Long)

spearmen unwisely exposed themselves on the shore, and Stanley, bringing his little fleet of canoes into position, delivered a broadside with his guns. Those of the enemy who were not killed or wounded scattered and fled.

Continuing northwards again Stanley joined Mutesa himself at the Ripon Falls, where a second battle was fought against another mutinous island.

There is something naïve about all Stanley's dealings with Mutesa, and one pauses here to wonder why it was that he got so heavily involved with a man who was at once so savage and so crudely cynical. Perhaps he was bound to seek Mutesa's alliance in order to complete his circumnavigation of the lake, but the reward he received for his intervention in the Buganda wars was as empty as Mutesa's profession of interest in Christianity: the promised reinforcements naturally bolted at the first opportunity, leaving the explorer to continue on his own.

One must remember of course that Stanley was still only 34 and that Livingstone's

Mutesa's war canoes must have looked very similar to those of Kabarega which attacked Chaillé-Long.
'. . . their hideous faces illumined with savage, devilish glee at the prospect of blood and booty, they advanced
to the attack.' (Chaillé-Long)

brief spell of influence upon him had to contend with all the experience of his earlier years in which he had found the world a harsh and ruthless place. Yet when he came to write about the Bumbire massacre – and he had ample time to reflect before doing so – he related the story almost with truculence, almost with an air of defying the reader.

'. . . The savage,' he wrote, 'only respects force, power, boldness and decision . . .'

No one was going to dispute the fact that life *was* very tough in Central Africa, and that often violent methods were needed if the explorer was going to survive; but it was not wise to make a virtue of this, and to many people in England it seemed that the Bumbire incident bore a strong resemblance to the massacre Livingstone had witnessed at Nyangwe; and it was an additional cause for offence that he had gone into action in these skirmishes carrying the Union Jack as his banner. Only the most insensitive of men could have failed to see that all this was going to cause an outcry in England. But then insensitiveness was part of Stanley's strength; he simply did not care. And certainly in his plain work of exploration he was superb.

He accepted with equanimity the loss of the escort which Mutesa had given him, even though this meant that he failed to determine the extent of Baker's Albert Nyanza and of Lake Edward, which lies just below the Equator, and instead he turned south into Karagwe. Here he spent a month with Rumanika at Bweranyange. Rumanika was growing old – indeed, Stanley was the last white man to see him alive, for he died soon after this. Apparently his mind became overwhelmed by the death of a favourite son and by the misery caused by an infliction in his eye, and he committed suicide.

Rumanika flits through the Central African story as a genial but not insubstantial ghost. One has the feeling that one knows him very well. He had been kind to Speke and Grant, and now once again he received Stanley with every form of hospitality. It was with some pride that he produced the gun which Speke had given him so many years before, and it is not difficult to picture him standing there holding it in his hand, a giant of a man, well over six foot in height, dressed a little pathetically in a red blanket. It was not easy to make the jump out of the Stone Age into the nineteenth century. Rumanika had been cruel enough in his time, in destroying other claimants to his throne, but he was less scheming and less brutal than Mutesa (whom he never met), and he possessed a dignity that did not depend upon his strutting about in imitation of a lion.

Restored by his month's rest in these surroundings, Stanley pushed on southwards to Lake Tanganyika, and in June 1876 he launched the *Lady Alice* at Ujiji. In under two months he was back again bringing with him certain evidence that the lake had no outlet which could possibly be described as the source of the Nile. With this, Burton's theories finally collapsed, and Speke at last was master of the field.

There remained now the third and final matter to clear up: what was Livingstone's Lualaba River and where did it flow? If it was not the Nile, then how did it fit into the great pattern of the Central African rivers? In August 1876, two years after he had left the coast, and with his expedition reduced to less than half its original size, Stanley set out on this last and greatest adventure of all.

The story of Stanley's voyage in the *Lady Alice* down the Lualaba and the Congo to the Atlantic is one of the great epics of African adventure. For many months he had no notion of where the river was eventually to take him – it might have been northwards into Egypt or anywhere into the vast unexplored regions to the south – but having once started he had to go on. Stanley's account of the voyage in *Through the Dark Continent* reads like some chronicle of the early Spanish conquistadors in South America, for he was overtaken by every possible disaster: shipwreck and starvation, the attacks of the riverside tribes and the loss of all his supplies, and finally the drowning of his last surviving white companion, Frank Pocock. Nine hundred and ninety-nine days after leaving Zanzibar the survivors emerged like ghouls from the jungles at the mouth of the Congo, and here a little community of European traders brought them back to life again. Of Stanley's original 356 followers only 114 remained (including 13 women and their children) and these were taken back by sea to Zanzibar.

Prior to Stanley's journey the course of the Nile from the Ripon Falls to the present border of the Sudan had been plotted by Gordon's lieutenants. Chaillé-Long had gone down from the source as far as the Karuma Falls in Central Uganda, and had discovered Lake Kyoga on the way, and the Italian, Romolo Gessi, had circum-navigated Lake Albert and had followed its outlet to the north as far as the border at Dufilé.

But Stanley's had been by far the main achievement. All the essential questions had now been answered: the Lualaba joined the Congo and flowed across Africa into the Atlantic. The Nile rose in Lake Victoria and flowed north to Egypt and the Mediterranean. The blank space on the map was a blank no longer. It could still be argued, of course, that the ultimate source of the Nile must be at the headwaters of the main stream that feeds Lake Victoria – the Kagera – and in fact there is a just perceptible drift of water from the mouth of the Kagera across the north-western corner of the lake to the Ripon Falls (or rather what used to be the Ripon Falls before the hydro-electric dam was constructed there in the nineteen-fifties). And if we follow the Kagera and its tributaries upstream for some hundreds of miles we find that its ultimate beginning lies in mountains over 6,000 feet high to the north of Lake Tanganyika. Thus Burton was very nearly right when he argued that the true source of the river would be found in these regions. But surely this is too fine a definition: if the argument were carried to its logical conclusion it must be admitted that the river begins in the rains of the sky itself and that Homer was right when he spoke of the 'Jove-descended Nile'. For ordinary purposes it would seem most sensible to accept the site of the Ripon Falls as the source, since it is only from there that the mighty river confines itself to a definite course, at first northward through Lake Kyoga to Central Uganda, then westward over the Karuma and Murchison Falls to Lake Albert, then generally northwards again through the rapids of Equatoria, the swamps of the Sudd and the deserts of the south Sudan to its junction with the Blue Nile at Khartoum; then on again for thousands of miles through a vast waste of sand until it reaches the pyramids and green delta of Egypt.

With Stanley's return to Zanzibar in 1877 it could be said that the exploration of the White Nile was virtually ended. It remained now to be seen what the political and religious forces of the world were going to do with this new eldorado that had been put into their hands.

Mutesa: 'He appears scarcely more than thirty-five years of age; certainly more than six feet high; his face is nervous but expressive of intelligence. From his large restless eyes, a gleam of fierce brutality beams out that mars an otherwise sympathetic expression; his features are regular, a complexion a light copper tint.' (Chaillé-Long) A painting by Lady Stanley from a photograph by H. M. Stanley.

PART TWO

THE EXPLOITATION

The Khedive Ismail.

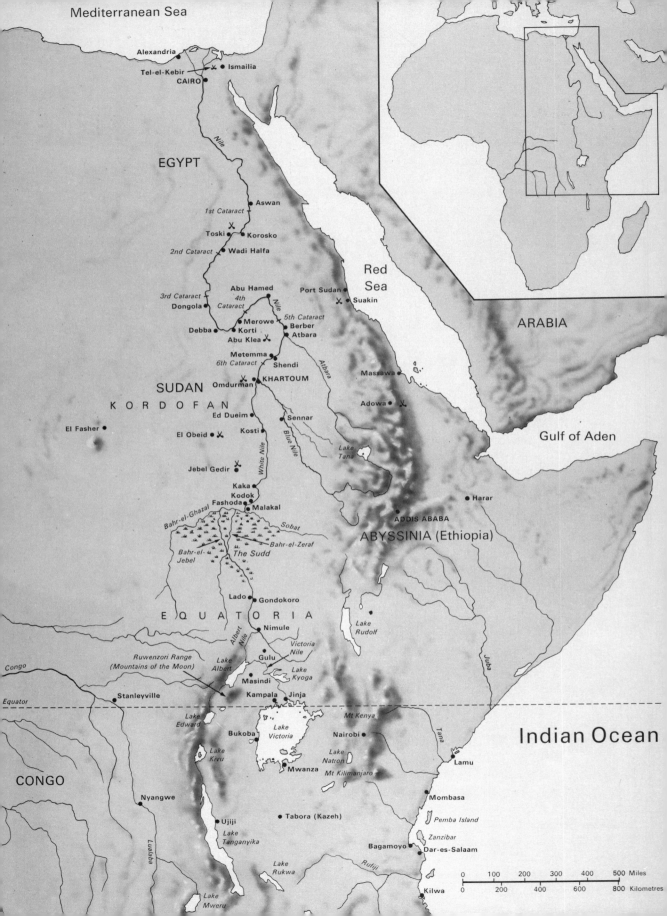

Mediterranean Sea

Alexandria
Tel-el-Kebir
Ismailia
CAIRO

EGYPT

Nile

Aswan
1st Cataract
Toski
Korosko
2nd Cataract
Wadi Halfa

3rd Cataract
Abu Hamed
4th Cataract
Dongola
Merowe
Debba
Korti
Abu Klea
Metemma
6th Cataract
Shendi
Omdurman
KHARTOUM

Red Sea

Port Sudan
Suakin

ARABIA

5th Cataract
Berber
Atbara

Massawa

Gulf of Aden

SUDAN
KORDOFAN

El Fasher

Ed Dueim
El Obeid
Kosti

Adowa

Sennar

Lake Tana

Jebel Gedir

White Nile
Blue Nile

Atbara

Kaka
Kodok
Fashoda
Malakal

Harar

Bahr-el-Ghazal
Sobat
Bahr-el-Zeraf
Bahr-el-Jebel
The Sudd

ADDIS ABABA

ABYSSINIA (Ethiopia)

Lado
Gondokoro

EQUATORIA

Nimule

Lake Rudolf

Albert Nile
Victoria Nile
Ruwenzori Range
(Mountains of the Moon)
Gulu
Lake Albert
Masindi
Lake Kyoga
Kampala
Jinja

Juba

Congo
Stanleyville

Equator

Lake Edward

Bukoba

Lake Kivu

Lake Victoria

Mt Kenya

Nairobi

Tana

Mwanza

Lake Natron
Mt Kilimanjaro

Indian Ocean

CONGO

Nyangwe

Ujiji
Lake Tanganyika

Tabora (Kazeh)

Lualaba

Lamu

Mombasa

Pemba Island

Zanzibar
Bagamoyo
Dar-es-Salaam

Lake Rukwa

Rufiji

Lake Mweru

Kilwa

0   100   200   300   400   500 Miles
0   200   400   600   800 Kilometres

8

Beggar on Horseback

By the end of the eighteen-sixties the Khedive Ismail of Egypt had arrived at the crest of his highly prosperous career. He looks out at us from the photographs taken at the time with the quickness and complacency of a sleek and shining seal. His black frock-coat is of that peculiar type which was known in the Near East as a Stamboulina, his fez is perched slightly sideways on his head, his reddish-sandy whiskers harmonize splendidly with the decorations on his plump chest, and he sits, a little incongruously, cross-legged on a divan. Behind him there is a carved lattice-work which no doubt gives on to the inner rooms in the palace, and it conveys a suggestion of harems and oriental banquets. And yet he is not entirely oriental; you might just conceivably describe him as a new type of ruler, an occidentalized oriental potentate. In 1869 he was 39 years of age, and now, after six years in power, he was the absolute monarch of Egypt. Technically he was still a vassal of the Sultan in Constantinople, and Egypt was still a part of the Ottoman Empire, but in fact Ismail had unquestioned authority over the Nile Delta, and he was as rich as only a new-made multi-millionaire can ever hope to be.

He felt rich. He spent his borrowed piastres in billions. In the manner of Pope Leo X Ismail might have exclaimed, 'Since Allah has given us the vice-royalty let us enjoy it.' Sir Evelyn Baring might have found him 'utterly uneducated' but he was also bound to agree with everybody else who knew the Khedive that he had remarkable charm and an energy in handling his affairs which was unique in the East and even astonishing in a man who had been brought up as a spoilt child in Paris.

Most Europeans who served under Ismail liked and admired him, at any rate in the early stages of his reign. Both Baker and General Gordon trusted him and believed that he was sincere when he said he meant to abolish the slave-trade; he touched a spark of enthusiasm in their natures and he treated them very well. They were excellent agents for the great design he had in view: the westernization of Egypt and the creation of a new Egyptian empire in East Africa.

When Ismail succeeded his uncle Mohammed Said in the vice-royalty in 1863 Egypt was financially sound and even prosperous. The American Civil War had caused a sharp rise in the price of cotton, and the Egyptian crop had increased in value from £5,000,000 to £25,000,000. Ismail transferred his private debts to the state, increased the taxes, and got to work. He spent money with an abandon which eclipsed anything the oil sheikhs of the Middle East have achieved in the twentieth century. It was not only honest men like Baker and Gordon who were attracted to his

The course of the Nile.

service; a plague of speculators descended upon Egypt as well and they easily contrived to get rid of Ismail's money even faster than he borrowed it. In round figures the Egyptian national debt was £3,000,000 at Ismail's accession, and before long he managed to convert this into a deficit of £100,000,000 – and this at a time when the pound was worth two or three times what it is today. Egypt in short was bankrupt, and Ismail the Magnificent was also known as the impecunious millionaire.

By 1869, however, when disaster was still some years ahead, Ismail already had a good deal to show for his money. His westernization of Egypt included every kind of internal reform, new canals and water-works, the remodelling of the customs system and the post office, the creation of a new sugar monopoly and a dozen other commercial enterprises. He maintained a new and expanding army and Cairo itself was partly rebuilt. In place of the foul streets and the rickety wooden houses a new commercial and residential quarter built of stone grew up around the Abdin Palace – the palace itself just one of the new residences which Ismail had constructed for his own use. A theatre and an opera house appeared, and the Bedouin were treated to the wonderful sight of a railway train steaming across the desert. Ismail's personal spending was equally sumptuous: with the gift of a steam yacht, a diamond-studded dinner service and a large sum in money he got a *firman* from the Sultan in Constantinople by which he became Khedive or Viceroy and virtually independent; and then there were his lavish trips abroad (he was received by Queen Victoria in 1867), his enormous households of women and slaves, his jewels, his *objets d'art* and his furniture brought from France.

In 1869 he was ready to make his greatest display of all. The Suez Canal was finished and he was determined to celebrate the opening with a series of entertainments which would establish Egypt's reputation as a new and important power in the world. The canal, of course, was not an Egyptian enterprise, but the Khedive was heavily involved in it. Ferdinand de Lesseps had formed his Compagnie Universelle du Canal Maritime de Suez in 1854, and had obtained from Mohammed Said a concession that was to run for 99 years from the opening date (after which time the canal was to become Egyptian property). From the beginning de Lesseps had run into difficulties on every side. The project itself was believed to be impossible, despite the fact that more than one such canal had existed on the site in ancient times. Napoleon had ordered a survey to be made at the time of his invasion of Egypt in 1798, and his engineer had estimated that there was a difference of 33 feet in the sea-levels of the Mediterranean and the Red Sea; an absolute obstacle to the construction of a canal. (In fact there is practically no difference at all in the sea levels.) The expenses of the undertaking – in the end, 287,000,000, gold francs – proved to be far higher than the original estimate and ten years were needed to complete the work instead of six. British investors would have nothing to do with the scheme and the money was obtained mostly from French and Turkish sources, Egypt receiving four-tenths of the shares.

Then, too, there was massive opposition to the canal on political grounds, chiefly from Britain. It was claimed that if a canal were to be built it would immediately become a political target and a battlefield – a point, incidentally, that has been all too amply demonstrated in the last fifty years.

But de Lesseps' pertinacity was endless. He got his money, he drew up his plans (a canal 100 miles in length with a depth of 8 metres and a bottom width of 22 metres, with a secondary fresh-water canal coming in from the Nile), and the Khedive supplied him with an army of forced labourers. Many technical difficulties had to be overcome as the work went forward. A cholera epidemic held up the work and there was a fearful death-roll caused by the hardships of life in the eastern desert of Egypt, one of the worst deserts in the world. But at the end of 1869 the main structure of the canal was completed, and most of its critics had fallen silent. It was apparent now that no maritime nation could afford to ignore or boycott the enterprise, least of all the British. The journey from Western Europe to India and the Far East had been reduced by one half, both in time and distance, and this was a vital economy now that coal-burning steamships were everywhere replacing sail. The cutting out of the long

BELOW *Labourers at work on the construction of the Canal.* OVERLEAF *The banquet for the opening of the Suez Canal, by Edouard Riou (1833–1900). Those at table include the Empress Eugénie of France, fourth from left (facing), with the Austrian Emperor on her right, and members of the Dutch and Prussian royal houses. The Khedive is fifth from left (facing away), and de Lesseps is second from left (facing away). From the* Album des Souverains.

journey round the Cape of Good Hope also meant that the whole pattern of the British Empire's defence was altered, since troops and men-of-war could now so quickly be transferred from the Atlantic and the Mediterranean to the Indian Ocean.

It was apparent too that the breadth and depth of the canal would affect ship-building design, and that all kinds of neglected territories would be opened up to Western civilization. Stanley's newspaper, the *New York Herald*, made the editorial comment: 'The . . . Suez Canal brings all these late discoveries around the equatorial sources of the Nile of Speke, Grant, Baker, Burton, Livingstone within a convenient distance for English colonization.'

There was one other point: the canal was part of the French bid for power in Egypt, and of their general campaign to dislodge the British from their position of increasing influence in East Africa and the Near East. A Frenchman had built the canal, French money had financed it, and the French were now determined to exploit their advantage to the full. Henceforth they could claim that they had a vital stake in Egypt and an established right to intervene in Egyptian politics.

Ismail's arrangements for the opening, which was fixed for November 17, 1869, had the Haroun-al-Raschid touch. The festivities were to continue for four days, and were to take place both at Cairo and on the Canal itself. In Cairo he built his opera house, and Verdi was commissioned to write *Aïda* for its inauguration (although, in fact, the opera was not performed in Egypt until later on). Plots of land were sold off in the centre of the city to raise money, and the pyramids were illuminated with magnesium light. At Port Said three pavilions were built, one for the more illustrious guests, one for the Moslem hierarchy, and another for the Christians. An arsenal of fireworks was prepared for an opening salute, and 500 cooks and 1,000 servants were imported from France and Italy to cater for six thousand guests. The best of wines and the most expensive food were of course provided without stint.

At Ismailia, the half-way point on Lake Timsah, a new town was built with a palace, hotels and kiosks; it was here that the fleet carrying the chief guests from Port Said was to meet a smaller flotilla sailing north from Suez, and thus the Mediterranean and the Red Sea were to be joined for the first time.

Such lavish preparations could not have been expected to go off without a hitch, especially in such a country as Egypt; at Port Said the fireworks dump blew up and very nearly demolished the town; and at the last moment a ship became grounded and blocked the canal. De Lesseps galloped off to the scene and had the vessel blown up.

The morning of November 17, however, found all ready for the start, with a great assembly of ships at Port Said, and both town and ships bedecked with bunting. The canal was blessed by Moslem, Greek Orthodox, Coptic and Roman Catholic priests, every available cannon and gun was fired off, twenty military bands struck up, and through the drifting smoke of gunpowder the Empress Eugénie of France in the imperial yacht *Aigle* led the way into the canal. She was followed by Ismail aboard the *Mahrousa* (his royal scimitar blazing with jewels), the Emperor of Austria (in white tunic, scarlet pantaloons and a cocked hat with a green feather), and a number of minor royalties and officials aboard two Austrian and five British ironclads, a Russian

ABOVE *Ferdinand de Lesseps.* BELOW *The first ships sail through the Canal, by Edouard Riou.* OVERLEAF
The three pavilions at Port Said, by Edouard Riou. From the Album des Souverains.

sloop-of-war and a great number of ships partly under steam and partly under sail — an armada of some 70 vessels in all.

At Ismailia the flotilla coming from Suez was met at sunset, and amid great ceremony Africa was now declared to be an island. The guests went ashore to attend a banquet, a fireworks display, and a ball illuminated by ten thousand lanterns. During her stay at Ismailia the Empress Eugénie had the excitement of riding a camel while the local Bedouin tribesmen fired off their muskets, and the fleet then steamed on to the Red Sea.

The British Royal Family were absent from this spree, but in fact they had anticipated it; some months beforehand the Prince and the Princess of Wales (who more than thirty years later were to become King Edward VII and Queen Alexandra), had come out to Egypt on an official visit and had been present when the sluices had been opened into the Bitter Lakes towards the southern end of the canal. It had been something of an occasion for a naturalist, since great quantities of fish from the Mediterranean swept in with the tide, while all the fish from the fresh-water canal, which there joined the lakes from the Nile, were instantly killed.

It was this visit that brought Samuel Baker and his wife back to Africa. Baker, with his knowledge of Arabic and of Egypt, was invited to accompany the tour as an interpreter. At a fancy dress ball given by de Lesseps Ismail drew the explorer aside and put before him a momentous proposition: he had decided, he said, to mount a military expedition which was to annex the Upper Nile to Egypt and suppress the slave-trade there. Would Baker take command?

The terms were generous, even for Ismail. Baker was to become a pasha, a lord of the Ottoman Empire, and a major-general. He was to choose his own staff and he himself was to have a salary of £40,000 spread over the four-year tenure of his office. The force he was to command was to consist of some 1,700 men, and Baker Pasha was to be given a free hand in the purchase of their equipment.

A more politically minded man than Baker might, of course, have regarded these proposals with a certain scepticism. It was extremely doubtful, for instance, that Ismail was sincere in his wish to abolish the slave-trade. He himself was one of the largest slave-owners; the fellaheen who worked on his enormous estates, and the hordes of servants in his palaces might have been given the appearance of free men, but in fact they were tied to their jobs as completely as any Russian serf, and Ismail exercised the power of life and death over them. As for the slavery in the Sudan, Ismail was perfectly well aware that all his officials there were deeply involved in it, and he himself had actually given state contracts to private traders authorizing them to exploit the Upper Nile. In Egypt as in Zanzibar slavery was part of the Moslem way of life and the government benefited very greatly from it.

But the abolition of the traffic had now become the great political cry in both Europe and America, and Ismail realized that he would have to make at least an outward show of joining the anti-slavery campaign if he was to continue to receive the support of the Western world. That support was quite essential to him. He needed more money from Europe, and he needed political backing for the larger aims he had

The Empress Eugénie riding in the desert. Detail from a painting by Frère.

in view: the extension of his power through the South Sudan, East Africa and Abyssinia. All was to be done under the banner of civilization; the new Egypt was to bring the blessings of the modern world to these savage areas in the south.

Baker accepted the commission and threw himself into the arrangements with method and gusto – and, it may be added, without much regard to the cost. His first journey up the Nile had turned him from a big game hunter into an explorer. Now the explorer was to develop into the soldier and the administrator.

The European staff was to number ten: Baker's nephew, Lieutenant Julian Baker, R.N., was engaged at a salary of £500 a year to act as personal assistant to the com-

In this cartoon headed 'Apostles of Liberty', the ghost of Wilberforce is saying to Sir Samuel Baker 'receive a nation's thanks, with mine, for fighting freedom's cause.'

mander; then there were Dr Joseph Gedge, the physician, two engineers, Higginbotham and McWilliam, Marcopolo, the storekeeper and interpreter, and Jarvis, the shipwright, with four assistants. Lady Baker was to be the only white woman to accompany the expedition.

Next, the entire force had to be organized on a proper military basis. There were to be two regiments, one of Sudanese soldiers and the other of Egyptians (who turned out to be mostly felons from the Cairo gaols), and from these Baker later selected a personal bodyguard of forty-eight sharpshooters. He put them into fezzes and scarlet uniforms and called them the Forty Thieves. In addition, there was to be a contingent of 200 cavalry and two batteries of artillery.

Next, the equipment, and it was to be of the best. In England Baker ordered the construction of a flotilla of boats all of which could be taken to pieces so that they could be dragged or carried by camels across the desert and then reassembled and launched on the Nile above the cataracts. The largest of these was a 100-foot paddle-boat of 251 tons and 20 horse-power, and in addition there were two smaller twin-screw steamers, one of 108 tons and the other of 38, and two 10-ton lifeboats.

At a cost of £9,000 general stores were also bought in England and were expected to last four years: four galvanized iron sheds 80 feet long and built in sections, 200 Hale's rockets and 50,000 rounds of Snider ammmunition, medicines, uniforms, 'Manchester goods', several saw-mills, tools and camping kit of every kind – 'any-

'The flotilla was ready for the voyage. We had engaged sailors with the greatest difficulty, as a general stampede of boatmen had taken place. Everyone ran from Khartoum to avoid the expectation. This was a dodge of the slave traders.' (Baker)

thing from a needle to a crowbar, or from a handkerchief to a boat's sail' – and finally, to impress and amuse the natives, toys, drums, musical boxes and a magnetic battery.

The main body of the expedition was to go up the Nile in relays while Baker himself and his wife travelled ahead to Khartoum on the Red Sea route (which meant crossing to the river from Suakin), and the transport arrangements were formidable. Hundreds of camels were engaged and in the end a fleet of nine steamers and fifty-five sailing boats was required to bring the soldiers and their equipment up from Cairo. Such a force had never been seen or even dreamed of in Central Africa before.

Naturally there were delays and it must be regarded as something of a marvel that by February 1870, hardly a year after receiving his commission, Baker had assembled the bulk of his force at Khartoum and was ready to set out for Gondokoro, which was

'After the capture of the slave boats the governor of Fashoda at once ordered the vessel to be unloaded. We discovered one hundred and fifty slaves stowed away in a most inconceivably small area. The stench was horrible when they began to move. Many were in irons; these were quickly released by the blacksmiths, to the astonishment of the captives, who did not appear to understand the proceeding.' (Baker)

to be his main base of operations. It was apparent at once at Khartoum that his presence was desperately needed. The slave traffic had been bad enough at the time of his earlier expedition and now it was ten times worse. The whole country was in ruins. Khartoum itself had been so taxed and despoiled by the Egyptian officials that the population of 30,000 had been reduced by half. In the surrounding villages the Africans had given up the hopeless work of tilling the land only to see their crops seized from them, and now there was desolation everywhere along the river, nothing but idle water-wheels and fields that had lapsed back into desert. Some 50,000 slaves were being brought down from the Upper Nile every year, and a gang of at least 15,000 Arabs was engaged in the trade. All these traders looked on Baker as their enemy. There was nothing he could do to touch them in the vicinity of Khartoum since his commission gave him no powers there, but he was bound for the Upper Nile which was the main source of the slave supply, and there the Khedive had conferred on him absolute authority. He could stop a slaving boat on the river, release the victims stowed away between decks and arrest the dealers regardless of whether they were officials or not. He could exercise summary justice and even impose the death penalty. On February 8, 1870, he sailed south from Khartoum with well over

'For a few moments they looked around them, as hardly believing the good news. In another instant, as the truth flashed across their delighted minds, they rushed upon me in a body, and before I had time for self-defence, I found myself in the arms of a naked beauty who kissed me almost to suffocation, and with a most unpleasant embrace, licked both my eyes with her tongue.' (Baker)

a thousand armed men, and they were strong enough to deal with any opposition they encountered on the river.

But it was the river itself that was Baker's real enemy now. In the five years that had elapsed since he had been on the Upper Nile nothing had been done to keep a clear channel through the Sudd, and by 1870 the stream at many places had disappeared beneath a spongy mass of tangled vegetation. For two dreadful months Baker's soldiers hacked a channel into this morass, but they succeeded in penetrating only a few miles. Islands of floating debris kept closing round behind the boats so that they looked 'as though frozen in an ice-drift in the Arctic'. Meanwhile the level of the river, unseen beneath the reeds, was rapidly falling. At the beginning of April Baker decided to back out and establish a base camp on hard ground near the present town of Malakal, while he waited for the annual flood to come down at the end of the year.

By the beginning of December 1870 he was ready to try again. The river was now in flood, a strong breeze blew from the north, and 59 vessels with 1,600 men and women and Lady Baker on board struck out once more for the hateful swamp. Two months later they were still creeping forward yard by yard along the Bahr-el-Jebel and the same monotonous scenes were repeated every day, the reluctant soldiers hacking with billhooks at the matted barrier of reeds. The heat was appalling and many collapsed with fever and sunstroke. One after another the sailing boats sank or were stranded on the mud, and by night there was no escape from the mosquitoes. Nowadays the Bahr-el-Jebel channel has been cleared, and the Nile paddle-steamers pass through this part of the Sudd in less than three days, but even so this journey is a tedious and oppressive business. To have lingered there for months on end in that claustrophobic green prison with no certainty that one would ever emerge must have been an experience to test the sanity of any ordinary man.

Towards March 1871 even Baker's nerve was beginning to fail. 'It is quite impossible to say where we are,' he wrote in his diary; and then again he records that there appeared to be no hope – the Egyptian soldiers had now ceased to care whether they lived or died. And many did die. Gedge, the doctor, had long since collapsed and had been sent off to Khartoum, and now there was no one to treat the hundreds who came down with malaria and dysentery. Baker himself and his wife seemed miraculously to be the only ones who were able to remain in health. Early in March the Nile began to fall again at an alarming rate, and on March 9 Baker records that the entire fleet 'was hard and fast aground'. But it was on that same day that, in a light reconnaissance

'Who would believe the change? Some evil spirit appears to rule in this horrible region of everlasting swamp. A wave of the demon's wand, and an incredible change appears. . . . The fabulous Styx must be a sweet rippling brook, compared to this horrible creation.' (Baker)

boat, he went ahead and reached the clear water where the Bahr-el-Jebel comes in to join the Bahr-el-Zeraf from the north. This was a tremendous moment, and Baker summoned his exhausted men to make one more effort. 'I at once determined,' he says, 'to make a dam behind the vessels so as to enclose the position in which we lay like a millpond. . . . I had a great quantity of fir timber in the shape of beams and rafter for building purposes. I therefore directed Mr Higginbotham to prepare two rows of piles which were to be driven across the river.'

For the next two days 1,500 men were employed in filling sacks with sand and clay and in tying together large fascines or bundles of reeds. All this material, at a given signal, was to be packed around the piles so as to form a continuous barrier across the river, and by March 13 everything was in readiness.

'I stood on one of the stranded boats only a few yards from the row of piles,' Baker says. 'The buglers and drummers stood upon another vessel ready to give the signal. At the first bugle every two men lifted the sacks of sand and clay. At once all the drums and bugles then sounded the advance, and 500 heavy sacks were dropped into the row of piles, and firmly stamped down by the men. The troops now worked with intense energy . . . while some stamped frantically and danced upon the entangled mass, all screaming and shouting in great excitement, and the bugles and drums kept up an incessant din. . . . At 3.30 the water had risen to an extent that obliged men in some places to swim. The steamer that had been hopelessly stranded, and the entire fleet, were floating merrily in the pond.'

Now at last their troubles were over. One by one the boats were sailed out into the clear water, and a month later they were tying up on the banks below the ruined Austrian mission house at Gondokoro.

The place if anything was more dismal than ever, but Baker at once set about landing his stores and building a fort there. It was enough to revive hope just to be out of the Sudd at last, and by the end of May an orderly line of huts had sprung up and these were surrounded by vegetable gardens and newly-sown fields of maize. On May 26, Baker indulged himself in a ceremony which might have been pathetic had it been conducted by any other man. He paraded twelve hundred of his men in clean uniforms, ran up the Ottoman flag on an 80-foot pole, and solemnly annexed the surrounding country to Egypt. Henceforth it was to be known as Equatoria, and Gondokoro, the little capital, was renamed Ismailia in honour of the Khedive. That night the Bakers had a dinner of roast beef, Christmas pudding and rum.

There remained now two years of Baker's contract to run and the story of these two years is, very largely, a story of colonial warfare. This had ceased to be an expedition; in a small way it was a military campaign that was designed to 'pacify' the country – and that word 'pacification' had sinister connotations. Strong liberal and humanitarian feelings were stirred up in England when the details of Baker's campaign became known. And yet it is difficult to see how, having once embarked on this adventure, he could have acted in any other way. He was caught up in a pattern of expansion which has since become labelled with the word 'colonialism' – the exploitation of the weak by the strong.

But it would be wilful and sentimental to dismiss colonialism in these terms, especially in Central Africa. Here was a vast area that supposedly had been left untouched through the centuries, and perhaps it might have been well to have left it so; the local tribes had worked out a Stone Age system of life which was perfectly valid despite its brutality, uncertainty and suffering. But it had not been left untouched; Arab traders had gone in with no other object but private gain and by 1870 this primitive Eden had become soiled, debauched and finally vile. To Baker and men like him it seemed that it was a moral duty for civilized governments to restore order once again, to throw out the ruthless foreign slavers and to teach the natives to live in peace and on a far higher standard than they had had before. Eventually, he found that he had to occupy the ground and impose good laws by force. And so, willy-nilly, another new colony was formed.

A great deal depended, of course, upon what means were used to achieve these worthy objects; Baker undoubtedly, within himself, was wise, strong and patient; it was simply his misfortune that he entered the colonizing process in Central Africa under the dubious patronage of the Khedive, and at its roughest and crudest moment. His expedition had to fight for its life and that made all the difference; unless he used strong-arm tactics he not only failed, he died.

And so when the Bari tribes attacked him at Gondokoro with poisoned arrows he drove them off with guns; when they refused to sell him cattle and grain he went off on raids and seized the food he needed for his men. None of this was very simple or easy. The Egyptian gaolbirds in Baker's little army were not men of great moral fibre. Baker came back to Gondokoro from one of his raids one day to find that 1,100 of them had seized thirty of his sailing vessels and had decamped down the river to Khartoum. This disaster left him with barely 500 men. However, he decided to push on into Bunyoro, the kingdom of Kamrasi. The Forty Thieves had become an efficient bodyguard, the Sudanese soldiers were loyal, and by now they had amassed a store of grain and large herds of cattle and sheep – an ample supply of food for the journey. A small garrison was left behind in Gondokoro under the command of an Egyptian officer, Raouf Bey, and this man was instructed to keep an eye open for Dr Livingstone and to look after him well if he turned up during Baker's absence. Livingstone at that moment was hundreds of miles away to the south on Lake Tanganyika, but Baker had had no news of him or indeed of anyone for a year or more.

It was a steady and well-organized march. They set out on January 22, 1872, Baker, his wife and the nephew, Julian, leading the way on horseback, and they arrived on the frontier of Bunyoro in the middle of March. Everywhere along the route, even so far south as this, the slave-trade had created desolation, and Fatiko, the outpost which the Bakers had visited in 1864, had now expanded into a compound covering at least thirty acres. A healthy young girl was valued at 'a single elephant's tusk of the first class' (worth from £20 to £30 in England but of course very much less in Bunyoro). She could also be purchased for a new shirt or for 13 English sewing needles, and these things were so much desired that parents frequently sold their children.

The Sudd.

Baker pushed on steadily southwards, and now with his little army he had no need to ask permission of the king to enter Bunyoro. On April 25, 1872, he arrived at the capital, and saw 'some thousands of large beehive-shaped straw huts' on the site of the present town of Masindi. Kamrasi was dead and Baker did not care for his successor: 'This,' he says, 'was Kabba Rega, the son of Kamrasi, the sixteenth king of Bunyoro, of the Galla conquerors, a gauche, awkward, undignified lout of twenty years of age, who thought himself a great monarch. He was cowardly, cruel, cunning and treacherous to the last degree.'

The young King advanced on Baker's camp, walking like a giraffe, at the head of a horde of some 2,000 of his followers, and Baker did not like his demeanour at all. He says that Kabba Rega was drunk most of the day except for a couple of hours when he conducted business in the early afternoon, and that the capital was a bedlam of dancing, shouting, horn-blowing and drinking all through the night.

Kabba Rega, or Kabarega, is of some importance in the Central African story, and Baker's judgment upon him can certainly not be taken as the last word. From the first Baker's own behaviour was designed to precipitate a crisis in Bunyoro. He made no pretence at all of what he had come to do, and that was to dominate Kabarega, by friendship if possible, and if not, by force.

He pitched his tent under a huge banyan tree and then proceeded to build himself, close by, a 'government house, and a private dwelling adjoining for myself'. Only the barest outlines of these structures remain today among the green lawns and the jacaranda trees in Masindi, but we have Baker's description of them and it is given with some justifiable pride: the government house was of one room, measuring 18 feet by 14 feet with a roof 20 feet high, the walls being made of canes and hung with red blankets. A remarkable gallery of pictures was displayed on these walls to impress the Africans – photographs of Queen Victoria and the Princess of Wales, coloured fashion-plates of 'very beautiful women, with very gorgeous dresses', and a number of sporting prints. The musical box was unpacked and rugs were spread on the floor. In these surroundings Baker Pasha, the new viceroy of the Khedive, prepared to receive official visits. Later on, a circular fort of heavy upended logs with an earthen roof and a surrounding ditch was constructed beside Government House. Gardens of cucumbers, melons, pumpkins and cottonseed were planted, and if Kabarega was still in any doubt about the strangers' motives the position was made absolutely clear to him on May 14, 1872; on that day Baker publicly annexed Bunyoro to the Khedive.

Now Kabarega, even at this early stage of his career, was a great deal more than a drunken lout. He had had to fight for his throne on the death of his father two years before, and already he had shown signs of those qualities which, later on, were to make him the most resourceful guerrilla leader in Central Africa. At this stage he was very inexperienced and very greatly in need of good advice, but one can hardly blame him for resenting Baker's intrusion into his kingdom. It was quite evident to him that he would have to get rid of Baker if he was going to remain King of Bunyoro, and because he was rash and aggressive he decided to set about the business at once. The

ABOVE 'On 25th December the fort of Fatiko was completed . . . my men had been four months engaged in the work, owing to the extreme hardness of the subsoil which was a compact gravel resembling concrete.' (Baker) BELOW 'On 18th July the natives held a great consultation and ended with a war-dance; they were all painted in various patterns with red ochre and white pipe-clay.' (Baker) Watercolours by Baker.

drum-beatings and horn-blowings that Baker heard through the night, and even the drinking bouts, were not merely a savage debauch, they were the primitive man's way of working up his spirit for war.

Through the last days of May, while Baker pushed on with the building of his fort, Kabarega's threats increased, and on June 8 the Battle of Masindi broke out. It was preceded by a little strategy of Kabarega's which immediately distinguishes him from the general run of other African chiefs, and might well have been applauded by the ancient Greeks; he sent over a gift of poisoned cider to Baker's troops, and many of them were feeling desperately ill when the fighting began.

The Battle of Masindi lasted just an hour and a quarter, and Baker describes it very vividly:

'Suddenly,' he says, 'we were startled by the savage yells of some thousand voices, which burst unexpectedly upon us . . . ! "Sound the taboor!" Fortunately I gave this order to the bugler by my side without a moment's delay. The Forty Thieves had just the time to grab their rifles and open up a point-blank fire upon the mass of Africans charging down on them through the cover of the tall grass.' Perhaps for a few minutes Kabarega might have had a chance of success but it was gone directly Baker got his 'blue lights' – the Hale Rockets – into play. Before long he was able to

'. . . *a general action was growing hotter every moment, the yells of the natives and the din of their horns became louder. I was momentarily expecting to hear the sound of cannon . . . but to my astonishment not a gun was fired. Simply the roll of muskets continued.' (Baker)*

lead his men into the enemy camp and set fire to the straw buildings there.

'In a few minutes the conflagration was terrific, as the great court of Kabarega blazed in flames 70 or 80 feet high. . . .' Soon 'not a house remained of the lately extensive town; a vast open space of smoke and black ashes . . . were the only remains of the capital of Bunyoro. The enemy fled. Their drums and horns, lately so noisy, were now silent.'

With so many dead and wounded Africans lying about in the thick grass it was impossible to arrive at an estimate of Kabarega's losses, but Baker heard reports that nine chiefs had been killed and 'a larger number of common people'. He himself had lost only four men. The vultures in hundreds settled down around the ruined town.

But this was merely the first round of an affair that grew steadily more serious for the little expedition. The Banyoro did not retire, they kept skirmishing about Baker's lines from the heavy cover of the grass, and presently it became obvious that it was impossible for him to stay where he was. Every day there were losses and no hope of reinforcements. Food was beginning to run short. In brief, the invaders had won the battle but lost the war.

On June 13 Baker decided that there was no help for it but to beat a retreat to Foweira, a traders' station on the Nile some sixty miles to the north-east, and there

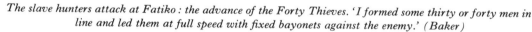

The slave hunters attack at Fatiko: the advance of the Forty Thieves. 'I formed some thirty or forty men in line and led them at full speed with fixed bayonets against the enemy.' (Baker)

regroup so that he could return and fight Kabarega on another day. The return march began in drizzling rain on June 14. Day by day Baker's wretched men were harried by spearmen, every other swamp and turn in the track was an ambush, and the war drums continued relentlessly all around them throughout the night. Lady Baker, as can be imagined, was magnificent throughout this disaster, but the native wives were a terrible hindrance to the march, since any who fell behind could face only instant death. The horses and donkeys were soon all dead, and the wounded had to be carried on stretchers. Presently it became necessary to abandon the cattle together with a further quantity of stores, and indeed it was remarkable in every way that on June 24 Baker was able to lead the remnants of his exhausted and wretched column into Foweira. Their losses on the march were ten dead and eleven wounded. Of the advance guard 200 strong which had gone to Masindi, only the three Europeans, 97 men and 51 women and servants remained.

Soon Baker was able to strike up an alliance with Rionga, the traditional enemy of the Bunyoro Kings, who lived a little further up the river. August 1872 found Baker back at Fatiko, and here, after more fighting, he decided to establish his main headquarters.

It was an admirable place to choose, and from the moment he settled in, Baker's fortunes began to improve. Before the end of the year he was even strong enough to attack Kabarega from the north and eventually put him to flight. This seems to have been the signal for a general collapse of the opposition of the tribes south of Gondokoro. For the last six months of his tenure of office Baker was able to concentrate without disturbance upon the building of his fort at Fatiko, and from here, in a rough and ready fashion, he was able to rule, by the mere threat of his presence, the little kingdom he had conquered. Half of it, including the Nile valley itself, was still unexplored, all of it was still savage, but while Baker remained it was at least in peace.

By the time he and his wife and nephew came to leave in March 1873 he was able to write:

'In the end every opposition was overcome: hatred and insubordination yielded to discipline and order. . . . The White Nile, for a distance of 1,600 miles from Khartoum to Central Africa, was cleansed from the abomination of a traffic which had hitherto sullied its waters. Every cloud had passed away, and the term of my office expired in peace and sunshine. In this result, I humbly traced God's blessing.'

A garrison of soldiers under an Egyptian officer was left behind at Fatiko and the Bakers reached Cairo in August 1873. By the end of the year they were safely ensconced in England where the untouched salary of £40,000 was awaiting them in the bank.

Fatiko was the chief monument Baker left behind in Africa, and even today the place still bears the stamp of his rugged and determined personality; it is an admirable expression of Victorian England in the heart of Africa. Except for a few African farmers no one lives there now, but the general outlines of the fort have been maintained more or less as they were in Baker's time. From here the African bush, with its immemorial stillness, spreads away: to the west, just visible to a practised eye, the green valley of the Nile; to the north, the road to Gondokoro; and to the south and east the vast plain that gently rises to the great lakes and the mountains of Ethiopia. Baker loved this country and dreamed of the creation of a great civilization here. But things have not really altered very much in the past ninety years. This is still a world of thatched huts and silence, and the general impression is one of enormous space and enormous emptiness.

The fort itself is a large square compound with a surrounding ditch, and it is anchored on the Nile side to a huge pile of rounded granite boulders. Upon these Baker built his storehouses of broken stone, using the local anthills for cement, and the visitor at the present time will find there a plaque which reads:

FATIKO 1872–88
FOUNDED BY SIR SAMUEL BAKER
OCCUPIED BY GORDON AND EMIN

The strange myopic figure of Emin we have yet to meet, but the name of Gordon, here as everywhere in Central Africa, evokes an instant sense of gallantry and adventure, and it is pleasant to know that he followed Baker here, and that both men, no doubt, often looked down from these battlements towards the Nile, which was so strong a theme in their lives, and that they heard, as one hears now, the rustling of the borassus palms beside the fort and saw, in the evening, these same flat-topped acacia trees which spread in the plain below and make a convenient perch for the migratory birds settling down there for the night.

9

To Go in Peace

Central Africa had no part in the great migrations that poured out of Europe through the middle of the nineteenth century. The push of the potato famine and the pull of gold brought hundreds of thousands of immigrants to Australia, California and other distant parts of the world, and having once arrived at their new homes most of these people turned their backs upon Europe for ever. But up to the end of the eighteen-seventies nothing of the kind had happened in Central Africa. It had remained explorers' country, and no one, with the exception of the missionaries who were preparing to enter the field, dreamed of making a permanent life there. It was thought that the opening of the Suez Canal would lead to a great expansion of trade along the eastern seaboard of the continent, but no such movement took place: most of the ships continued on to India, the Far East, Australia and New Zealand, and it was left to the only two local powers of any consequence, Egypt and Zanzibar, to struggle against each other for the possession of the vast hinterland. It was not a struggle which could continue for very long – the European powers were bound eventually to step in and take charge of the situation – but in the eighteen-seventies the Khedive of Egypt and the Sultan of Zanzibar still had a few more years of independence to run.

Zanzibar, of course, was much the weaker of the two states, and her little population of half a million had been badly hit, at first by another cholera epidemic in 1869, and then by a hurricane that all but levelled the city and the port in 1872. Yet the Sultan was still undisputed master of the three islands of Zanzibar, Pemba and Mafia, and of about a thousand miles of the coastline on the mainland. The slave-trade was beginning to feel the pressure of the international blockade, but other exports such as indiarubber were proving even more profitable. The clove harvest, which was sent largely to Java (where the fruit-buds are still used to give a flavour to cigarettes), brought in an increasing revenue: and places like Dar-es-Salaam, Mombasa and Lamu on the mainland were developing into considerable towns.

In 1870 the Sultan Majid had died, and had been succeeded by Barghash, the same man who, with the aid of a pro-French party, had raised a revolt some years before. It was a move for the better, since Barghash was a robust and forceful man. The photographs of him now in the little museum at Zanzibar reveal a plump and genial Henry the Eighth in the ceremonial robes of the East, and they suit him. He is not soft like his powerful antagonist to the north; where the Khedive is urbane, Barghash has a more simple dignity, and he carries about him still the atmosphere of the rocks and the hard spaces of Oman.

When Barghash was asked one day what determined the succession in Zanzibar, he replied with some truth, 'the length of one's sword'; and yet he was a great deal more than a swashbuckler and an adventurer; he was a shrewd and skilful negotiator and a man who kept his word. Kirk who was in charge of the British Agency with the rank of acting consul was already proving himself to be the ablest British representative on the island since the death of Hamerton and he liked Barghash. There began that intimate relationship between the two men that was to continue for the next sixteen years and was to lay the foundations of British power in East and Central Africa.

It was never an easy relationship, because in the very nature of things the two men were obliged to be opponents; Barghash wanted to rule his little empire in his own way, and that included the continuance of slavery, while the British were determined upon abolition. The issue came to a head over Livingstone's revelations of the horrors being committed by the Arab traders in the interior, and Kirk's handling of it was masterly. Under the terms of a new treaty the slave-market in Zanzibar was to be closed and the shipping of slaves anywhere inside the Sultan's dominions was to be abolished. Barghash twisted and turned and would not sign, but tactfully and firmly — always keeping the threat of a naval blockade in the background — Kirk persuaded him that he had no choice in the matter, and in the end Barghash gave way and put his signature to the hated document.

In point of fact the new treaty was not at once effective: the Zanzibar slave-market was closed in June 1873 and a new Christian church rose on the site, but slaving still went on as before on the mainland and the smuggling of human cargoes across the Indian Ocean continued as relentlessly as ever. Yet this treaty made it possible for the British to take more definite action later on.

Barghash, who had been defeated and somewhat humiliated by the affair, could reasonably expect some *quid pro quo* in return. What he got was Kirk's determination to keep his little empire intact. From this time forward the new consul (Kirk was confirmed in the office) turned all the force of his patient logical mind upon the work of persuading the British Foreign Office that Barghash must be supported against all encroachments from outside, especially from Egypt. Kirk was ready to go to the limit in this matter. He was even willing, illogically, to support the slave-traders in Central Africa since they were to some extent the agents of the Sultan, and could serve a useful purpose there in keeping the Egyptians at bay. In particular, though not of course very publicly, he made a friend of Mohammed bin Sayed, who was the greatest trader of them all. Mohammed bin Sayed, who was generally known as Tippu Tib (a nickname that referred to an affliction in his eyes that made him blink), is not a character who can be understood in Western terms, for he was a gangster of the most brutal kind with all the attributes of a scholarly and distinguished gentleman. He was tall, dark-skinned, black-bearded and very good-looking, an authoritative figure, beautifully dressed, intelligent to talk to, a pirate of considerable charm and delicacy.

This gentle ruffian — and we shall see his kind repeated later in the Sudan — was a

Barghash, Sultan of Zanzibar.

Tippu Tib.

man of immense wealth, and his splendid house in the centre of Zanzibar (which still stands) was the terminus of a network of caravans that were already working up to the borders of the Congo and beyond. In the past he had been one of the slave-masters who had saved Livingstone from destitution in the interior, and he had furnished Stanley with porters on his march across Africa. And now, provided his own pocket was well lined, he was quite ready to put his resources at the disposal of Barghash and Kirk in their struggle against Egypt.

It must have been a curious little community on the island at this time, at once intimate and antagonistic. Bishop Steere, of the British Universities Mission to Central Africa, was at work designing and building his new cathedral on the site of the old slave-market; the crucifix on the pillar at the left-hand side of the chancel is made from the wood of the tree which marked the place where Livingstone died south of Lake Bangweolo, in Central Africa. Kirk had his chapel and his house on a little promontory just outside the town, and there he indulged himself in his passion for planting exotic flowering trees. Then there were Barghash's various palaces and kiosks, with his retinue of wives, relatives, slaves and hangers-on; and the narrow hectic streets running down to the port; and, in the port itself, the brigs of Salem, the dhows, the India merchantmen, and the new steamers with their paddle-boxes and their thin vertical funnels sticking up like chimney pots among the rigging.

Despite the cholera epidemics and the restrictions upon slavery the town had grown busier and more prosperous in recent years. A group of shops had sprung up behind the palace: coppersmiths, goldsmiths and ivory-dealers with their piles of tusks. The wealthiest people of all were the money-lenders who charged enormous rates of interest. There was no one coinage: Indian rupees, English pounds, American dollers, French francs, and Egyptian piastres were all in circulation, but the Maria Theresa Austrian dollar, worth about five shillings, was the chief currency. Great caravans setting out for the interior made a constant stir of movement on the waterfront, and throughout the day coolies kept up a monotonous chant as they trotted with their burdens between the dhows and the godowns on the docks.

It was a complex little beehive of widely differing manners, religions and politics, the East struggling against the West, Islam against Christianity, the worst of poverty surviving under the utmost luxury, and it was all too fragile and too disordered to last. Yet in the early eighteen-seventies Zanzibar was capable of making one more effort to maintain its independence, and Barghash and Kirk between them were still a match for the Khedive in Egypt.

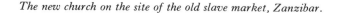

The new church on the site of the old slave market, Zanzibar.

Cairo through these years was becoming very grand. The days when travellers like Kinglake could speak of the open market of slave-girls, of unpaved streets, of no fine buildings other than the mosques, and of lions tied up like dogs in the citadel, were gone, or at any rate, rapidly going. The opening of the canal had brought a great influx of Western ideas into the capital. We have Winwood Reade's description, written about 1873: 'Cairo, like Rome and Florence, lives upon tourists, who, if they are not beloved, are welcome; the city is lighted by gas; it has public gardens in which a

The Khedive Ismail's country drive.

native military band performs every afternoon; an excellent theatre for which Verdi composed *Aïda*; new houses in the Parisian style are springing up by streets, and are let out at high rents as soon as they are finished. No gentleman wears a turban . . . As for the Soudan, it was formerly divided among a number of barbarous chiefs almost incessantly at war. It is now conquered and at peace, and trade is seldom disturbed . . . The traffic in slaves is abolished . . .' He goes on to describe the Khedive, now in his early forties, as possessing 'marvellous intelligence and energy'.

Perhaps Cairo really did seem like this to a passing tourist in the eighteen-seventies but to anyone who knew the real facts about the Khedive and the Sudan his account is absurd. The Sudan was not at peace, trade there was on the point of ruin except in one department – the traffic in slaves, which was flourishing more strongly than ever; and in Cairo the Khedive was using all his remarkable intelligence and energy in the desperate pursuit of money.

He quadrupled the land-tax, gathered one-fifth of Egypt's arable land into his own hands and extorted money from the fellaheen with the use of the whip; but still it was not enough to keep pace with his own spending or to satisfy his creditors. With the ending of the Civil War in America the price of cotton fell, and this still further increased his difficulties. Egypt was becoming bankrupt, and in 1875 he was driven to the expedient of selling his Suez Canal shares to Britain for £4 million. The canal was a great success; in the first year after its opening 500 vessels passed through, but from now on Egypt received very little financial benefit from it.

None of these difficulties however deterred Ismail from his plans for the conquest of the valley of the Nile.

'The audacity manifested in all these projects of empire,' Stanley wrote, 'is perfectly marvellous – almost as wonderful as the total absence of common-sense.' But then common-sense had never been a mainspring at the Abdin Palace; Ismail was out for the full, rich life, and if his course led downhill he was still determined to proceed at speed. With Baker's return to Europe he cast about for another European who would take charge of his campaign into Equatoria and the regions round the sources of the Nile, and his choice fell on Colonel Charles George Gordon of the British Royal Engineers.

Gordon was 41 and already a famous man: he had served with great bravery in the Crimean War, and had led the Ever Victorious Army through its hazardous adventures in China. Even the six anonymous years he had just passed in garrison duty at the mouth of the Thames in England had not really diminished his reputation as an eccentric adventurer and Bible-soldier, one of the long line of British military mystics that leads on to such generals as Orde Wingate in the last of the great world wars.

One of the strangest aspects of Gordon is the changing nature of the reputation that has overtaken him since his death. He dies as a national hero more loved and pitied than any other figure in the Victorian age, not even Livingstone excepted. There can seldom have been, at any one time, such a widely read book as his posthumous *Khartoum Journals*; they were known to every literate adult in England and established a legend which seemed to his contemporaries to be as noble as the classic heroism of St George. Then, most unexpectedly, a quarter of a century after his death, a homosexual intellectual revives the story, and all at once Gordon takes on a new reputation in Lytton Strachey's detached and ironical essay in *Eminent Victorians*. Here we have Gordon as the pious toper who likes a 'b. and s.' for breakfast, and then again more brandy and more soda when he retires, sometimes for days on end, into his tent in a fit of melancholy depression. This Gordon is still brave, still the mystical man-of-action, still quixotically generous and kind, still an erratic sort of saint, but definitely a little mad.

For a later generation, however, this brilliant denigration of the hero will not do at all. We are told that Strachey was all wrong about the b. and s., and that the stories of his drunken bouts of black depression were nothing but libels put about by Chaillé-Long who was an unreliable person, and whom Gordon certainly despised. The character that now emerges is a concentrated and highly efficient soldier, a man of great piety and simplicity who put aside all the normal distractions and comforts of life in order to serve his fellow-men. There is something scoutmasterish about this figure, with his spartan life, his deep interest in the welfare of boys, his proficiency in playing games and his emphasis upon duty; and if he is a little too vain, a little too fond of publicity, then this is only part of his flair for leadership and his genuine, courageous faith in himself.

Yet who will ever understand General Gordon? No matter how much evidence is compiled, both for and against him, an elusive quality remains, and it is strange that, being so unlike other men, he yet should strike such an instant chord of recognition in our minds, so that we laugh with him at his most reckless jests, and feel that we comprehend something of his mystical strivings. When he is being most difficult and hobgoblinish in his dealings with officialdom, we are, irrationally, nearly always on his side. He can switch his loyalties in twenty different directions and still he seems to us to be utterly loyal to the fundamentals of his own nature and to mankind; he worships in no church but he is an intensely religious man just the same. It is no wonder that almost without exception everyone who served him loved him. He was a most moving man; he could charm the birds out of the trees with those bright blue eyes in the sunburnt face, with his boyishness (despite the touch of grey in his hair) and his absolute sincerity. It is useless for him to protest that he loses his temper at times and gives way to occasional attacks of 'the doles'; and again, 'No man in the world is more changeable than I am.' We know him very well (which is not quite the same thing as understanding him); he is the man who is completely selfless, who is always interested in us no matter who we may be, and who always wants to help. Here is *baraka* a hundredfold.

Gordon was at Constantinople in 1872 when Nubar Pasha, the Egyptian Prime Minister, met him in the British Embassy and asked him if he could recommend a man to replace Baker as Governor of Equatoria. Gordon replied that he himself would accept the post if he could obtain leave from the British army, and the matter was finally settled on his return to England in the following year. On January 28, 1874 – the same day that the news of Livingstone's death was received in England – he set off to take up the appointment, and arrived in Cairo ten days later. Gordon liked the Khedive at their first meeting, and the Khedive, on his side, was delighted to find that Gordon entirely approved of his plans for expanding the Egyptian empire to the great lakes in the centre of the continent. The details of the appointment were quickly settled: Gordon was to establish a chain of military stations down the White Nile from Gondokoro to the source of the river in Buganda, to annex Buganda itself and then to launch Baker's steamers upon Lake Albert and Lake Victoria. The usual worthy clause about abolishing the slave-trade was added to his instructions and he was to acknowledge in a general way the authority of Ismail Pasha Ayoub, the Governor-General of the Sudan, who had his headquarters in Khartoum.

Gordon must have seemed a rare bird in the predatory world of the Cairo officials, and they can hardly have approved of him. He rejected Baker's salary of £10,000 a year – £2,000, he said, was all that was necessary – and there was a brisk and authoritative air about the way he made his arrangements. The selection of his staff presented no particular difficulty; from every part of the world at this time adventurous young men were making their way to Egypt in the hope of obtaining employment with the Khedive or of getting themselves attached to one or other of the expeditions setting out for the interior. There were Americans like Chaillé-Long, Colonel Prout, Major Campbell and Lieutenant-Colonel Mason, whose zest for action had not been satisfied by the Civil War in the United States; young Englishmen like Lieutenant Chippindall and Gordon's nephew, Willy Anson; Frenchmen like Auguste and Ernest Linant de Bellefonds, and the Italian Romolo Gessi, who were already familiar with Egypt and the Middle East; and a number of others, naturalists, botanists, anthropologists and geologists, upon whom Africa cast a spell because they hoped to make discoveries which would open up a new world for science.

Then there were in addition the native Turks, Egyptians and Sudanese who provided the bulk of the officers and men for the expedition, and were ordered by the Khedive to go. Gordon was a rapid and spontaneous chooser of men. Baker, in England, observed with indignation that one of the principal posts on the staff was to be given to the notorious slaver, Abu Saoud. But everyone was grist to Gordon's mill; if he thought he could use a man he believed he could reform him; and he argued that Abu Saoud, in the manner of a poacher turned gamekeeper, would have a valuable knowledge of the local conditions, and would help him to deal with the Arab slavers on the Nile.

Some of these men were already in the Sudan, others were to join Gordon later, and for the moment it was decided to split the force into two halves; while the Italian Gessi and one or two others remained behind to organize the stores and bring them up the Nile to Khartoum, Gordon and Chaillé-Long were to go ahead by the Red Sea route and make contact with the garrisons Baker had left behind in Equatoria. Gordon required just two weeks to complete these arrangements and then he was off at that breakneck pace which was to characterize all his journeys in Africa. He travelled by sea from Suez to Suakin and then, mounting a camel for the first time, he rode across the Nubian desert, arriving at Khartoum in the record time of twenty-one days. Strachey describes his reception:

'On his way up the Nile, he was received in state at Khartoum by the Egyptian Governor-General of the Sudan, his immediate official superior. The function ended in a prolonged banquet, followed by a mixed ballet of soldiers and completely naked young women, who danced in a circle, beat time with their feet, and accompanied their gestures with a curious sound of clucking. At last the Austrian Consul, overcome by the exhilaration of the scene, flung himself in a frenzy among the dancers; the Governor-General, shouting with delight, seemed about to follow suit, when Gordon abruptly left the room, and the party broke up in confusion.'

Gordon delayed only nine days in Khartoum before embarking by steamer for his capital at Gondokoro, a thousand miles away in the south. He was fortunate to find an open channel through the Sudd, and after a voyage of twenty-five days the *Bordein* brought him to his destination. A year had now elapsed since Baker had left Equatoria, and the province had gone to ruin. At Gondokoro the garrison had long since lost

Romolo Gessi, after the campaign in Bahr-el-Ghazal.

all discipline; the soldiers were paid either in spirits or slave-girls shipped up the river to them from Khartoum, and the old corrupt control of the Egyptian officials governed all. Within five days Gordon reached a series of drastic decisions: the officials he found dealing in slaves were dismissed, Chaillé-Long was dispatched to Buganda to make contact with Mutesa, and he himself sailed directly back to Khartoum. Here he demanded of the Governor-General that Equatoria henceforth should be separated from the rest of the Sudan and treated as an independent state. When Ismail Pasha Ayoub naturally refused, Gordon got through on the telegraph to Cairo and obtained the Khedive's consent. Next, with a boat-load of Austrian dollars (with which he proposed to pay his soldiers in lieu of their spirits and slave-girls), he sailed north to Berber, where he met Gessi and the remainder of his staff coming up the river. By the end of May he had his whole party together, and he sailed south once more for Gondokoro with four steamers and their attendant barges.

Now finally Gordon began to realize that he had embarked upon an enterprise that was infinitely more hazardous than anything he had undertaken in China. South of Gondokoro the river had never yet been navigated or mapped, and much of the territory he proposed to invade was still unexplored. His Egyptian soldiers had antagonized the tribes for miles around with their ruthless pillaging and no traveller could move in any direction except with an armed guard. The climate was unbearable; to avoid the mosquitoes it was necessary to go to bed before seven in the evening, and one after another the Europeans succumbed to malaria and the fearful heat. Before the end of the year three of them were dead, others were ill and others again had to be invalided home. Gordon alone remained miraculously unscathed — perhaps because he never allowed himself for a moment to be idle.

In these terrible circumstances — and it is safe to say that no modern traveller in Africa can have any inkling of how bad they were — the true nature and capability of his companions soon began to reveal itself. Chaillé-Long went down with fever on his return from Buganda and had to be sent to Khartoum to recuperate. Gordon cannot have been sorry to see him go, for he was proving to be a braggart and a complainer. Abu Saoud by natural instinct returned to his slave-dealing and his treachery the moment he reached Gondokoro, for he knew no other way of life, and Gordon was forced to get rid of him. Ernest Linant de Bellefonds, whose brother had already died, was the next to go; he was speared in an action against the Bari tribe. In the same skirmish Baker's Forty Thieves, the corps d'élite of Gordon's little army, were practically wiped out. Of the other officers on his staff only Gessi seemed to be able to rise above the appalling hardships which oppressed and unnerved them all from time to time.

It is strange that Romolo Gessi is not better known either in Africa or in his own country (a street has been named after him in Ravenna, but there is little else in Italy to recall his memory), for he is the greatest of Italian pioneers on the Nile. Of all Gordon's lieutenants Gessi was the toughest, the most cheerful, the most determined and the best. Gordon described him thus: 'Italian subject, aged 49 [in 1881]. Short, compact figure; cool, most determined man. Born genius for practical ingenuity in mechanics. Ought to have been born in 1560 not 1832. Same disposition as Francis Drake. Had been engaged in many petty political affairs. Was interpreter to Her Majesty's Forces in the Crimea, and attached to the headquarters of the Royal Artillery.'

Gessi, who had been born of an Italian father and an Armenian mother in Constantinople, was almost the same age as Gordon, and the two men had much in common; while Gordon was leading the Ever Victorious Army in China, Gessi was fighting with Garibaldi for the liberation of Italy, and they had served together in the Crimea. Both were at their best in irregular guerrilla warfare, and neither of them had much time for the regular peacetime soldier's world of parades, uniforms and promotions. In sum, they were men of the commando type, and they complemented one another very well: where Gordon was sensitive, solitary and ascetic, Gessi was warm-hearted and gregarious, and both were impulsively brave. They were equally prone to violent outbursts of anger, but that too may have been a bond; always in a crisis they were loyal.

Now, however, amid the strains and setbacks of the opening of his expedition, Gordon felt it was necessary to send this most reliable of all his men back to Khartoum so that he could hasten the dispatch of his steamers up the river. Thus he was left almost alone with his native soldiers to open up the route to the south.

'I have been a good deal worn,' Gordon wrote to a friend at the end of 1874, 'and I fear my temper is *very very* bad, but the people are trying and it is no use unless one is feared.'

It was during these early days that he gave way to his fits of melancholy. According to Strachey (who picked up the story from Chaillé-Long), he sometimes sat in his tent 'with a hatchet and a flag placed at the door to indicate that he was not to be disturbed for any reason whatever; until at last the cloud would lift, the signals would be removed, and the Governor would reappear, brisk and cheerful'. In one such crisis Chaillé-Long says that he nerved himself to enter the tent and there he found Gordon silently sitting with an open Bible and a bottle of whisky.

Whether or not these stories be true (and their implication that Gordon was a drunkard is certainly a lie) they cannot affect the fact that Gordon, during these early years on the Upper Nile, accomplished far more than he ever did in his last fatal stand in Khartoum eight years later. He was not a shooter of Africans and he made raids upon the tribes only under the direst necessity. He coaxed and persuaded the African chiefs, he infused the blaze of his energy into his own men, and he was adamant; he simply would not accept defeat.

One of his first acts on his arrival in Equatoria was to move his headquarters from Gondokoro to a healthier climate some miles further downstream at Lado. Next he tackled the problem of the river itself. A little above Gondokoro it broke into rapids, followed by a fairly smooth stretch of some thirty miles, then again more rapids that came racing down through steep, heavily-wooded banks from regions that were quite unknown. Even today no steamer attempts to make the passage through this dangerous and turbulent section of the river – and it runs for about a hundred miles from the present-day town of Juba to Dufilé on the Uganda border – but in 1874 Gordon believed he could manage it. He had three steamers, the 251-ton paddle-boat *Ismailia*, which Baker had left behind in sections in Khartoum and which Gessi was now assembling in the dockyards there, the 108-ton *Khedive*, a still smaller vessel the 38-ton *Nyanza*, and two steel boats. In Gordon's phrase he 'prayed' these vessels up the river, and a fantastic amount of ingenuity and of physical labour was

General Gordon, by Lady Abercromby ; a posthumous portrait.

involved. He himself went ahead carefully mapping the stream and establishing military outposts at regular intervals along the banks. The *Khedive* was the first vessel to come up behind him, partly sailing under her own steam, and partly being winched up by gangs of natives towing on long lines from the bank. By September 1875 she had covered barely half the distance to Dufilé and then one day she broke from her moorings and stuck fast upon a rock. The prospect of even worse disaster lay ahead; advancing up the Nile Gordon for the first time came in sight of the Fola Falls which are the last and most serious obstacle in the Nile before Dufilé is reached. 'It is all over,' he wrote. '. . . I fancied for some time I heard a voice like thunder, which increased as we approached the river. At last we stood above it on a rocky bank covered with vegetation, which descended abruptly to the stream, and there it was appalling to look at, far less to think of getting anything up or down, except in splinters . . . it boiled down, twisting into all sorts of eddies, while the banks, steep and precipitous, prevented a great length of view. These shoots last two miles.'

He resolved now to abandon the *Khedive* for the time being and to send for Gessi, who was to bring up the smaller vessel, the *Nyanza*, and the two steel boats as far as possible under their own power. Below the Fola Falls they were to be dismantled and a thousand men were to carry them in pieces overland to Dufilé, where they were to be put together again. Gordon himself meanwhile pushed ahead on foot to establish more stations to the south and to complete his conquest of Buganda. Walking at the rate of 16 miles a day in intense heat he made first towards Baker's old outposts at Fatiko and Foweira.

Dropping off soldiers at Fatiko and Foweira he continued on again to the south, and in a final forced march of thirty miles reached Mrooli, which is about ten miles east of the modern Masindi Port on Lake Kyoga, and here still another outpost was set up. There had been occasional skirmishing with the natives along the way, but Kabarega had fled before Gordon's advance, and now at last the expedition was within reach of Lake Victoria and the source of the Nile. Nuer Agha, one of the best of Gordon's native officers, was sent on with a force of 160 men to establish a base in Buganda, while Gordon himself turned back to see how things were progressing at the rapids. He reached Dufilé on February 8, 1876, after covering 400 miles in 40 days. Here he learned that the *Khedive* had been floated off the rocks but was far down the river, and the *Nyanza* was still in the process of being reassembled above the Fola Falls. However, the two steel boats, each of ten tons, were afloat at Dufilé, and Gordon decided to dispatch them up the river to explore the unknown section that presumably led on to Lake Albert.

This was a moment of great triumph, for it seemed now, with the sailing of these two boats, that the conquest of Central Africa lay clear before them. Gordon, of course, would not permit himself the pleasant and exhilarating experience of taking charge of this voyage himself; that would have been self-indulgence. He handed over the command to Romolo Gessi and Carlo Piaggia, another Italian explorer who had just arrived, and on March 6, 1876, they sailed away. Gordon walked back to Lado, a hundred miles away, to await their return.

The mosque El Mooristan in Cairo, by David Roberts, from Egypt and Nubia.

Steel boats that could be transported in sections were important items of equipment on Central African expeditions. Gordon used two and Stanley had employed this technique: 'Arriving at the first river the Advance *was already jointed, and we were ferried over to the other bank in fifties, and camped.' (Stanley)*

Gessi was back at the end of April, to be followed soon afterwards by Piaggia, and they had news that was both exciting and disturbing. Above Dufilé the Nile, they had discovered, did in fact lead on to Lake Albert without rapids or obstacles of any sort. At the entrance to the lake Gessi had continued around its shores and had discovered it to be much smaller than Baker had thought, while Piaggia had struck out eastwards in canoes, carrying them around the Murchison and Karuma Falls, and had reached Lake Kyoga. All this was a solid geographical gain, but the disturbing thing was that both men claimed that on their journeys they had discovered new branches of the Nile; Gessi said that he had seen a stream flowing out of the river to the west a few miles above Lake Albert. Piaggia said a similar river flowed out of Lake Kyoga to the north-east. What then was the true course of the Nile; which the main stream?

Gordon decided now to investigate the matter for himself, for he was determined to map the river accurately from Gondokoro to its source. The *Nyanza* was now afloat at Dufilé, and on July 20, 1876, he went on board and steamed to the south, towing the two steel boats. He soon established that Gessi's new river, north of Lake Albert, was a fiction, and then steamed east as far as the Murchison Falls, where he disembarked and continued on foot along the bank of the river until he reached Foweira for the second time in six months. It was now clear that he had no hope whatever of getting the steamers up the river past the Murchison Falls, and in a further journey to the south as far as Lake Kyoga he discovered that Piaggia's alternative outlet to the north-east failed to exist. A further disappointment was awaiting him; at Foweira Nuer Agha met him with the news that, far from his having annexed Buganda, Mutesa had virtually imprisoned the Egyptian garrison there. Gordon wrote grimly in his journal, 'Mutesa has annexed my soldiers; he has not been annexed himself,' and another officer was sent south to extract the garrison from Buganda.

Gordon had now been for two and a half years in Central Africa, and if he had failed in his grand design – the annexation of the Nile from Gondokoro to its source and the launching of his steamers on Lake Victoria – he had only just failed. The river was accurately mapped and explored for the first time to within sixty miles of its source, the *Nyanza* was afloat on Lake Albert and the *Khedive* was soon to join her there; the Arab slavers had been driven out of Equatoria, and his military forts held a secure control from one end of his province to the other. Even more important, perhaps, than all this, he had prevented his own soldiers from pillaging the inhabitants, and had converted the tribes along the river from enemies into friends. It was now possible for a single traveller to move about armed with nothing more than a walking stick. That was something of a marvel for Central Africa.

The forts alone had been a remarkable achievement. Already they had begun to take on the appearance of settled townships. There were about a dozen of them in all forming a connected chain stretching for some 600 miles from Fashoda on latitude 10 N. almost as far south as the Equator, the principal ones being Lado, the new capital of the province, Dufilé and, later, Wadelai, on the Upper Nile to the north of Lake Albert. These places were very much alike. Each enclosed an area of about half a dozen acres at some convenient spot on the river bank where there was a good crossing, free of papyrus, and a clear line of vision both upstream and down. One side was open to the river, and here, as a rule, a landing stage and a little shipbuilding yard were constructed so that the steamers could be assembled and repaired. The other three sides consisted of a high, thick, earthen embankment surrounded by a ditch. From the river's edge neat streets of straw huts ran inland, and in the centre of the fort were the brick buildings of the principal officers, the storehouses and the ammunition dump. Cannon were posted round the embankment and the Khedive's red flag floated overhead.

Gordon had imposed his own strict notions of discipline on the garrisons: a bugle sounded reveillé at 5.30 a.m. when the day was breaking – a strange sound in this wilderness. (The tribesmen remembered it in after years; in the Murchison Game Park in Uganda there is still a place called Bugili. It stands on the river opposite the ruins of Gordon's old fort at Magungo, and was so named by the natives because a man standing there could hear the sound of the garrison bugles, and thus be warned that he was getting too close for comfort.)

The streets were then swept and the soldiers turned their women out to work in the fields through the day. At 8 p.m. the gates of the fort were locked for the night and the evening meal was cooked and eaten.

It was a monotonous existence, of course, since the steamers and the supplies and letters they brought were the lifestream of the garrisons, and often weeks and months would go by before the sound of a distant whistle would send everyone rushing to the river bank. But then Central Africa, like any other tropical place, had its own torpid methods of enhancing life. The soldiers fished for the Nile perch and the tilapia, they brewed their native beer, they found wives among the local tribes, they danced at the full moon, and they turned towards Mecca for their daily prayers. If the steamers failed then there were always couriers passing along the jungle paths that linked one garrison with the next, and in their isolation in this green world of the river they produced their own gossip and their own crimes. It was an intimate, organized, ant-heap sort of life, and at least it provided security where there had been nothing but uncertainty and savagery before.

But Gordon was tired. In all his two and a half years on the Upper Nile he had never taken so much as a day's holiday, and he had driven himself to the utmost. Although he had never been seriously ill he had been surrounded from the beginning with the sickness and death of his men, and the unrelenting climate of the Nile had, for the moment, undermined his strength. Often too he had been in physical danger, and it is a sign of his exhaustion that about this time he quarrelled with Gessi: it was the quarrel of two men who had been strained too much.

According to Gessi's son, who wrote an account of the incident many years later, Gessi was aggrieved because the other officers on Gordon's staff received higher rewards than he did. Matters came to a head when Gessi returned from his circum-navigation of Lake Albert and Gordon, delighted with his achievement, was incautious enough to remark, 'What a pity you are not an Englishman.' At that Gessi took off his cap, threw it on the floor, and gave in his resignation.

This obviously is not the whole story, but there is no doubt that some such scene took place, and Gessi certainly departed. However, they must have made things up soon afterwards because Gordon, too, was determined to resign, and the two men made their way down to Cairo together at the end of 1876.

Perhaps Gordon's very success had disheartened him, for his work in Equatoria had revealed the enormity of the problem of the whole Sudan. Gordon, in short, was like a surgeon who, in performing a local operation, discovers that the whole body of his patient is diseased.

In Cairo he told the Khedive that he did not want to go back, and although Ismail persuaded him to reconsider the matter he went off on leave to England full of misgivings; and from England he sent in his definite resignation. It was something more than the gesture of a tired and disillusioned man; he was oppressed by an overwhelming sense of his own inadequacy. 'I have a sort of wish,' he was to write later to his sister, 'that I could get rid of Colonel Gordon.'

10

The Camel Rider

The Sudan covers an area of nearly a million square miles, and in the eighteen-seventies it still possessed no towns of any size except Khartoum and El Obeid, the capital of Kordofan, virtually no railways, no roads, no means of transportation other than the boats on the Nile and the caravans of mules and camels in the desert. Almost the only link with the outside world was provided by the newly-made telegraph line that ran from Khartoum to Cairo. It was estimated that nine million people lived in this enormous space, but it may have been a million more or less, since it was impossible to count them, and no one as yet had defined the borders of the country. There were no borders. To the east a sort of boundary was provided by the Red Sea and the mountains of Abyssinia, and it was generally conceded that the northern frontier with Egypt lay somewhere in the neighbourhood of Wadi Halfa, just south of the Tropic of Cancer. But to the west the unmapped plains spread away into the wilderness which came to be known as French Equatorial Africa, and to the south Gordon's forts had established only a rough and ready border on the Nile above Buganda.

The Sudanese were a mixed race, an intermingling of the Arabs with the black indigenous tribes. Apart from the pagan negroes on the Nile most of the people were Moslems. A network of Egyptian military garrisons, most of them many hundreds of miles apart, was established in the country, but whenever there was trouble the soldiers were hardly more than prisoners within their own forts. It was like the sea: the desert kept the inhabitants constantly on the move in search of pasture and water for their animals, and every trading-post was a kind of port where the caravans rested for a while and then went on their way again.

Outside Khartoum the Egyptian government had no real authority. The tribes and the slave and ivory traders made their own law, and it was the law of force. Equatoria, of course, was now in a different case, but then Equatoria was only a small corner of the Sudan, and the authority that Gordon had established there had very little hope of surviving so long as an Egyptian governor-general sat in Khartoum. Until that official was supplanted by an honest and efficient man and the whole Egyptian system was uprooted, there was no hope for the Sudan. Gordon had seen this very clearly. That was why he had resigned.

Once again the real issue was slavery. Baker had been altogether too optimistic, if not downright misleading, when he declared that he had abolished slavery from the Nile: all he had been able to do was to drive the traffic off the river, and now it was flourishing more strongly than ever in the open desert. The traders had found very little difficulty in developing new overland routes to Egypt and the Red Sea, and in the provinces of Bahr-el-Ghazal, Darfur and Kordofan a vast manhunt was going on. At least 5,000 traders were operating there. Gessi estimated that since 1860, when the traffic began, more than 400,000 women and children had been taken from the area to be sold in Egypt and Turkey, and that many thousands more had died. Baker, he thought, had done very little to improve the situation, and his methods had been unnecessarily harsh.

This was a cry that had already been taken up in England. On Baker's return home in 1873 he had been attacked as a dupe of Ismail's, and there had been a hot correspondence upon the matter in the columns of *The Times*. Julian Baker had written strongly in reply but he was not the best man in the world to defend his uncle, for he had very little love for the Africans himself. In his journal he writes of 'the treachery of these brutes of niggers'.

Dr Schweinfurth, the Baltic explorer and naturalist, was perhaps the most reliable witness of what had been happening, for he had been travelling for years in the remote Bahr-el-Ghazal province and he had no axe to grind for anybody. The

'Probably the . . . slave trade along the roads of Kordofan had never been so flourishing . . . neither Baker nor the Government accomplished anything like a practical supervision over the local authorities.' (Schweinfurth)

Zobeir Pasha.

picture he gave of the slaving there was appalling. He said that the traders who had been driven off the Nile swarmed through the region, and they ranged from the small man who went about the country on a couple of donkeys buying up three or four slaves at a time, to great merchant princes who dealt with their victims in tens of thousands; unless something was done the African tribes would be entirely wiped out.

The case of Zobeir Pasha was really spectacular. Zobeir was the Tippu Tib of the Sudan, and he lived upon an even grander scale than the Zanzibar nabobs. Like Tippu Tib he was a man of distinguished appearance and courtly manners. When Winston Churchill, as a young man on his way to the Battle of Omdurman, met him in Cairo many years later he was dressed in a frock-coat and shiny boots, and he dispensed an air of great wealth and political authority. The huge spaces of Bahr-el-Ghazal and Darfur were his hunting ground. Here, in the dry clear antiseptic air of the desert and the Marra mountains, he disposed of a private army of Arab horsemen whose faces had the beauty and the predatory cruelty of hawks. They raided like Mongols for hundreds of miles into the interior and spread that special sort of terror which is fanatically Moslem, and absolutely ruthless. By 1874 Zobeir could fairly claim that he had conquered all Darfur and no one – certainly not the Egyptian officials – would have dreamed of contesting his authority. Schweinfurth visited his headquarters: 'Seebehr [Zobeir],' he writes, 'had surrounded himself with a court that was little short of princely in its details. A group of large well-built square huts, enclosed by tall hedges, composed the private residence; within these there were various state apartments before which armed sentries kept guard day and night. Special rooms, provided with carpeted divans, were reserved as ante-chambers, and into these all visitors were conducted by richly-dressed slaves, who served them with coffee, sherbet, and *tchibouks*. The regal aspect of these halls of state was increased by the introduction of some lions, secured, as may be supposed, by sufficiently strong and massive chains.' The master himself reclined on a couch behind a curtain in the inmost hut, outside which fakirs sat murmuring prayers, and domestic slaves stood waiting to be called.

About the time of Gordon's resignation Zobeir had left his young son Suleiman in charge of his slaving empire, and had gone down to Cairo to claim from the Khedive a *firman* which would establish him as the legal governor of Darfur.

Ismail, as ever, was in a difficult position. He had poured money into the Sudan, and except in Equatoria everything had gone wrong. It was too late for him to re-trench. Too much money had been expended on the Sudan, and too much prestige was involved for him to abandon the country altogether. He was like a man who has expanded his business far beyond his resources, and who faces bankruptcy in the midst of apparent prosperity; and so he must somehow go on and hope that the tide will turn one day. Even if the profits of the slave-trade were eluding him there were other natural resources in the Sudan which could be made to pay. Nominally he had a monopoly in the ivory trade, and although the elephants had been butchered in tens of thousands there were still further hunting fields to be exploited. The inexplicable craving of the outside world to have billiard balls, piano keys and statuettes of ivory was just as strong as ever, and nobody cared how many elephants were destroyed. The ostrich-feather and gum-arabic trade also brought in a revenue, and there were other commercial products in the Sudan as well.

But how to manage all this? How to collect the revenue, come to terms with Abyssinia, clean up Khartoum, keep Equatoria going, and at the same time put Zobeir in his place? There was one man who might just conceivably accomplish all this, and that was Gordon.

In Gordon Ismail had found a paragon, a governor who really governed and who was spectacularly uncorrupt. Gordon of course would make difficulties over the slave-trade, but even if he destroyed that valuable business or at any rate a large part of it, Gordon was still worth employing. He was the one available soldier who could conquer the Sudan and bring it under the direct control of the Abdin Palace. He, more than any other man, could prevent the bribery and wastage among the Egyptian officials on the Nile and guide the taxes safely back into the viceregal treasury. But would Gordon come back?

Ismail knew his man. On January 17, 1877, he telegraphed to Gordon in London: 'I refuse to believe that, when Gordon has once given his word as a gentleman, anything will ever induce him to go back on his word.' The telegram was signed, 'Your affectionate Ismail.'

Gordon's exploits on the Nile had been enthusiastically described by the newspapers in England, and he was once more in the public eye. *The Times* had proposed that he should be appointed 'Governor of Bulgaria' – the country was then in the midst of its struggle for independence – and there was an alternative plan (which Gordon himself favoured) that he should lead an expedition against slavery inland from Zanzibar. But Ismail's telegram was compulsive, and after barely a month in England Gordon returned to Cairo. He arrived in February 1877 and named his terms: he must have the governor-generalship of the whole Sudan – all the million square miles of it – he must have full powers to treat with the Negus of Abyssinia and to suppress the slave-trade. Ismail agreed at once. Gordon describes the interview in the laconic style that presently the world was going to know so well: 'Then I began, and told him all; and then he gave me the Sudan, and I leave on Saturday morning.' The salary of the Governor-General of the Sudan was £6,000 a year. Gordon reduced it to £3,000. He did, however, accept a present of a fine gold-lace coat worth £150, and it proved most useful in impressing the tribesmen in the Sudan.

Sir Evelyn Baring (the future Earl of Cromer), who had just taken up his career as a British representative in Cairo, remarks dryly, 'Even assuming that Ismail Pasha was sincere in his desire to suppress slavery and to govern the Sudan well, nothing is more certain than that he was powerless to do so.'

Yet there is at least an air of sincerity in Ismail's dealings with Gordon. He had made things easier for him in Darfur by putting Zobeir under a form of house-arrest in Cairo. He gave him all the arms and men he wanted. He even wrote to the new viceroy as he was setting off to take up his post, 'Use all the powers I have given you. Take every step you think necessary; punish, change, dismiss all officials as you please.'

That was precisely what Gordon intended to do.

First he travelled down the Red Sea to Massawa, and there came to an agreement with the local Abyssinian chieftains for a suspension of hostilities. A long camel ride through the Red Sea provinces of the Sudan brought him to the Nile, and he burst in upon Khartoum on May 4, 1877. There had been some apprehension about his coming, and the whole town was waiting on the river bank to receive him. He did not keep them waiting long. 'With the help of God,' he declared, 'I will hold the balance level.'

There then followed a stream of new statutes and decrees that were aimed at breaking up the power of the officials and making life more bearable for the poor. Flogging in the prisons was abolished, taxes upon the peasants were lightened or remitted altogether, a box for petitions was set up at the Palace door, the privileges of the Ulema (the Moslem teachers) were stopped, and the worst of the army officers and civil servants were sent packing to Cairo.

Gordon through these days presents himself at his best. He speaks little Arabic but it does not matter; interpreters and secretaries are available, the orders go out, and presently Khartoum begins to learn something of the direct approach, of power exerted steadily and persistently from one central and unbribable source.

The Governor-General lived alone in his Palace on the Nile, and he was to be found there at all hours of the day receiving callers, a trim and alert figure in his red fez and his white uniform, his secretaries at his side, and the inevitable tobacco jar close to his hand. One of his contemporaries describes him as 'a strange little unpretending man with eyes like blue diamonds', and others speak of his 'superhuman energy', his marvellous resistance to the fatiguing climate.

It had always been Gordon's way to be generous and to keep nothing for himself. The Manchus in China had offered him a large sum of money and he had refused it. The gold medallion with which they had presented him had long since been sold to provide funds for charity in England, and most of his army pay had gone the same way. But now as Governor-General he had a great deal to give in the way of rewards and promotions for his staff, and every traveller arriving at Khartoum refers to his hospitality and kindness. European officials arrive to take up the vacant places on the staff, and one and all are enchanted by the new Governor-General. It is true that the meals at the Palace are very frugal and very fast – ten minutes is the usual time allowed for lunch – but Gordon is a lively and amusing host, and of his private anxieties the casual caller sees no sign whatever.

He was not, however, very often in Khartoum. The true picture of Gordon at this time is not that of an administrator in an office, but of a soldier riding on a camel. His journeys are prodigious. He covers distances which would make quite a respectable excursion for a modern car. He rides on and on for weeks and months at a time until it becomes second nature for him to be perched up there on the hard hump, nothing but the empty desert around him, with the brilliant stars by night and the pitiless sun by day, and no doubt it is a wonderful background for those solitary musings upon the Bible which are the obsession of his life.

Whenever a crisis occurs his immediate impulse is to get on a fast camel and ride to the scene of the disturbance at once. He astonishes them all with his sudden appearances, and there is something about his bearing so absolutely confident that he manages to impose his will where he might just as easily get a bullet through his brain. At one moment he is off to Darfur, accompanied only by an interpreter, to settle an insurrection which is brewing with Suleiman, Zobeir's son; then in Abyssinia, travelling as far as Harar to treat with the Negus; next he is back in Cairo to preside over a financial conference, and within a matter of months we find him once more in Darfur. It is bewildering, and the results are bewildering too.

Trade flows again, and Khartoum with its new shops and buildings begins to look like a modern city; it reminded Gessi of Milan. A channel through the Sudd is cleared, and Baker's steamer, the *Khedive*, is dragged in parts to the head of the Fola Falls where it becomes the flagship of the little fleet on the upper reaches of the river. Abyssinia is quiet and Darfur remains the only serious centre of disturbance. Even with Darfur Gordon is fortunate, for he finds the one man who is supremely fitted to lead an expedition there: Gessi had returned in 1878.

Gessi was still aggrieved. He came back to the Sudan at the head of a private expedition which was to explore the Sobat River up to its source in the Abyssinian mountains, and presently we hear of him complaining that the new Governor-

General is refusing to give help to private expeditions. Gessi was wrong there. Gordon received him very kindly, offered him *carte blanche* to go wherever he wished, and soon charmed him back on to the staff again.

Gessi was by no means eager to go off fighting against the Arab slavers, but Gordon managed to persuade him. Perhaps it was the very magnitude of the undertaking that attracted him, for by the summer of 1878 the situation in Darfur and in Bahr-el-Ghazal had become extremely dangerous. Suleiman was in secret correspondence with his father in Cairo, and had raised a force of Arab chieftains against the government. He retreated south through Darfur into Bahr-el-Ghazal beyond the reach of the Egyptian soldiers – and in fact the soldiers had no reach, they preferred to remain locked up in their garrisons and to wait there passively until help arrived. Gessi sailed south from Khartoum in the *Bordein* with a contingent of Government troops, and fought a series of pitched battles against Suleiman in Bahr-el-Ghazal. In the end he ambushed the young man and put him to death with all his leading sheikhs. Ten thousand slaves were released. It was a fast and brilliant operation, the first of the great guerrilla battles in the Sudan, and the only one in which the European commander showed any real understanding of the nature of war against the Arabs. Its effects were remarkable. For the first time in twenty-five years the Western Sudan was freed from the tyranny of Zobeir and his family, and for the moment at

The Bordein *in 1930.*

least the wholesale traffic in slaves was checked. Gordon, following up in Gessi's rear, mopped up the isolated pockets of resistance, and it seemed that at last he was in sight of bringing the whole of the Sudan under his control.

By now a new staff had been established, and the provinces were parcelled out among them. Gessi was appointed Governor of Bahr-el-Ghazal, with the rank of Pasha, and a young Viennese officer named Rudolf Carl von Slatin was sent to Darfur. (Gordon previously had offered Darfur to Burton, but Burton had replied: 'I could not serve under you, nor you under me.') Frank Lupton, an Englishman who had been serving as first officer on a cargo boat in the Red Sea and had been recommended by the missionaries as a steady man who did not drink, was being trained at Khartoum; and there were others as well, Egyptians and Arabs among them, whom Gordon had picked up at random on his travels and had liked and trusted. Equatoria after Gordon's departure had been governed in turn by the two Americans, Prout and Mason, but their health had failed, and they were now replaced by a German doctor named Eduard Schnitzer who had already been for some years in the Turkish service. Schnitzer had travelled widely through the Middle East, and had become so enamoured of it that he had adopted the Moslem faith and had changed his name to Emin, which means 'The Faithful One'. These men seem without exception to have been devoted to Gordon, and Emin was probably speaking for them all when he wrote in a letter from Equatoria that the province was at peace – 'thanks to Gordon Pasha's eminent talent for organization, thanks to his three years of really superhuman exertions and labours in a climate which very few have hitherto been able to withstand, thanks to his energy which no hindrances were able to damp. . . . Only one who has had any direct dealings with negroes . . . can form a true estimate of what Gordon Pasha has accomplished here.'

Thus it went all the way down the river, past the Fola Falls to Gondokoro, and on through the Sudd and the desert to Khartoum and the Egyptian border. East of the Nile to the Red Sea, and west to Darfur, another network of outposts and trading routes was spreading out, and everywhere the new governors were making it possible for the inhabitants to live without war. Gordon was probably justified in writing, as he did later on, 'No man could lift his hand or foot in the land of the Sudan without me.' The country was being better governed than it had ever been before.

And yet, in the midst of all this success, strange evolutions were taking place in Gordon's mind, and they were soon to make it impossible for him to continue. There was something in his nature that impelled him to find disillusionment and failure at the heart of all his best achievements. With him, every arrival is another departure, his reach forever exceeds his grasp, and nothing in this world can fulfil his hunger for perfection. And so, all at once, his enthusiasm evaporates, he detests the object he has been so desperately striving for, he sees another point of view and rushes away into the most bewildering complications and contradictions. This happened to him now in the Sudan.

It is clear from Gordon's letters and journals that about this time he began to hate his own Egyptian soldiers. They were ruthless with the negroes, just as ruthless as the Arabs were, and in using them Gordon felt he was bringing, not progress, but perfect misery to the Upper Nile. The time was to come, of course, when Gordon was to give his life for these same Egyptian soldiers, but now in 1879, after five years in the Sudan, he was discovering that many things about the country were more complicated than he had imagined. The Arab slave-dealers, for example, were not quite so heinous as they had been made out to be. There were even virtues to be found in Islam. 'I like the Mussulman', he wrote, 'he is not ashamed of his God. His life is a fairly pure one. Certainly he gives himself a good margin in the wife line, but at any rate he never poaches on others'. Can our Christian people say the same?' It was a question too as to whether or not you could really abolish slavery in a Mohammedan country, since it was a fundamental of the Moslem way of life, and on closer acquaintance it was not all bestiality: many of the slaves did very well for themselves and would not have exchanged their masters for freedom. Suddenly to uproot the system could lead only to chaos. And so he goes on and on turning over these points in his mind, and this is a dangerous business because Gordon, unlike other men, cannot quietly accept a compromise, he has to act and say precisely what he thinks.

A further disillusionment had overtaken Gordon in Cairo. Ismail's financial dealings were now entering their final downslide into ruin; there was an £80 million debt owing to European creditors and a board of inquiry had been set up to discover means by which Ismail could pay the next instalment of interest at 7 per cent. De Lesseps was on this board, and so was Baring. In March 1878 Ismail had had the strange notion of bringing Gordon up to Cairo to preside at the meetings of the board. He knew he could be sure of Gordon's loyalty, and at the same time he hoped no doubt that Gordon's reputation in the world would help to smooth things over.

Now there was only one way for the Khedive to raise more money, and that was to extort it from the peasants with the use of the whip, and the peasants had already been taxed into abject beggary. It seemed to Gordon (and of course to the Khedive) that the only rational thing to be done was for the European creditors to forgo their interest for the next few months. He also wanted to exclude from the board of inquiry the representatives of the European creditors, since they were interested parties. On both points he met implacable opposition: the European investors were adamant and they were not concerned to know how the money was to be raised provided they got it. Baring, de Lesseps and the others were also quite determined that the representatives of the European creditors should be present at the inquiry so that they could keep an eye on the proceedings and also, probably, upon Gordon himself.

Inevitably Gordon quarrelled with them all. Baring he disliked on sight: 'He has,' he wrote, 'a pretentious, grand, patronizing way about him. We had a few words together. I said, "I would do what His Highness asked me." He said, "it was unfair to the creditors," and in a few moments all was over. When oil mixes with water we will mix together.' He resigned from the inquiry and returned to Khartoum.

By now he was suffering increasingly from nervous exhaustion, and the campaign against Suleiman that followed his return from Cairo had drained his last reserves of energy. The hot summer months in Khartoum in 1879 must have been a misery to him, and one catches here a glimpse of the momentous tragedy that lay ahead. He was aware of a growing hostility. It mounted up against him from the officials he had dismissed and from the slave-traders he had ruined. In Cairo as well as Khartoum the Egyptian Pashas were his enemies. Zobeir was not likely to forget the death of his son. And then there was Baring.

Baring certainly was not an enemy, but at that brief first meeting with him in Cairo Gordon had had a sharp and chilling reminder that, when all the crises are over, it is officialdom that really rules the world, and Baring *par excellence* was an official. Baring was seven years younger than Gordon and not nearly such a great name with the public, but he represented a force which Gordon had recognized at once and from which he instantly recoiled.

Nowadays we would say that Baring was a member of the Establishment (which Gordon certainly was not). He represented the *status quo*, and by breeding and instinct he defended it with a steady, unemotional discipline. The eccentricities of a man like Gordon were not at all likely to dismay him, and he was prone neither to hero-worship nor to jealousy. In a world of untidy, adolescent enthusiasms he stood for precision and the middle course, and in a detached and desiccated way he threw out an air of privilege and of adult firmness.

He had been trained in the army, and it was not until he was 31 that he was sent out to India as private secretary to his cousin, the Viceroy, Lord Northbrook. His ability was then quickly recognized and now eight years later he was on the verge of his tremendous career as the virtual ruler of Egypt. A reputation for rudeness held him back, but Baring was a great deal more than a stuffed shirt, and any balanced judge of him in his dealings with Gordon will admit that, throughout the tumultuous years that lay ahead, it was he and not Gordon who was fair, patient, loyal and very sensible. Spontaneity Baring lacked, and perhaps also Gordon's flair for seeing into the simple truth of things – his was the official's world of caution and the safe negative – but he was a remarkable administrator and he was not afraid. In all honesty one ought not to take Gordon's side in this dispute, and yet one does.

It was Gordon's loneliness that was gaining on him now. The young governors he had appointed were far afield, and in Khartoum there was no one to confide in. Gessi just possibly might have helped him, but then Gessi was too impulsive and too ignorant of politics, and in any case was involved in his own problems in Bahr-el-Ghazal.

There is a certain pent-up desire for understanding and communication in Gordon's correspondence at this time. He rages against 'official dinners' in society in London, what bores they are, what a waste of time. Again and again he declares that he is 'dead to honours and riches'. Marriage he rejects: 'What a blessing it is that one was never married! Marriage spoils human beings, I think: if the wife is willing the husband is not, and *vice-versa*.' Apart from his great interest in the training and activities of boys (which was certainly innocent) there is no evidence that he had homosexual inclinations; rather, he is a neuter. But still he must communicate; and so he turns to religion and finds perhaps a palliative to his loneliness in the universality of human suffering. And of course he exhausts his strength, arouses jealousies, makes enemies and finally recoils upon himself. Hence the 'doles', the sudden rages, the recourse to the occasional 'b. and s.' and the inevitable self-disgust. All these things now beset him once again at Khartoum, and he was much less able to withstand them than he had been when he first came to the Sudan in 1874. Five years in that climate had made a very great difference. It needed only a small additional set-back to push him to the end of his resources, and presently that set-back was supplied.

The Khedive Tewfik. 'His highness is most amiable and good-looking.' (Stanley)

In June 1879 word arrived that Ismail, the friend to whom he had been able to 'tell all', the man who had 'given him the Sudan', had been deposed.

Ismail, after sixteen years of glorious spending, had had one final spree. After the failure of his board of inquiry he had engineered a military riot against European interference with his affairs, and had set up an autocratic government of his own. It had sailed along dizzily for a few months, but then the tide of debts had washed over him again. Baring and his colleagues, with the backing of their European governments, had supervised the final sinking of the Khedive with diplomatic skill. The Sultan in Constantinople, who was still the nominal overlord of Egypt, was induced to send Ismail a telegram in which he addressed him as the 'ex-Khedive' and informed him that his eldest son Tewfik had succeeded to his place.

*'I have a splendid camel – none like it; it flies along, and quite astonishes even the Arabs. I came flying
into their station in marshal's uniform, and before the men had had time to unpile their arms, had arrived
with only one man with me.' (Gordon)*

Ismail had departed in much the same way as he had come in the beginning; he
had cleaned out the cash in the treasury, gathered together his valuables, and with a
sum of about £3 million had boarded his yacht *Mahrousa* and had sailed away. He
was to console himself for the remainder of his life in a palace on the Bosphorus,
and cannot have been too much saddened by his fall.

But to Gordon his going was a deep and final break; the only Sudan he knew was
the one that Ismail had given him and he did not wish to continue there under any
other master. Even with Ismail he was disillusioned, and he wrote in one of his
letters, 'Do not fret about Ismail Pasha – he is a philosopher and has plenty of
money. He played high stakes and lost . . . I am one of those he fooled but I bear him
no grudge. It is a blessing for Egypt that he is gone.'

Now finally he was disgusted. 'I may indeed say,' he wrote, 'I have lost every desire
in a material way for the things of this life, and I have no wish for eating, drinking, or
comforts. If I have a wish for anything it would be for a dreamless sleep.'

In July 1879 he decided to resign his governor-generalship. His last act before
returning home was to make another of his prodigious rides into Abyssinia – he had
now travelled in all some 8,000 or 9,000 miles on the back of a camel – in an attempt to
obtain a final settlement between Egypt and the Negus. The Abyssinians, however,

arrested him and ignominiously turned him out, and after a terrible forced march he struggled back to Cairo on January 2, 1880. Hardly anyone in authority was sorry to see him go. 'Some,' Wilfrid Scawen Blunt says, 'thought him mad, others that he drank, and others again that he was a religious fanatic;' and for the moment there was no place for such a man in either Europe or Africa. General Gordon was too headstrong and too erratic.

It was also thought typical of this difficult man that he should have chosen to make still another powerful enemy on his way home to England. Passing through Paris he told the Ambassador, Lord Lyons, who had the ear of the British cabinet, that unless the British found a successor for the governor-generalship of the Sudan he would go to the French and suggest that they should fill the place. Lord Lyons demurred, and Gordon wrote to him: 'I have some comfort in thinking that in ten or fifteen years' time it will matter little to either of us. A black box, six feet six by three feet wide, will then contain all that is left of Ambassador or Cabinet Minister, or of your humble and obedient servant.'

Lord Lyons was not amused; surely this man was mentally unhinged.

Soon too another link between Gordon and the Sudan was broken: Gessi was dead. He had hung on for a year or more in Bahr-el-Ghazal after Gordon's departure, but the Nile had killed him in the end, and perhaps the ingratitude of the Egyptians also had a hand in it. Gessi was one of the best servants the Egyptians ever had, but they recalled him in 1881 and degraded him from the rank of governor to the status of a minor official. On his way downstream to Khartoum he was blocked for three frightful months in the Sudd, and most of the 400 men in his escort died of starvation; some of them had even been reduced to cannibalism before they were rescued. Gessi himself survived only long enough to reach Egypt.

Gessi could no more have divorced himself from Africa than Gordon could have done. They had suffered too much there to put the country out of their lives; like Livingstone they had to continue in Africa to the end. It required, however, a major catastrophe to get Gordon back; but then catastrophes were never absent from the Nile for very long, and the one that overtook the river in the eighteen-eighties was fundamental and drastic in the extreme.

PART THREE

———

THE MOSLEM
REVOLT

A dervish outpost. The Mahdi called his followers 'Ansár' (helpers); the word 'dervish' was British soldiers' slang imported from the Middle East and India.

11

Suez 1882

The British invasion of Egypt in 1882 bears a depressing resemblance to the abortive Anglo-French campaign on the Suez Canal in 1956, except that the earlier adventure was handled so much more efficiently and was successfully carried through. In 1882, as in 1956, the cry of Egypt for the Egyptians was raised, and Colonel Arabi, like Colonel Nasser, emerged from the obscurity of the Egyptian army to become the leader of the nation against the Western invader. Then, as later, Britain was divided against herself except for a short time when the hostilities were joined. It was the familiar pattern; all at once the national blood mounts up on either side, the national honour is engaged, and a thousand reasons are discovered for military action. In Egypt the British become rapacious bullying monsters. In England the Egyptians are described as 'terrorists' who break all pledges and murder innocent European civilians, and it becomes an imperative necessity that troops must be landed to restore law and order. And so the crisis sweeps on from riots to ultimatums, and finally to war.

The Egyptian grievances were very real and they were not all of their own making. After the removal of Ismail it should not have been difficult for the British and the French to have given the country a breathing space so that it could recover from its bankruptcy. But the European creditors still demanded their interest, and only the smallest efforts were made to reduce taxes upon the fellaheen. Turks and Circassians still held a privileged position in the government and the army, and no real parliamentary reform was attempted because it was believed that the Egyptians were not fit to govern themselves. Tewfik's every move was overlooked and guided by Baring and de Blignières, the French representative in Cairo. These two men controlled the revenue and the expenditure, and although for a little time they did succeed in improving the administration they were resented as foreigners and infidels. They were given responsibility without power, and the way was open for the ancient animosity of the East towards the West to flare up again.

Since Napoleon's invasion at the end of the previous century Egypt could look back upon hardly anything but defeat and humiliation at the hands of the Christians. At the first sign of trouble British and French warships were sure to appear at Alexandria, and the possibility of outright invasion was always in the air. In May 1881 the French took possession of Tunis, and that was one more stronghold of Islam in Africa that had collapsed. This steady encroachment was bound to arouse hostility. Even as early as 1868 Schweinfurth had noticed that everywhere, even in the depths of the Sudan, the Franks (a term that applied to other Europeans beside Frenchmen) were detested, and in the years that had elapsed since then this xenophobia had increased. It had been kept underground, its spirit had faltered because of the natural lethargy of the Middle East, but still it continued to expand.

In Paris and in London politicians had begun to talk of a dangerous Pan-Islamic conspiracy, a resurgence of fanatical Mohammedanism. In Cairo it seemed to the Egyptians that things were the other way about: they were being encircled by a Pan-Christian movement that was becoming more menacing every day.

Ahmed Arabi.

The crisis began, as Middle Eastern crises often do, at the height of the summer, when the Nile comes down in flood, and the humid, oppressive air is a wonderful stimulant to exasperation. A group of young Egyptian army officers had been becoming increasingly restless and defiant of discipline, and on September 8, 1881, they were ordered to take their regiments out of Cairo. Instead they marched their men to the Abdin Palace. Tewfik capitulated at once and completely. He agreed to the formation of a nationalist ministry, and Ahmed Arabi, the leader of the mutinous officers, was soon installed as secretary of state for war. Arabi does not quite resemble his reincarnation in Colonel Nasser seventy years afterwards, for he was a rather slow and rustic figure, and as things turned out not a very aggressive soldier; yet he was a good public speaker, he was undoubtedly sincere and – what was more important – the masses were more than ready to support him. They wanted a hero, a man who would symbolize and express their dislike of the foreigners, and they found it in this tall impressive-looking soldier who had been born the son of a sheikh in the provincial town of Zagazig forty-two years before.

Even if Arabi did not at first know where he was going, events soon decided the matter for him. The British and the French protested at his appointment, and that was bound to make him more popular than ever. The army was in a state of near-mutiny, Europeans were spat on and insulted in the streets of Cairo and Alexandria, and throughout the Delta Arabi was acclaimed as a national leader. A group of Egyptian sympathizers in England had by this time come out in open support of the insurgents, and they did nothing to ease the tension by warning Arabi in a telegram that he must keep the government and the army together or 'Europe would annex Egypt'.

The British now resorted to the course of action which had served so well in the past: the Mediterranean Fleet, under the command of Sir Beauchamp Seymour, was ordered to Alexandria, and Tewfik was presented with a joint Anglo-French note which demanded the resignation of the national government and the expulsion of Arabi. On May 27, 1882, the government resigned, only to find itself reinstated again at the head of a popular rising in Cairo. Arabi's position was now that of a dictator in a country where all the usual forms of government were disintegrating. There was panic in the European community. All who could leave packed up their belongings and made for Alexandria, where some twenty-five warships of the Western powers were waiting to take them on board. By June about 14,000 had been embarked, and 6,000 more were preparing to follow.

Through the first week of June conditions on shore became steadily worse. Agitators ran through the streets calling out, 'O Moslems, kill the Christians.' The vernacular press took up the cry for the regeneration of Islam and an independent Egypt. And Arabi, who was surrounded by a violent and persistent clamour wherever he went, began to prepare for war. Gangs of workmen started to set up gun emplacements around Alexandria harbour, and on June 11 savage rioting burst out in the town. By the end of the day several hundred people had been killed or wounded, some fifty Europeans among them. The British Consul, Sir Charles Cookson, was badly hurt, and a mob was running through the streets, looting shops and setting European houses on fire. Although some effort was made at the end of June to get a peaceful settlement it was now apparent that it was war or nothing.

Gladstone in England had done all he could to put off the evil day. He had chopped and changed and delayed. He had foreseen that as soon as war broke out British and French interests would come into collision in Africa, and he had declared, 'My belief is that the day which witnesses our occupation of Egypt will bid a long farewell to all cordiality of political relations between France and England.' He did not want to

Guns in Alexandria harbour after the bombardment.

take responsibility for Egypt, he did not want to enter the Sudan and he wanted no commitments whatever in East Africa. But Gladstone could no more keep England out of Africa than he could cause the Nile to dry up. The British explorers and missionaries had already committed him there with their hue and cry against the slave-trade. Disraeli with his purchase of the Suez Canal shares had committed him still further, and so had the people who had invested money in Egypt and were determined not to lose it. And now with this rioting and the murder of British subjects he had reached the point of no return, and in the worst of circumstances: the French would not join him, neither would the Italians, but the British public pressed him on.

On July 10 Admiral Seymour sent a message to the commandant of the Egyptian garrison in Alexandria saying that unless the shore batteries were dismounted he would open fire on the following morning. The Egyptians replied that they were prepared to make a partial demolition, but it was late at night before their messenger managed to find the Admiral, and Sir Beauchamp, in any case, was not satisfied with the offer. At 7 a.m. on July 11 he gave the order for the action to commence, and the bombardment continued until five in the evening. By that time all the Egyptian batteries were silenced (though they had managed to get seventy-five hits on the British fleet), and most of the inhabitants of the town were streaming in confusion

Bird's-eye view of the Battle of Tel-el-Kebir, September 13, 1881.

into the desert. On the following day the mob which had remained behind took over, and a great part of the city was pillaged and burned. It was not until late on July 13 that a small party of marines and bluejackets was landed to start the work of restoring order again.

Arabi meanwhile retreated with his army towards Cairo, declaring that he would blow up the Suez Canal and cancel Egypt's foreign debt.

The ensuing events can be quickly described. In mid-August General Sir Garnet Wolseley landed in Egypt with a force of about 20,000 men, and he proceeded at once to occupy the Suez Canal. He then struck inland from Ismailia, and after a series of

RIGHT *General Sir Garnet Wolseley at Alexandria, 1882, by Orlando Norie.*

skirmishes brought the Egyptian army to battle at Tel-el-Kebir, about sixty-five miles from Cairo, on September 13. The action was over in an hour or two, and the Egyptians scattered over the desert, leaving some thousands of dead and wounded on the field. Arabi, who had not commanded his troops himself, reached Cairo on horseback but was captured there when the British entered the city on the following day. On September 25 Tewfik, who had taken refuge in one of his palaces outside Alexandria, returned to the capital.

As a military operation it had been a resounding success, and it committed Britain to a political position the end of which no one had as yet begun to see. Having opposed the building of the Suez Canal she was now the master of it. Having used every expedient to control Egypt without the use of force she was now obliged to occupy the country with her army, and to rule it with a government of her own choosing. France, as Gladstone had foreseen, had been turned from a partner into an enemy, for she was intensely jealous of this sudden expansion of British power in the Near East. 'From that moment [the Battle of Tel-el-Kebir],' Baring wrote, 'until the signature of the Anglo-French agreement in 1904, French action in Egypt was more or less persistently hostile to England.' Baring could speak with authority on this matter, since he was the man who was selected to govern Egypt.

There remained still another problem, and that was the valley of the Nile itself. Did the conquest of Egypt mean the conquest of Egypt's possessions as well? Had the Sudan also to be occupied? This was a question that was answered very directly by the Sudanese themselves: they rose in the name of Islam and threw the foreigners out.

Even today the traveller on the Nile must be struck by the power of Islam in the North and Central Sudan. It would seem that there is little enough to thank God for in these appalling deserts, and yet the poorest and most wretched of the inhabitants will be seen throughout the day to prostrate themselves upon the sand with a simple concentrated fervour that is hardly known in the green delta of Egypt. No village lacks its minaret even if it be nothing more than a ramshackle scaffolding of poles, and the muezzin, calling the people to prayer, at once brings to a halt all sound and movement on the ground below. Here every precept of the Prophet, every injunction that governs the great fasts and feasts, appears to be observed to the letter.

Perhaps it is the very austerity of life in these arid wastes that predisposes the people to worship. An immense silence possesses the surrounding desert. The heat is so great it stifles the appetite and induces a feeling of trance-like detachment in which monotony dissolves into a natural timelessness, visions take on the appearance of reality, and asceticism can become a religious object of itself. These are ideal circumstances for fanaticism, and a religious leader can arouse his followers with a devastating effect. All at once the barriers are swept aside, revolt becomes a holy duty, and it can be a shocking and uprooting thing because it makes so sharp a break with the apathy that has gone before. The long silence is broken, the vision is suddenly translated into action, and detachment is replaced by a fierce and violent concentration.

In the very nature of things, then, the revolt in the Sudan was bound to be at once more drastic and more fundamental than the rising in Egypt. Had Gordon been able to continue as Governor-General it might have been another story, but directly he went the authority of the government disintegrated and revolt became inevitable. Emin continued in Equatoria, Slatin continued in Darfur, and Frank Lupton, the British sailor, replaced Gessi in Bahr-el-Ghazal, but there was nothing really effective these white men could do to hold the Sudan together so long as an Egyptian Governor-General ruled in Khartoum – and Raouf Pasha, the man who followed Gordon in that office, was the worst possible choice. Gordon had actually dismissed him from the Sudan service because of his inhumanity to the Africans. Raouf, like a good party boss, lost no time in restoring his old cronies to office, men of the calibre of Abu Saoud, who had swindled both Baker and Gordon in his day, and in very little time bribery once more became the normal method of conducting business in Khartoum, flogging and torture were resumed in the prisons, and the slave-traders everywhere took heart again. In 1882 Abd-el-Kader, the soldier who had once commanded

Raouf Pasha.

Baker's Forty Thieves, succeeded Raouf as Governor-General, and he was a better man. But by then it was too late: the Sudan was ready for chaos.

Hatred of the Egyptians was the first motive of the rebellion. There were about 28,000 of them stationed in the various garrisons throughout the country, and their behaviour towards the Sudanese had become unbearable. Taxes were gathered with extreme harshness, and every Egyptian official was known to be corrupt. Gordon himself had foreseen trouble, even as far back as 1879, when he wrote, '. . . If the present system of government goes on, there cannot fail to be a revolt of the whole country.'

MONTBAR

Early in 1881 the general air of unrest in the Sudan began to crystallize around the name of a strange personality who had appeared on Abba Island in the Nile, about 150 miles upstream from Khartoum. This man was said to have set himself up as a new religious leader, a Mahdi. The Sudan, he declared, was to be purged of the corrupt Egyptians, and her people were to be brought back to the austerities of the true faith.

There was no great alarm at first. Abu Saoud and a force of 200 men were dispatched to Abba Island with instructions to bring the rebel into Khartoum for punishment. But it was soon apparent that the Mahdi was something more than another provincial fakir with visions of glory. His followers on the island obeyed him with a fanatical reverence. They butchered Abu Saoud's soldiers with terrible ease, and presently there was news that the Mahdi, retreating into the deserts of Kordofan, had raised the cry for a Jihad, a Holy War.

Mohammed Ahmed Ibn el-Sayyid Abdullah, the Mahdi, follows the true tradition of the warrior-priests of Islam. Like a sandstorm in the desert he appears, suddenly and inexplicably out of nowhere, and by some strange process of attraction generates an ever-increasing force as he goes along. Confused accounts were given of his origins: some said that he came from a family of boat-builders on the Nile, others that he was the son of a poor religious teacher, others again that he was the descendant of a line of sheikhs. It was generally accepted, however, that he was born in the Dongola province in the North Sudan in 1844 (which would make him 37 years of age at this time), and that quite early in life he had achieved a local reputation for great sanctity and for a gift of oratory that was quite exceptional. His effects, it seemed, were obtained by an extraordinary personal magnetism. To put it in Strachey's phrase: 'There was a strange splendour in his presence, an overwhelming passion in the torrent of his speech.' He was a man possessed. Mohammed had promised that one of his descendants would one day appear and reanimate the faith, and Abdullah now declared, with an unshakable conviction, that he himself was that man. His hatred of the Egyptians was intense.

We have several first-hand descriptions of the Mahdi, the best of which perhaps is that given by Father Joseph Ohrwalder, the Austrian priest who for seven years was his prisoner. 'His outward appearance,' Father Ohrwalder says, 'was strangely fascinating; he was a man of strong constitution, very dark complexion, and his face always wore a pleasant smile.' He had 'singularly white teeth, and between the two upper middle ones was a vee-shaped space, which in the Sudan is considered a sign that the owner will be lucky. His mode of conversation, too, had by training become exceptionally pleasant and sweet.'

Slatin, the Governor of Darfur, who spent an even longer period as the Mahdi's prisoner, bears this description out. The Mahdi, he says, was forever smiling. He smiled when he prescribed the most brutal tortures for some wretch who had blasphemed or had taken a glass of liquor. He was a smiler with a knife.

There is an element of fantasy in the progress of this inspired and highly gifted man, and even now, after the passage of eighty years, it is difficult to assess him.

Mohammed Ahmed Ibn el-Sayyid Abdullah, the Mahdi.

Certainly he was not an adventurer in the ordinary sense. Even if it is assumed that he was not sincere, that his religious protestations were simply a bogus cover for his personal ambition, it still has to be admitted that his followers worshipped him; they never, now or later, questioned his authority, they thought him semi-divine, and from the most powerful Emir to the humblest water-carrier they were ready to die for him. His success was astonishing. To begin with, in Kordofan his men were hardly armed at all, except for spears and sticks, and yet they routed a column of Egyptian soldiers sent against them, and in August 1882 (the same month that the British landed on the Suez Canal) they laid siege to El Obeid, which was a town of 100,000 people, protected by a strong Egyptian garrison. The Egyptians knew that they could expect nothing but death from these madmen, and so they held on for six months. Famine defeated them in the end; it was so frightful that every rat and dog was eaten by the garrison, and a single camel fetched the price of two thousand dollars. In January 1883 the city fell, and when the ensuing massacre had subsided it was found that a large store of arms and a sum of money equal to about £100,000 had fallen into the Mahdi's hands. From this point onward the revolution became a civil war.

At the centre stood the Mahdi, the new reincarnation of the Prophet, and he was attended by his inner ring of disciples: the three Khalifas who were his principal lieutenants. Beneath these were the Emirs, the Mukuddums, and the leaders of the tribes. Finally came the wild horde of tribesmen themselves, with their camp followers and their herds of domestic animals. They had their uniform – a *jibbeh* with square patches sewn on it as a mark of virtuous poverty, and a turban; their emblems – the flags of the Emirs inscribed with texts from the Koran, and the green flag of the Mahdi himself; and their military parades – usually a headlong cavalry charge across the open desert.

The following proclamation was published by the Mahdi from his new residence at Government House in El Obeid:

'Let all show penitence before God, and abandon all bad and forbidden habits, such as the degrading acts of the flesh, the use of wine and tobacco, lying, bearing false witness, disobedience to parents, brigandage, the non-restitution of goods to others, the clapping of hands, dancing, improper signs with the eyes, tears and lamentations at the bed of the dead, slanderous language, calumny, and the company of strange women. Clothe your women in a decent way, and let them be careful not to speak to unknown persons. All those who do not pay attention to these principles disobey God and His Prophet, and they shall be punished in accordance with the law.

'Say your prayers at the prescribed hours.

'Give the tenth part of your goods, handing it to our Prince, Sheikh Mansour [the new governor of El Obeid], in order that he may forward it to the treasury of Islam.

'Adore God, and hate not each other, but assist each other to do good.'

These precepts were ferociously enforced. Flogging to death and the cutting off of the hands were the penalties for the most trivial offences. Marriage feasts and festivities of every kind were abolished. No man might swear, or take an alcoholic drink, or even smoke, unless he cared to face the instant pain of death. There was but one honourable way to die and that was in battle in the holy service of the Mahdi.

After the fall of El Obeid, Father Ohrwalder says that the Mahdi was venerated almost as the Prophet himself. The very water in which he washed was distributed to his followers who hoped in drinking it to cure themselves of their ills. No one doubted the success of his mission any longer, and his nightly dreams and visions were regarded as a direct revelation from God.

The Mahdi smiled and a sublime confidence radiated from him. He was not at all dismayed when he heard, in the summer months of 1883, that an Egyptian army commanded by a British general was advancing upon him from the Nile.

Egypt had taken a full year to bestir herself. From month to month it had been hoped that the Governor-General in Khartoum would have been able to handle the situation with the soldiers already under his command. But with the fall of Kordofan, the richest province in the Sudan, it had become plain that a military expedition would have to be sent from Cairo if the revolution was to be suppressed. But who was to raise this expedition? The British would have no part in it. In England a reaction had set in after the Battle of Tel-el-Kebir. Gladstone wanted no more conquests in Africa, and would no doubt have retired the British soldiers from Egypt had Baring been able to rule the country without them. It remained then for the Egyptian government to find the arms and the men, and in this, miraculously, they succeeded. The command was given to Colonel William Hicks of the Bombay Army, who was yet another of the footloose soldiers who had joined the Egyptian service, and he had with him a staff of over a dozen Europeans, including a correspondent of *The Times* and another from the London *Graphic*. When the force was finally assembled and despatched up the Nile to Khartoum it numbered some 7,000 infantry, 1,000 cavalry, and the usual horde of camp followers. More than 5,000 camels were required to carry supplies into the desert, and the equipment included both mountain and machine guns with a million rounds of ammunition. On paper it was a formidable array, but there were ominous weaknesses. Many of the soldiers were men who were serving terms of imprisonment because they had taken part in the Arabi rebellion – they were actually sent off in chains to Khartoum – and Colonel Hicks was a long way from being another Gessi. He was a thorough-going British officer who was not at all lacking in courage, and he might have done very well had he been leading an expedition in Europe. But this was Africa. 'In three days,' the *Times* correspondent wrote from Khartoum, 'we march on a campaign that even the most sanguine look forward to with the greatest gloom.'

There is no need to linger over the painful details. After a series of preliminary skirmishes the expedition ascended the Nile as far as el-Dueim, about 100 miles south of Khartoum, and then marched westward across the dry plains towards El Obeid. The guides either deliberately or through carelessness lost their way, the commissariat was hopeless, the soldiers unwilling, and the supply of water virtually non-existent. It was a wonderfully obsolete cavalcade. Despite the terrible heat some of the wretched soldiers were wearing chain armour and antique helmets, which looked as though they might have dated from the times of the Crusaders. In battle they were ordered to form a square with the guns pointing outwards from each corner while their camels were herded together with the baggage in the centre. Each soldier carried with him a contraption made of four iron spikes known as a crow's foot, and this he threw down in front of him on the sand so as to make a barrier against the charges of the enemy.

From El Obeid the Mahdi and his Khalifas watched the approach of this cumbersome and helpless column with a predatory joy. Long before the inevitable end there was a despairing note in the dispatches which Hicks sent back to Khartoum: the water has failed, in increasing numbers his men and his camels are dying every day, the Mahdi's horsemen have cut off his line of supply to the Nile and he does not know where he is. On November 5, 1883, the expedition was wandering in the depths of a dry forest thirty miles to the south of El Obeid when 50,000 Arab warriors burst upon it. No one knows the exact details of the battle, since the Arabs kept no written records and few if any prisoners were taken. Of the original ten thousand two or three hundred men may have survived, and Hicks and his European staff were not among them. Two weeks elapsed before the news of the disaster filtered through to Khartoum and the outside world, and months were to go by before its full implications were realized.

In the Sudan it was as though a dam had burst. In a tremendous wave the cult of Mahdiism swept outward, and there was hardly a corner of the huge country that was not engulfed. In Khartoum a panic began and many of the wealthier families fled down the Nile to Egypt. In Darfur Slatin was completely cut off. He fought a series of hopeless battles with the Arabs and then surrendered. In Bahr-el-Ghazal Frank Lupton hung on desperately into the New Year, and then he too collapsed. Emin in Equatoria retreated up the Nile. And far away to the east a Turkish-Sudanese slave-dealer named Osman Digna rose for the Mahdi on the Red Sea coast. Here and there, at strongholds like Sennar and Kassala, an Egyptian garrison remained like an island above the tide, but they were islands of sand rather than of rock.

At the end of 1883 it might then have been argued that the honours in the struggle between Islam and Christianity were fairly equal. The British had won Egypt but they had lost the Sudan. Gladstone no doubt would have been glad to have left the matter at that — in fact, he was determined to do no more. Khartoum, he declared, must look out for itself, and the Egyptians in the Sudanese garrisons must fend for themselves as best they could. But there were others in England who believed that nothing as yet had been settled, that all that had happened to date was merely a prelude to a much more intensive struggle on the Nile. These people believed that, having gone so far in Africa, England could not go back, and they began in the winter of 1883 to look about for a man who would force the government into action. They found him in General Gordon.

12

Sarawaking the Sudan

Nothing very satisfactory had overtaken Gordon since his retirement from Khartoum in 1879. Ill and exhausted as he had been, he had plunged, one of his contemporaries says, into 'a series of abortive undertakings, accepted in haste and repented of at leisure'. For some months after his return to England he had busied himself with the Sudan question and had written anonymous articles and reports for the Anti-Slavery Society. But he had refused to be lionized.

In the spring of 1880 he paid a brief visit to the King of the Belgians in Brussels. It was Stanley's idea that he and Gordon between them should govern the newly discovered Congo under Leopold's patronage, and Gordon told the King he was very ready to fall in with the plan if it ever came to maturity. Then Lord Ripon, the new Viceroy of India (after whom the falls at the source of the Nile had been named), had wanted him as a private secretary, and so he had gone off to Bombay, only to resign after three days because he could not tolerate his lordship's habit of saying that he had read his letters when he had not actually done so. Gordon, one feels, would never have made a really satisfactory private secretary. But now China was in the news again – there were rumours of her going to war with Russia – and so within two days he was off to Pekin. Then he was back in England offering to help the South African government in its campaign against the Basutos. Eventually he went to Mauritius for a year in command of the Royal Engineers, and before he returned to England he contrived to have a quarrel with the South Africans.

In 1882 he was in the strange position of being promoted to the rank of major-general with no employment, and he applied for a year's leave of absence so that he could go to Palestine and there immerse himself in the study of the Bible.

All through these years he had been thinking of the Sudan; again and again in his correspondence he refers to the subject, often with a feeling of anger and regret at what was happening there. At the end of 1883, however, King Leopold offered him definite employment in the Congo under Stanley, and Gordon decided to accept. The arrangements with Leopold were soon made, and on January 7, 1884, he arrived at his sister's house at Southampton determined to resign from the British army. It was then that he discovered that the Sudan had blown itself up into a political storm in Whitehall and that he himself was in the thick of it. He could hardly have arrived at a better moment.

The Hicks disaster, Gladstone was discovering, was not an event that could be conveniently forgotten, nor was it really possible to abandon Khartoum and the

Egyptian garrisons to their fate. His own Cabinet was divided on this issue. Both Lord Hartington, the Minister for War, and Lord Granville, the Foreign Secretary, were in favour of some form of intervention, and so was Samuel Baker, who was now living in retirement in the country but was still regarded as an authority on the Nile. On January 1, 1884, Baker had written a strong letter to *The Times* suggesting that British or Indian troops should be sent to the Sudan to fight the Mahdi and that Gordon should have command. *The Times* had backed this up in a leading article and a day or two later the *Pall Mall Gazette* (which had hitherto favoured evacuation) also came out for a much stronger hand in the Sudan.

W. T. Stead, Editor of the Pall Mall Gazette, *1888.*

The *Pall Mall Gazette* was edited by William Thomas Stead, who was the most vigorous political journalist of his day, and it was not in his nature to let a split in the Cabinet wither away to nothing. He himself had introduced the 'interview' into British journalism, and he saw here an opportunity for an interview of the most effective kind. He took a train to Southampton and nobbled Gordon at his sister's house. What, he asked, did the General think about the Sudan? The General thought very strongly indeed about it. There could be no question of getting out. The Mahdi, who was he? Simply another Arab rebel who could be dealt with just as Zobeir and his son Suleiman had been dealt with in their time. But unless he was dealt with, he could be very dangerous. Khartoum must be held at all costs, and perhaps it might be

Gladstone's 1880–5 Cabinet. The figure seated on the far left is the Marquis of Hartington, Minister for War, and next to him is Lord Granville, Foreign Secretary.

useful to have a couple of million pounds to put the Egyptian army in the Sudan on to a proper footing. All that was really needed was the presence of a strong commander on the spot.

Stead published these views together with a leading article in which he said, 'Why not send General Gordon with full powers to Khartoum to assume absolute control of the territory, to relieve the garrisons, and do what can be done to save what can be saved from the wreck in the Sudan?' In Sarawak, on the northern coast of Borneo, James Brooke had been given a free hand in somewhat similar circumstances. Could not the same procedure be adopted with Gordon on the Nile? Stead called it 'Sarawaking the Sudan'.

After the publication of Stead's interview with Gordon there could be no doubt about the way the public's mind was drifting: it wanted action of some kind, some gesture that would at least assuage the humiliation of the Hicks defeat. Gordon could hardly be accused of blowing his own trumpet – in his talk with Stead he had suggested that Baker, and not himself, was the best man to Sarawak the Sudan – but it was now clearly desirable that the two men should meet. The rendezvous took place very quietly in Devon. Gordon, by arrangement, went by train to Newton Abbot station where Baker was waiting for him in his carriage. As they drove along the country lanes to Baker's house, Sandford Orleigh, near Exeter, Baker urged Gordon to forget about the Congo and the King of the Belgians and to return to the Sudan instead. We are told that Gordon was silent, but that his blue eyes gleamed with elation. That night he wrote Baker a letter in which he set out once more his views for intervention, and Baker passed this letter on to *The Times*. It appeared on January 14.

With the publication of this letter it was not politically possible for Gladstone to ignore the matter any longer. Granville, the Foreign Secretary, was urging him to change his mind, both Hartington and Wolseley at the War Office thought something had to be done, and most of the London papers were in full cry. There was one man, however, who kept his head, and that was Baring in Cairo. When Granville sounded him out on the possibility of using Gordon in the Sudan, Baring replied that the General was 'quite unfit'. He said he had talked to both Tewfik and to the Egyptian Prime Minister, and neither of them wanted Gordon. Baring still held his ground when Granville pressed him a second time.

But now opinion in London was running far ahead of Gladstone and his minister in Cairo. Gordon's name was everywhere. In Whitehall, in Fleet Street, in the West End clubs and in the provincial cities, it was suddenly apparent to everyone who took an interest in the matter that Gordon was the perfect man to employ. Why on earth had they not thought of him before? He knew the Sudan intimately, his authority there was very great, he had the necessary dash, he was available, he knew what was wanted, he would cut the red tape and put an end to this ridiculous indecision.

But how to persuade Gladstone? Lord Granville and his friends at the War Office believed they knew a way: Gordon would go out to the Sudan not as military commander or as a governor but merely to report. Once on the spot he would be in a position to advise them about getting the garrisons out, and perhaps through his personal influence he could bring about a peaceful settlement of the whole affair. And so, without expense, without really involving the British government, you would put an end to the public clamour and everyone would be satisfied.

It was an absurd notion, for it was based upon a wishful ignorance of both Gordon and the Mahdi. Anyone who thought that Gordon, once out of the range of Whitehall, would be content to sit still and passively make 'a report' simply did not know him. The underestimation of the Mahdi in London was even more serious. Gordon himself was just as deluded as everybody else; he was quite unable to see that in the four years that had elapsed since he had been in the Sudan the situation had entirely changed. The Mahdi was not another local agitator with a rabble of lawless tribesmen at his back. He was the leader of a national religious rising and he was very dangerous. There was only one way of dealing with him, and that was the way that Arabi had been dealt with in Egypt: by sending out a properly organized military expedition from England. Yet the idea that Gordon could go out to the Sudan and work miracles was very attractive in London at this moment, and Gladstone himself finally agreed that Gordon should be brought to London and sounded out upon his willingness to go, but only of course as a 'reporter', nothing more.

It was Wolseley who interviewed Gordon in the War Office on January 15, and Gordon at once said he was ready to go. Granville now felt he could put a little pressure on Cairo. He sent a third telegram urging Baring to reconsider the appointment, and Baring saw that he could resist no more. In his *Modern Egypt* Baring says that he never thereafter ceased to regret that he gave his consent to Gordon's mission to Khartoum. He says he yielded simply because everyone was against him. Even at that time he made very definite stipulations in the reply he sent to Granville; Gordon was to take his orders from Cairo (that is, from Baring himself). Gordon was to make it clear that he understood perfectly that his duties were to report on the Sudan and get the garrisons out if he could, but that was all. Baring, in brief, did not trust Gordon. Granville saw the point and agreed.

One is constantly astonished at the precipitancy with which political action is taken in Victorian England. There may be enormous and often fatal delays while the argument goes round and round for months or even years on end. But then, abruptly, a decision is taken, special trains and ships are pressed into service, the Cabinet assembles, and within a matter of hours there is another fateful traveller with a half-packed bag and a dispatch-case of hurriedly written instructions departing from Charing Cross Station.

On January 16 Gordon went over to Brussels and got Leopold to agree to the postponement of his Congo appointment. On January 17 he was back, and on the following day he had his first and final meeting with the Cabinet. Gladstone was ill and did not come to the meeting; in fact, it was attended only by Granville, Hartington and one or two others. Gordon's account of what took place is as follows:

'At noon he, Wolseley, came to me and took me to the Ministers. He went in and talked to the Ministers, and came back and said: "Her Majesty's Government want you to understand this. Government are determined to evacuate the Sudan, for they will not guarantee future government. You will go and do it?" I said, "Yes." He said, "Go in." I went in and saw them. They said: "Did Wolseley tell you our ideas?" I said: "Yes, he said, 'You will not guarantee future government of Sudan, and you wish me to go and evacuate it.'" They said: "Yes," and it was over, and I left at 8 p.m. for Calais.'

The S.S. Tanjore *in Victoria Docks.*

So all was decided and everyone was delighted. The press the following day acclaimed the decision, Whitehall was satisfied, Gladstone acquiescent. The Prime Minister after this, Blunt says, 'was powerless to draw back, and, putting a good face on the matter as long as the sun shone, he went in for the gamble with the rest.'

Gordon was off within a few hours of his meeting with the Cabinet. Wolseley, Granville and the Duke of Cambridge were at Charing Cross Station to put him in the train at 8 p.m., and they were joined on the platform by Colonel J. D. H. Stewart, who was also to make the journey as Gordon's second-in-command. At the last moment it was discovered that Gordon had only a few shillings in his pocket, and Wolseley pressed upon him his own spare cash together with his watch and chain. Then the train was off, carrying him out of the London winter into the sunshine of the Mediterranean. The Brindisi Mail took him down to Southern Italy, and from there he went on to Egypt in the S.S. *Tanjore*.

On the voyage down the Mediterranean Gordon was hardly able to contain the cataract of ideas and plans that came whirling through his brain. No traveller was ever so beset with anticipations about his journey's end. He had a sudden memory of his old enemy Zobeir. Zobeir was dangerous. He might be in communication with the Mahdi. Gordon sent off a message to Granville suggesting that Zobeir should be watched and, if possible, removed from Cairo to Cyprus. Next there was the question of his getting across the desert to Khartoum. He would by-pass Cairo, he decided, and proceed directly down the Red Sea to Suakin and then strike inland to the Nile on camels. And the Sudan itself? What was the best way to settle the country once one had got the garrisons out? Why should not the Sudanese sheikhs be set up as nominally independent rulers when the Egyptians had gone? That was the system that had been adopted with the maharajas in India. He wrote a memorandum about it. But first the Mahdi had to be dealt with. Well, he had had a way of handling rebels in the past, and why should he not put it into practice again? He would ride off to see the Mahdi in his stronghold in the desert and there he would reason with him, persuade him to get his tribesmen to disperse. One final thought: if he was to carry out his mission in Khartoum successfully he must have an official position of some kind. Tewfik must appoint him Governor-General once again. But then he had quarrelled with Tewfik. All the more reason then for him to avoid Cairo – Baring could arrange the matter.

The *Tanjore* took but three days to carry its impatient passenger down the Mediterranean, but that was time enough for Baring to become aware of some, at least, of the plans that were coursing through Gordon's mind. He liked hardly any of them. He was prepared to have Zobeir watched and he had nothing against Gordon resuming the title of Governor-General, but he emphatically did not want the General to go riding off into the desert to see the Mahdi; if he did so he would probably never be heard of again. As for his planning to proceed directly to Khartoum by the Red Sea route, that was impossible: the Mahdists under Osman Digna had overrun the territory between the coast and the Nile, and no one could get through. The only way to reach Khartoum was to proceed up the Nile from Cairo. He must have a talk with Gordon, Baring decided; that was absolutely essential.

When the *Tanjore* arrived at Port Said a messenger came on board with a letter for General Gordon: he was requested to come at once to Cairo. Since he was under Baring's orders he could hardly refuse. He set off in a special train, a small solitary figure in a black overcoat, without servants and with practically no baggage, and a few hours later he was with the Consul-General. Nearly seven years had elapsed since their last meeting, and both men were prepared to make a fresh start. Certainly they had no time to indulge their mutual distrust of one another, even if they had wished to do so, and Baring, who was suffering from a sore throat at the time and could hardly speak, was anxious only to help. The events of the next forty-eight hours were bizarre. First there had to be an official call on Tewfik, and it passed off very well: Gordon apologized for the criticisms he had made in the past and was confirmed in his appointment as Governor-General. Next it was necessary for them to draw up the precise terms of his mission. A good deal had happened in the short period – it was barely a week – that had passed since Gordon had left London. From a mere 'reporter' he had become a Governor-General, and in London as well as Cairo it had gradually become apparent that the mere business of reporting would not meet the case at all; there had been reporting enough already. The time had arrived when the garrisons had to be got out of the Sudan at once or not at all, and Gordon, presumably, was the man to manage the evacuation. But he could not simply abandon the Sudan to the Mahdi: some form of government had to be left behind. To resurrect the ancient sheikhdoms and tribal leaders was hardly a sufficient solution: someone in authority would have to bind them together into a sort of confederation. Who should it be? Gordon now came forward with a proposal which, for the moment, left them all aghast: why not Zobeir?

But was not Zobeir Gordon's sworn enemy? Had he not described him as 'the greatest slave-hunter who ever existed'? Had he not wanted him removed to Cyprus? The General waved these points aside. He explained that an extraordinary phenomenon had happened and how everything was changed. Purely by chance he had come face to face with Zobeir in the course of one of his official visits in Cairo, and at once he had been overtaken by a mystic feeling that he could trust him. But eventually it was decided to defer the question of Zobeir's employment for the time being and his place on Gordon's staff was taken by another sheikh who was living in exile in Cairo, the Emir Abdul-Shakour. The Emir was a soft and unintelligent man, somewhat given to drink, but at least his political record was clean. He was a descendant of the original sultans of Darfur, and it was proposed now that he should be set up in the province as the first of the independent rulers. He was supplied with £2,000, an embroidered coat and the largest decoration that could be found in Cairo.

Gordon's second-in-command, Colonel Stewart, was a Scottish soldier who had already served in the Sudan. Blunt admits that Stewart was energetic and able, but describes him as 'a smart young cavalry officer of the Hussars, the 11th, with all the English officer's contempt for "natives".' Baring, on the other hand, found him admirable, a cool and patient man, with a very clear understanding of Moslem politics; in short, an ideal foil for Gordon. It was arranged that Stewart should report separately to Baring in Cairo.

The remaining arrangements were quickly settled. Gordon was given a credit of £100,000 and a promise of more if he needed it. Two *firmans* were drawn up: one announcing his appointment as Governor-General, and the other proclaiming the Khedive's intention of evacuating the Sudan; 'We have decided,' it read, 'to restore to the families of the kings of the Sudan their former independence.' It was left to Gordon's discretion as to when or if at all these *firmans* should be published to the Sudanese. Finally Gordon repeated his assurance that he approved of the policy of evacuation and that he would carry out such instructions as might be given him by Baring and the Egyptian government. The Red Sea route was abandoned. Instead he was to leave Cairo by special train for the south and then continue up the Nile valley by boat and camel until he reached Khartoum.

That same night, January 28, he was off, having spent just three days in Cairo. There was a moment of farce at the end. It was cold and the dim lanterns on the station gave very little light. Extra carriages had to be attached to the train to accom-

OPPOSITE *Sir Evelyn Baring (later Lord Cromer) by John Singer Sargent, 1902.*
OVERLEAF *Bird's-eye view of the Sudan and surrounding country.*

Khartoum

ARABIA

ROSSIER
MEDINA

EGYPT

ASSOUAN

KOROSKO
JEDDAH

WADY HALFA
MECCA

NUBIA

ABU HAMMED
SINKAT
SUAKIN

KORTI
BERBER
TRINKITAT

EDAB
SHENDY
TOKAR

TOUM
KASSALA

WHITE NILE
MASSOWAH

TIGRE
AMHARA
ANTALO

SENNAAR
GONDAR

KORDOFAN
ABYSSINIA
LAKE DEMBEA

EL OBEID
THE BLUE NILE
SHOA
PERIM I?
ADEN

TAKALE
ANKOBER

FASHODA
I? OF SOCOTRA

R. EL GHAZAL
CAPE GUADAFUI

MESHERA

SOMALI TRIBES

COAST OF AJAN

GONDOKORO

MUNZA
(SCHWEINFURTH)

GALLA

FT FATIKO
PALORO

UNYORO

ALBERT N'YANZA
VACOVIA
BAKER

COAST OF ZANZIBAR

MTESA'S
RIPON FALLS
JUBA

Mt KENIA

PORT DURNFORD

VICTORIA
N'YANZA

Zanzibar to Aden - 1630 miles - 8 days

INDIAN OCEAN

MUKAMBA'S

UVIRA
SPEKE GULF

STANLEY

UJIJI
URYANYEMBE
PEMBA I?

UMPETE

LAKE TANGANY
ZANZIBAR I?
AND TOWN

UGOGO

modate the Emir Abdul-Shakour's twenty-three wives and their baggage, and further delay was caused by the disappearance of the embroidered coat. At last it was found, and the train with its oddly-assorted passengers rolled away into the desert.

But Gordon out of sight, Baring discovered, was not Gordon out of mind. The telegraph was a two-edged weapon. It could be useful for issuing instructions to the new Governor-General, but then it also exposed one to the Governor-General's responses; and these were tumultuous. Gordon used the telegraph as most men use conversation. Hardly a thought danced through his brain without his dashing off yet another telegram to Baring. The party had hardly left Cairo before the first of these telegrams began to arrive and presently they began to number from twenty to thirty a day. Wearily, Baring let them pile up from early morning until afternoon, and then, with his other work finished, he opened all together, setting aside those that flatly contradicted one another, answering those that seemed to need an answer, passing on to London such fragments as he deemed worth saving from the torrent.

And yet, as Baring himself admits, there was often a good deal of simple truth and foresight immersed within the spate of Gordon's words, and often, too, he had important and even startling information to convey.

The party reached Korosko, close to the Sudan border, on February 1, 1884; Berber, beyond the great loop of the Nile, on February 11, and Khartoum a week later. At every staging-post there were crises. Before they had even reached the Sudan Gordon had quarrelled with both Stewart and with the Emir Abdul-Shakour. Stewart felt bound to stay on, but the Emir in a huff had disembarked with his wives at Assuan and was left behind. Eventually he struggled on to the Dongola province, but he soon retired to Cairo and was heard of no more.

The issue that arose at Berber was more serious. Berber was still holding out against the Mahdi, and it was a vital point of communications on the Nile. To keep Berber loyal was a first consideration, especially since the surrounding tribes were known to be wavering in their allegiance to Egypt. They needed encouragement and a firm declaration of Gordon's intention to resist the Mahdi. Instead he chose to assemble the leading sheikhs and take them into his confidence. He announced that Egypt was going to evacuate the Sudan, and at the same time he made it known that he would do nothing more to interfere with the slave-trade. 'Whoever has slaves,' he declared, 'shall have full right to their services and full control over them. This proclamation is a proof of my clemency towards you.'

According to Stewart, Gordon pondered all night before taking this drastic step, and he had his reasons – he believed that the sheikhs would be delighted at receiving their independence and would consequently be stiffened in their resolve to fight the Mahdi. The gesture about slavery was thrown in as a *bonne bouche* because it cost Gordon nothing – at this moment he was quite powerless to do anything to stop the traffic anyway – and at the same time he hoped that by his condoning it the sheikhs would be still further disposed towards him.

In actual fact, however, the effects were very different. The tribes had no wish to be exposed to the vengeance of the Mahdi when the Egyptians had departed. They

Arabian dromedaries and their young in the Sudan.

knew the power of the Mahdi (which Gordon at this stage did not) and they now began to gravitate towards him while there was still time.

Gordon, meanwhile, continued on to Khartoum, and he entered the city on February 18. He was received with fervour. Five years' absence had done nothing to efface the people's memory of his firmness, his liberality and the magnetism of his name. In this one respect the British government had been right in sending Gordon

The Sudan Express.

to Khartoum: no other man on earth commanded such influence in the city. He installed himself in the Palace once more, and it was as if the last five years had suddenly rolled away. Power, the British Consul in Khartoum, telegraphed to Baring: 'Gordon arrived here this morning, and met with a wonderful demonstration of welcome on the part of the population.'

The gates of the city were flung open and all those who wished to leave and join the Mahdi were invited to do so. Arrangements were set in hand for the evacuation of the first batch of Egyptian soldiers and a messenger was sent off to the Mahdi offering peace. In a second telegram to Baring Power reported further good news. Gordon had formed in Khartoum a 'Council of twelve Notables, Arabs, to sit with him. Burned all old records of debts against people, and instruments of torture in Government House. Colonel Stewart at prison striking irons off all prisoners of war, debtors, and men who have long ago served their sentences. . . . Everything is now safe here for troops and Europeans. He is giving the people more than they expected from the Mahdi.' Gordon himself had telegraphed a few days earlier, 'I believe you need not give yourself any further anxiety about this part of the Sudan. The people, great and small, are heartily glad to be free of a union (with Egypt) which only caused them sorrow.'

This then was the hopeful situation in Khartoum in February when the weather as yet was not too hot, and Gordon in the first flush of his arrival had instilled confidence everywhere. The Mahdi made no move – and that surely was a good sign in itself, perhaps even an indication that he realized that he had met his match at last and would come to terms. But then as February turned into March there was a less encouraging note in the telegrams that piled up on Baring's desk in Cairo. Gordon was beginning to have second thoughts about the policy of evacuation. Could you really abandon these people to the anarchy that would certainly ensue if they were left without a ruler? Was that humane? Was it wise? Directly he left the Sudan, the Mahdi would descend upon Khartoum and then it would be in his power to menace Egypt. The chances of coming to an agreement with the Mahdi no longer seemed quite so bright as they had been before. 'If Egypt is to be kept quiet,' Gordon now wrote, 'the Mahdi must be smashed up. Mahdi is most unpopular, and with care and time could be smashed. Remember that once Khartoum belongs to Mahdi the task will be far more difficult; yet you will, for safety of Egypt, execute it. If you decide on smashing Mahdi then send up another £100,000, and send up 200 Indian troops to Wadi Halfa, and send officers up to Dongola under pretence to look out quarters for troops. . . . I repeat that evacuation is possible, but you will feel effect in Egypt, and will be forced to enter into a far more serious affair in order to guard Egypt. At present it would be comparatively easy to destroy Mahdi.'

Fourteen years were to elapse before the prophecy contained in these words was to be made manifest.

Gordon now began to canvass a plan for abandoning Khartoum and for evacuating his force to Berber. In his heart he had no real intention of carrying out this design; it was simply another device with which to *épater* Baring and the deluded politicians in England. But then on March 13 there was a development that made it unnecessary for any of them to concern themselves with the question of occupying Berber; the tribes north of Khartoum rose for the Mahdi and blocked the Egyptian traffic on the river. The telegraph went dead. Khartoum was cut off.

13

A Roof with a View

From March 1884 until January in the following year – a period of ten months – a steadily deepening silence fell on the Sudan. It was known that Gordon was still in Khartoum, and that the town had not fallen, since he managed to send out native runners from time to time. But the messages they brought were written on tiny scraps of paper and gave only the briefest information. Presently it became known that Slatin in Darfur and Lupton in Bahr-el-Ghazal had surrendered to the Mahdi, and had escaped execution only by professing the Moslem faith. Father Ohrwalder and a group of priests and nuns who were attached to the Austrian Mission in Darfur were also believed to be prisoners of the Mahdi, together with a number of Greek traders who had been overrun in the distant outposts. Emin was still holding out in Equatoria, and so were the Egyptian garrisons in Kassala and Sennar, close to the Abyssinian border, but in May Berber fell and the Mahdi's empire now covered an area as large as all France, Spain and Germany combined.

Gordon's plight in Khartoum was not absolutely desperate. He had with him in the town about 34,000 people, of whom some 8,000 were soldiers, not really reliable soldiers perhaps, but they were armed with rifles and they had in addition twelve pieces of artillery and nine armed paddle-boats that were able to keep up a running fight along the river. Two million rounds of ammunition had been stored in the town before it was cut off, and the arsenal was capable of producing another 40,000 rounds every week. In March Gordon estimated that he had sufficient food to last six months, and with the Nile flowing by there was naturally no problem about water. The treasury was soon reduced to the equivalent of a few thousand pounds in cash, but Gordon printed a new paper currency of his own.

Khartoum was by no means an impossible place to defend. To the north it was protected by the Blue Nile, and to the west by the White Nile – and the White Nile, even at low water, was half a mile wide. By keeping to the centre of the stream the paddle-steamers with their light armour-plating were in no great danger from the Arab riflemen on the bank. A strong Egyptian garrison was posted in Omdurman Fort on the west bank of the White Nile, and the surrounding country was held by the Shaiqiya tribe which was still hostile to the Mahdi. The weak point in the defence was, of course, in the south where the town was exposed to the open desert, but here a deep semicircular trench four miles long had been dug from the White Nile to the Blue. From the first Gordon concentrated his attention upon this southern flank. Primitive landmines were sown in the sand, along with thousands of crow's feet and broken bottles — the Arabs had bare feet — and dyed cotton was used to imitate earthworks while new trenches and fortifications were being constructed further back.

After March some 30,000 Arabs laid siege to the town, but the bulk of the Mahdi's forces remained scattered through the Sudan, and through the hot summer months no serious attempt was made to break through the defences. The tribesmen were content merely to keep up a desultory rifle fire, and the raiding parties that Gordon sent out were often able to bring in cattle and maize. His steamers sailed as far north as Berber, and messengers were constantly passing through the lines. It was not exactly war nor was it peace, and there is almost a mediaeval flavour in the letters that

Fortifications at Khartoum based on a map from Wingate's Mahdiism and the Egyptian Soudan.

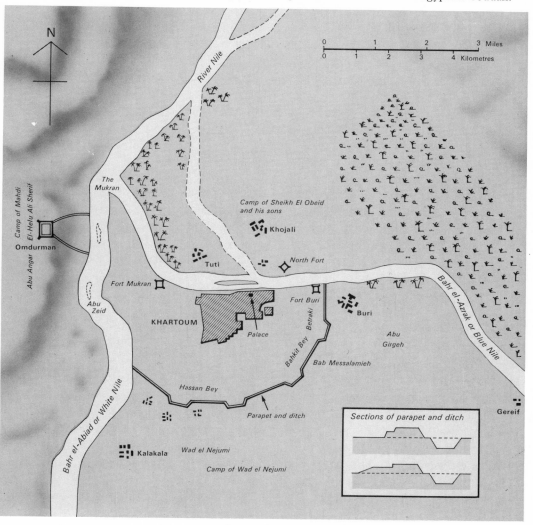

A village near Khartoum; ninety years later it presents much the same appearance as it must have done to Gordon.

passed between the besieged and the besiegers. On March 22 the Mahdi rejected Gordon's offer of peace. His envoys, on being admitted to the Palace in Khartoum, presented the General with a *jibbeh* and invited him to become a follower of the Mahdi. Gordon threw the bundle of clothing on the ground and declared he would never surrender. Later we find him sending out gifts of soap and other rarities to the Emirs who were encamped outside Khartoum. There is no hunger as yet, very few think of deserting to the Arabs, and the daily life in the town continues in a muted and fatalistic way but without real tension or alarm. Neither Gordon nor anyone else imagines that the situation can continue indefinitely; either they will have to be rescued by an expedition sent up from Egypt or they will be forced to surrender. But for the moment the expectation of rescue is very strong, and Gordon, who is forever on the move about the town, radiates a confidence which inspires them all, from the glummest merchant to the most miserable Egyptian soldier asleep on sentry duty in the lines. He promotes captains to majors, doles out special rations for the feast days, rewards the more daring soldiers with double pay, imprisons criminals and settles disputes with an air of absolute authority that nobody can deny. Gordon Pasha is now something more than the Governor of Khartoum, he is the will of Khartoum itself, and when he reads out to his Council of Notables the Mahdi's call for their surrender they unanimously and enthusiastically reject it. And so the long stifling days of April, May and June go by and no one has lost hope as yet.

In London meanwhile the government was becoming uncomfortably – and perhaps even indignantly – aware that they were being subjected to a form of blackmail by the Governor-General in Khartoum. Just conceivably, even at this late stage, it might have been possible to abandon the Egyptian garrisons to the Mahdi, but to abandon Gordon was altogether different; he was a public figure, he had gone out to the Sudan with the aura of a Christian knight-errant about him, and it was practically certain that the Press would raise an outcry unless something was done to rescue him. Even as early as March 24 Baring had seen this very clearly. He had telegraphed to Granville: 'The question now is how to get General Gordon and Colonel Stewart away from Khartoum.' Queen Victoria, who understood the emotions of her subjects rather better perhaps than any member of the Cabinet, was even more emphatic, 'It is alarming,' she wrote in a telegram to Lord Hartington. 'General Gordon is in danger; you are bound to try and save him . . . you have incurred fearful responsibility.'

Nor was it long before the public took up the cry. By May mass meetings were being held to protest against the 'betrayal of General Gordon'. Funds were raised for his rescue, prayers were said for him in the churches. But neither Gladstone, nor Granville at the Foreign Office was prepared to admit that their gamble had failed as yet. After all, Gordon was still perfectly safe in Khartoum and it was still quite possible for him to leave if he chose to do so.

In fact, Gordon himself was able to escape even as late as September, but he was wholly unwilling to leave his soldiers behind; either the garrison came with him or he stayed. This was precisely the point that the government would not accept. Gladstone was quite determined upon this issue. He declared that he would not send a military expedition, and he turned down a proposal of Baring's that a dash across to Berber should be made by the British forces on the Red Sea coast. Replying to a vote of censure in the House in May he stated calmly that he was not at all prepared to admit that General Gordon was cut off or in any real danger. He was 'hemmed in' for the time being perhaps, but that was all. There was no cause for alarm.

But this was merely playing for time. As the weeks went by Gordon's messages became fewer and fewer like a voice growing fainter in the distance, and by July the feeling of indignation in England began to take a much stronger hold. It was Lord Hartington who precipitated the crisis. At the end of July he told Gladstone that he would resign unless an expedition was sent to Khartoum. It was 'a question of personal honour and good faith,' he said, 'and I don't see how I can yield upon it.' Hartington's resignation was enough to bring the government down, and Gladstone gave way at last. On August 8 it was announced that an expedition would be sent to the Sudan and Parliament voted a sum of £300,000 to defray the expenses. Lord Wolseley, the victor of the Battle of Tel-el-Kebir, was appointed to the command.

There is a fated quality about the events of the next six months, an air of pure and certain tragedy that lifts the story out of time and space so that it becomes part of a permanent tradition of human courage and human helplessness. It can be repeated just as a Shakespearean tragedy can be repeated, and it never alters. Each of the three main protagonists – Wolseley coming up the Nile with his soldiers, Gordon waiting and watching on the Palace roof in Khartoum and the Mahdi with his warriors encamped in the desert outside the town – behaves precisely as he is destined to do, and it is wonderfully dramatic that these three men, who were so perfectly incapable of understanding one another, should have been thrust together in such desperate circumstances and in such an outlandish corner of the world. Each man is the victim of forces which are stronger than himself. The Mahdi, having raised a holy war, is bound to assault Khartoum. Gordon, having committed his word to the people in the town, is bound to remain there to the end. And Wolseley, the soldier, having received his orders, is bound to try and rescue him. None of these three really controls events, none of them can predict what will happen. From time to time they feel hope or despair, confidence or uncertainty, but in the main they simply hold on to their

1. *Daily News.*   2. *Times.*   3. *Standard.*   4. *Pall Mall Gazette.*

ABOVE AND OPPOSITE *Drawings from Gordon's* Journal.

predestined courses and they are like the pilots of three ships in a fog that are headed for an inevitable collision.

Wolseley arrived in Cairo on September 9, left Shepheard's Hotel with his staff for Wadi Halfa on September 27 and finally joined battle with the Mahdi's forces north of Khartoum in January 1885. It was not a very rapid progress, but it does not compare badly with the British march into the Sudan twelve years later. After all, Wolseley had to convey 7,000 men and their equipment 1,500 miles into the desert, and the memory of the Hicks disaster was very recent. The news Wolseley got from Khartoum did not indicate that Gordon was in such straits that an extra week or two would make a vital difference. Admittedly this news was very sparse, and eventually ceased altogether, but Wolseley's intelligence staff was not unhopeful. An energetic young major named Herbert Kitchener had gone ahead of the column into the desert, and as early as August had established himself at Debba on the loop of the Nile, barely 200 miles away from Khartoum. From this outpost Kitchener was able to send runners into Khartoum with news of the expedition's approach, and to receive the messages that Gordon sent out.

Nor was the Mahdi on his side to be greatly blamed for delaying his assault on Khartoum. El Obeid had fallen to him because he had starved out the inhabitants, and he had every reason to believe that the same fate would overtake Khartoum. It would have been the height of rashness to have launched his warriors on to the town's defences earlier than the New Year, since Gordon's guns and rifles were much superior to his own and the Egyptian garrison had not yet become demoralized by starvation.

As for Gordon himself, he had no choice; being who he was he had to hang on, using every conceivable device to keep up the morale of his people because the alternative – surrender – was unthinkable. Surrender meant massacre. The Mahdi's tribesmen took no prisoners in battle except women and young boys and girls, and all of these were destined for slavery.

Yet Khartoum, or more especially Gordon himself, remains the real focus of this

tragedy. He occupies throughout the centre of the stage, and the final scenes he dominates entirely. It is fortunate, therefore, that through his journal we know exactly what he thought and felt, we know all about his daily hopes and fears, and Khartoum in its death throes is almost as real to us as a catastrophe that has taken place in our own lives. The journal is an astonishing document. No other English soldier has revealed his heart so emphatically, so simply or so movingly as Gordon does in these wild jottings, sometimes written on telegraph forms and flimsy scraps of paper, sometimes heavily underscored or crossed out, sometimes decorated with oddly exact little maps and ribald caricatures, sometimes pathetic, ironical or recklessly unfair, but always absolutely honest.

By September (when, unknown to Gordon, the relief expedition was beginning to form up in Egypt), the situation in Khartoum was becoming critical. The supply of food was still holding out; indeed so many cattle had been captured by raiding parties that the price of meat had fallen from ten shillings to two shillings a pound. But the Egyptian soldiers were every day more lethargic, and on September 4 a serious reverse occurred: over eight hundred men were killed in a skirmish outside the town, and it was apparent that from now onwards the garrison must remain entirely on the defensive. But it was the absence of news that was the really under-

Khartoum, looking down the Nile.

mining factor – the feeling that they had been abandoned and that there was nothing definite to look forward to. Each successive day was a little more oppressive than the last, and even Gordon was forced to admit that unless help arrived within a month or two the town would fall.

He decided to send the steamer *Abbas* down the river with an Arab captain who was to take with him dispatches appealing for immediate help. It was a dangerous undertaking but it was not at all impossible that the boat could get through; once beyond the Mahdi's stronghold at Berber the crew would find themselves among friendly tribes who, no doubt, would agree to send on the messages by camel to Kitchener and Cairo.

There had remained with Gordon in Khartoum only a small group of Europeans – Stewart, his second-in-command, three consuls, Power the Englishman, Herbin the Frenchman and Hansal the Austrian, and a number of Greeks and others of European extraction. Directly it was heard that the *Abbas* was to sail applications were made to the Palace for permission to go with her. Herbin came first, and Gordon says he jumped at the offer: Herbin might be able to get the French government to move. Then Stewart offered to go provided that Gordon exonerated him from the charge of desertion. Gordon told him that he would not actually order him to go, since there was too much risk involved in the journey, but he would certainly give him an official letter which would make it clear that there was no question of desertion; indeed,

Stewart could perform a valuable service by going. He could reveal the true situation in Khartoum, and make a personal appeal to the European powers for assistance. Gordon had another idea; if England would not help perhaps others could. He wrote out an appeal to the Pope in Rome and another to the Sultan in Constantinople.

Power, the British Consul, now said that he too would join the party. Hansal, the Austrian, elected to remain behind.

There are some curious aspects about this matter, and they have never been satisfactorily explained. Among the papers which the party was to take down was the cypher that was used to decode official messages from Egypt. According to Gordon he let the cypher go because he feared that it might fall into the hands of the Mahdi if it remained in Khartoum. This meant presumably that he and all of them expected Khartoum to fall, and thus Stewart and the two consuls cannot altogether escape the charge of desertion. It is also a little difficult to understand just why Gordon would not order Stewart to go. Stewart had a long interview with Gordon before he left and pressed him to give the order. Gordon's explanation that he would not give the order because of the dangerous nature of the journey does not ring altogether true. He must have known that without the order to leave Stewart would have some trouble in clearing his name. Nor was it true, as Gordon later attested in his journal, that Stewart was serving no useful purpose in Khartoum. The plain fact was that Gordon very badly needed the assistance of another white officer, especially so experienced an officer as Stewart. It was simply impossible for one man to control so large and so reluctant a garrison without at least one reliable assistant. Nevertheless, he rejected Stewart's services now just as, for other reasons, he rejected Slatin's services later on.

The only conclusion that one can draw from all this is that Gordon wanted to be alone. He wanted them all to leave, and he would have liked Hansal to have gone as well. He did not like Hansal. The Austrian Consul was that same man who, if we can believe Strachey's story, had disgusted him so many years before when he had first arrived at Khartoum by flinging himself into an orgy of naked girl dancers at an official banquet. In his journal Gordon now wrote, 'I hear Hansal, the Austrian Consul, is disposed to go with his *seven female attendants* to the Arabs. I hope he will do so.' It seems unlikely that Hansal ever had any such intention. He had large properties and business interests in Khartoum, he had lived there many years, and no doubt had succumbed to the inertia of the place – these probably were his real reasons for staying: and no doubt by staying he clouded somewhat Gordon's subconscious wish for solitary martyrdom. If the two men were ever intimate during the last months of the siege there is no record of it in Gordon's journals; indeed he is at pains to say that he has no friends in the town, no one whom he can trust.

On September 10 all was ready for the others to go. They boarded the *Abbas* together with a party of Greeks and a small bodyguard of soldiers, and with two other steamers to escort them beyond Berber they set sail down the river to the north. The pilot of the *Abbas* was one of the most experienced men in the Nile service, and he was especially enjoined to gather firewood for the ship's engine only at deserted places outside the territory of the hostile tribes. Gordon watched them run the gauntlet of the Arab rifle fire beyond the limits of the town, and then, alone, turned back to his endless vigil on the lines and his solitary communings in the Palace.

'The Mahdi is still at Rahad [near El Obeid, about 200 miles from Khartoum],' he wrote in his journal that same day, September 10, and once again he allowed his mind to brood over the troublesome question of Slatin. He himself had enlisted Slatin in the Sudan service – that young, good-looking officer from Prince Rudolf's regiment, a Roman Catholic and a gentleman; he had written to him in Austria

Khartoum, the fort.

inviting him to join the Sudan service, had trained him, promoted him and had sent him off to Darfur. And now Slatin had surrendered to the Mahdi and had become a Moslem. 'It is not a small thing for a European, for fear of death, to deny our faith . . . If the Christian faith is a myth, then let men throw it off, but it is mean and dishonourable to do so merely to save one's life if one believes it is the true faith. . . . Treachery never succeeds, and however matters may end it is better to fall with clean hands than to be mixed up with dubious acts and dubious men.'

But then who was really brave? 'During our blockade, we have often discussed the question of being frightened, which, in the world's view, a man should never be. For my part I am always frightened, and very much so . . . It is not the fear of death, that is past, thank God; but I fear defeat, and its consequences . . . Thence I conclude no commander of forces ought to live closely in relation with his subordinates, who watch him like lynxes, for there is no contagion equal to that of fear. I have been rendered furious when, from anxiety, I could not eat. I would find those at the same table were in like manner affected.'

Now, at least, there was no danger of his private life being overlooked too closely. Except for his servants he lived alone at the Palace. He ate his meals alone. He watched the antics of his favourite turkey-cock in the court-yard, and the hawks flying by along the river. He stepped out alertly in the morning on his round of the forts, the

LEFT *Rudolf Slatin when Governor of Darfur.* RIGHT *Sister Thérèse Gregolini with her baby and Greek husband Kokorombo. Sister Thérèse had been Lady Superior of the convent at El Obeid and had been captured in 1883.*

arsenal and the ship-building yard, the barracks and the storehouses. He spent hours on the flat roof of the Palace with his telescope – 'by far the best glass I ever saw'. One could see so much from the roof; the wide sweep of the river to the north whence one day the relief expedition must arrive (Stewart must surely be past Berber by now); the great ocean of sand that lay around the town, and, moving across it, the Arab horsemen, the Arab tents and huts, the enemy. They were forever prostrating themselves in prayer. 'Another church parade,' he notes in his journal.

Then there was the question of those nuns with the Austrian Mission to Darfur; there was a rumour that they had been married to the Greek traders who had also been captured by the Mahdi. 'What a row the Pope will make about the nuns marrying the Greeks. It is the union of the Greek and Latin churches.'

It was strange stuff for him to be writing in what was supposed to be an official dispatch to the War Office in London, and yet he could not prevent his mind from running on. Nuns, Greeks, turkey-cocks, apostasy and Arab tribesmen praying on the sand – it was all part of this forgotten little world on the Nile, but it was worth recording for in the end human beings forgot everything. 'It is curious how quick the people forget their disasters and losses,' he wrote on September 14; 'it is only ten days ago that we lost in killed nearly one thousand men, yet no one speaks of it now; it takes about four to six days to obliterate the bitterness of a disaster.'

By the last week in September Gordon had definite news that the expedition was on its way. A native runner came in from Kitchener at Debba with a message saying that Lord Wolseley had left London, and that already in August (the message took nearly a month to reach Gordon) the vanguard of the column was moving out of Wadi Halfa into the Dongola province.

Gordon made the most of these tremendous tidings. All the forts were ordered to fire their guns in celebration, and presently pictures were pasted up in the streets showing British and Indian soldiers on the march. The men had the stamp of victory and success on their faces. Along the Blue Nile houses were rented for the incoming English officers, and a great to-do was made over the engagement of servants and the purchase of furniture and water jars. Contracts were signed with the Khartoum butchers and bakers to supply the soldiers when they arrived.

Other telegrams as well arrived, but they were in cypher and Gordon, having no means of decoding them, could only speculate about their contents. Speculations now filled half his day. Where was Stewart? By now he ought to be across the loop of the Nile and possibly in touch with Kitchener. Where was the Mahdi? When was he going to bring the main bulk of his army up to Khartoum?

On the whole Gordon was inclined to think that the Mahdi would wait until the Nile began to fall towards the end of the year before he made his assault. Would the expedition reach Khartoum before then? It depended upon how well Wolseley understood the tactics of fighting in the desert. Gordon's own notions on this matter were precise. 'I cannot too much impress on you that this expedition will not encounter any enemy worth the name in a European sense of the word; the struggle is with the climate and destitution of the country. . . . A heavy lumbering column, however strong, is nowhere in this land. Parties of forty or sixty men, swiftly moving about, will do more than any column. . . . The time to attack is the dawn, or rather before it (this is stale news), but sixty men would put these Arabs to flight just before dawn, which one thousand would not accomplish in daylight.'

Let them remember Hicks. Better still let them remember Cambyses and his army that was swallowed up in the desert. Gordon looked up the relevant passage in Herodotus and pasted it into his journal.

There is a note of firmness and hope in these entries, but as September passed into October the mood begins to change. He is constantly wondering what has happened to Stewart. He is worried about his armed steamers, his only lifeline with the outside world: 'My beautiful steamers, which used to be comparatively sweet, now stink like badgers.' Perhaps he will sail one of them up the White Nile into Central Africa and have done for ever with London and its hypocritical politics, its clubs and its frightful dinner parties.

Next he turns his thoughts once more to the hawks on the wing outside the window and a mouse – obviously a female 'judging by her swelled-out appearance' – that shares his solitary meals: 'A mouse has taken Stewart's place at table; she . . . comes up and eats out of my plate without fear.' Then there is the turkey-cock that has become 'so disagreeable that I had to put his head under his wing and sway him to and fro till he slept'. And then again, when will the British column arrive? 'It is, of course, on the cards that Khartoum is taken under the nose of the expeditionary force, which will be *just too late*. The expeditionary force will perhaps think it necessary to retake it; but that will be no use, and will cause loss of life uselessly on both sides. It had far better quietly return, with its tail between its legs.'

Towards the middle of October there was a sudden flurry of activity. News reached the Palace that a group of sixteen leading men in the town were planning to raise a revolt and go over to the Mahdi. With misgivings Gordon put them under arrest. 'I confess,' he wrote, 'I am more perplexed about these arrests than I like: is it a good thing? Or is it not?' No one could give him an answer as yet. The mass of the people in the town were becoming seriously hungry at last and could think of nothing but food. The long siege had broken their power to take decisions of any kind. Gordon himself was the one solid factor in their lives and what he willed they willed. They held on now because he held on.

About Slatin, however, Gordon had no hesitation whatever. On October 16 he wrote: 'The letters of Slatin have arrived. I have no remarks to make on them, and cannot make out why he wrote them.' In these letters, which had been brought into Khartoum from the Mahdi's camp, Slatin said that he had heard that Gordon had taken a harsh view of his surrender and he begged the Governor-General to listen to his explanation. He had merely professed to be a Moslem, while he was still fighting the Mahdi, he says, in order to gain the confidence of his troops: as for his surrender, he had had no choice; when his soldiers capitulated he was bound to follow suit. 'Does your Excellency believe that to me, an Austrian officer, the surrender was easy? It was one of the hardest days of my life.

'By submission and obedient behaviour,' he went on, 'I have attained a certain degree of confidence amongst the local magnates, and have thus received permission to write to you, because they are of the opinion that by these lines I am requesting your Excellency to surrender. . . . I am ready with or under you, for victory or death. My few faithful ones here, my fortune, etc., all – all will I gladly desert to die, if God so please, an honourable death.'

When this had gone unanswered Slatin had written again:

Your Excellency,

I have fought twenty-seven times for the government against the enemy, and they

OVERLEAF *The march out of Wadi Halfa into Dongola province.*

have beaten me twice, and I have done nothing dishonourable, nothing which should hinder your Excellency from writing me an answer, that I may know what to do. . . . If there are letters from Europe for me at the post I beg you to send them me, because it is almost three years since I have had any news of my family. I entreat your Excellency to honour me with an answer.

Your devoted and obedient servant
Slatin.

Gordon was more than adamant: he was contemptuous. 'He evidently is not a Spartan. . . . If he gets away I shall take him to the Congo with me, he will want some *quarantine*; one feels sorry for him.' Next day he returned to the subject: 'I shall have nothing to do with Slatin's coming in here to stay, unless he has the Mahdi's positive leave, which he is not likely to get; his doing so would be the breaking of his parole, which should be as sacred when given to the Mahdi as to any other power, and it would jeopardize the safety of all those Europeans, prisoners of the Mahdi.' He did however offer to ransom Slatin and the other Europeans from the Mahdi for a sum of 10,000 guineas. There was no reply.

But it was not Slatin who occupied Gordon's attention at this moment; another, much more disturbing matter had come up. In his second letter Slatin had declared that the *Abbas* had not got through; it had been captured below Berber, and Stewart had been put to death. Gordon had heard a similar report from another source only a few days before, but had refused to believe it. He reassured himself that such rumours were always flying about and they were always unreliable. And yet, on October 21, he confesses, 'I am very anxious about the *Abbas*: it would be terrible, if it is true, that she is captured.' Then on October 22, a letter from the Mahdi himself arrived. It was written on a single, very large sheet of paper to which had been affixed the Mahdi's square seal, and it began:

'In the name of God the merciful and compassionate: praise be to God, the bountiful Ruler, and blessing on our Lord Mohammed with peace.

'From the servant who trusts in God – Mohammed the son of Abdullah.

'To Gordon Pasha of Khartoum: may God guide him into the path of virtue, amen!

'Know that your small steamer, named *Abbas* – which you sent with the intention of forwarding your news to Cairo, by way of Dongola, the persons sent being your representative Stewart Pasha and the two consuls, French and English, with other persons, has been captured by the will of God.

'Those who believed in us as Mahdi, and surrendered, have been delivered; and those who did not were destroyed – as your representative afore-named, with the Consuls and the rest – whose souls God has condemned to the fire and to eternal misery.'

There followed a long and exact catalogue of all the papers and documents that had been taken from the dead men – Stewart's journal, the cypher, the appeals to the Pope and the Sultan, the statements which gave details of the amount of food and ammunition remaining in Khartoum, copies of all the telegrams that had passed between Gordon and Cairo, a census of the number of soldiers remaining in the garrison and of their arms, and Gordon's letters repeatedly asking for help.

'We have now understood it all,' the Mahdi wrote, and once again he invited Gordon to surrender before it was too late: 'For, after the beginning of the battle were you to surrender, it would be from fear, and not willingly, and that will not be accepted.'

A dispatch was enclosed from the Mahdi's commander in the south and it revealed that the Bahr-el-Ghazal province had fallen.

So Stewart was really dead and Lupton had surrendered. But no, it could not be true. The documents the Mahdi had seen must have been copies which he had sent out by an agent before the *Abbas* sailed. Perhaps one of the Greeks who went down the river had read Stewart's papers and had turned traitor.

To the Mahdi he replied: '. . . to me it is all one whether Lupton Bey has surrendered or has not surrendered. And whether he [the Mahdi] has captured twenty thousand steamers like the *Abbas*, or twenty thousand Stewarts Pasha; it is all one to me.

'I am here, like iron, and hope to see the newly-arrived English. . . .' It was impossible, he added, for him to have any more dealings with the Mahdi; from now on they had better communicate with bullets.

Yet the news was true, and within a few days Kitchener smuggled through a message to confirm it. Again and again Gordon asked himself how it could have happened. The *Abbas* was strong enough to ward off any Arab attack so long as she continued in the middle of the river; she could hardly have hit a rock and sunk for she was fitted with buffers. Only treachery could explain it; some traitorous sheikh must have led them into a trap while they were in search of wood for fuel on the bank.

What had actually happened was that on September 18 the *Abbas* had struck a rock and had been disabled when she was 60 miles below Abu Hamed and only 100 miles from Kitchener's outpost. Believing that they were beyond enemy territory Stewart went ashore and there met Suleiman Wad Gamr, the chief of the Monasir tribe, and other sheikhs. The Arabs were immediately friendly and when they offered to provide camels to take on the party overland Stewart presented them with two swords and an embroidered cloak. The sheikhs then pressed the Europeans to pass the night ashore and the invitation was accepted. In the night there was a rush of wild Arabs and all was over. Having massacred Stewart, Herbin and Power the sheikhs went on board the *Abbas* and killed all but fourteen of her remaining passengers and crew.

On October 21, the Mahdi, heartened by the information he had received from the *Abbas* papers, moved up to Khartoum with the main bulk of his forces and established himself in two camps close to Omdurman on the western bank of the Nile. He announced his intention to attack Khartoum in a letter to Gordon: '. . . I have taken pity on some of my men and allowed them to die so as to obtain . . . paradise.' The final stage of the siege had begun. In the Palace Gordon calculated his chances. He was not seriously worried about his ammunition – his arsenal continued to produce some forty thousand rounds a day – but the question of food was urgent. 'If they (the British troops) do not come before 30th November the game is up, and Rule Britannia. In this calculation I have given every latitude for difficulties of transport, making forts etc., and on the 15th November I ought to see Her Majesty's uniform.' He speculated very closely on the expedition's advance: having reached Debba or Merowe further upstream, Wolseley must send one column up the river to attack Berber while another struck directly across the desert to Metemma, a little over 100 miles north of Khartoum. Here Gordon could help his rescuers, for he still commanded the river thus far. He dispatched five of his steamers to Metemma with instructions to the captains that they must remain there until the vanguard of the British column appeared, and then they were to bring it on to Khartoum.

Early in November a batch of letters arrived and they included one from Samuel Baker and another, six months old, from Stanley in the Congo. Baker's letter had an official note written on the envelope, '*Communications avec le Soudan interrompées*', which gave Gordon a certain grim pleasure. 'I should think the communications were interrompées!!!' Kitchener had wrapped these letters in a newspaper, the London *Standard* of September 15, which Gordon's servants threw away in the Palace yard, and it was only by chance that he recovered it. He read it eagerly, for it was the first news of the outside world he had had for many weeks, but one report drove him into a frenzy: 'Lord Wolseley seen off at Victoria Station, for the *Gordon relief expedition*!!! NO! for the relief of the Sudan garrisons. . . . *I declare positively, and once and for all, that I will not leave the Sudan until every one who wants to go down is given the chance to do so, unless* a government is established which relieves me of the charge; therefore if any emissary or letter comes up here ordering me to come down, I WILL NOT OBEY IT BUT WILL STAY HERE; AND FALL WITH TOWN, AND RUN ALL RISKS.'

If Gordon had known the terms of Wolseley's orders he would have been even more furious. These orders had been drafted in Cairo and were as follows: 'The primary object of the expedition up the valley of the Nile is to bring away General Gordon and Colonel Stewart from Khartoum. When that object has been secured, no further offensive operations of any kind are to be undertaken.' So now, in overpowering heat, the long cumbersome column was slowly making its way up the Dongola province to rescue one man who was dead and another who did not wish to be rescued – not at any rate on these terms; not until the garrisons were got away and some reasonable form of government was set up in the Sudan.

Gordon began to give his mind more and more to this question of the future government. Zobeir of course was still the best solution. Set him up as Governor-General and let Gordon himself look after Equatoria. Failing that let the Turks come in and rule the Sudan. Failing that find some other competent man who would take control with a subsidy from Egypt. He had a new idea. Why not this fellow Kitchener? Kitchener, it was true, had made an awful mess of his intelligence service – hardly any of his runners got through to Khartoum – but Baker in his letter had spoken very highly of him. Baker had said:

'The man whom I have always placed my hopes upon, Major Kitchener, R.E., is

Major Kitchener.

one of the few *very superior* British officers, with a cool and good head and a hard constitution, combined with untiring energy . . .'

Well then, let them make this young officer Governor-General. Gordon sent off a letter to Kitchener himself suggesting the appointment.

This was an extraordinary piece of intuition, for Kitchener was by some way the most promising soldier, not only in Wolseley's force, but in the whole British army. He was aged 34 at this time, a man six feet two inches tall with piercing bright blue eyes, and already he had a reputation for cold, determined, machine-like precision.

He was a good horseman – he had raised a force of 1,500 irregulars on the Sudanese border earlier in the campaign – and there was a touch of daring in the young man that is hardly recognizable in the awesome figure of the general he was later to become. Being a friend of Stewart's he had pleaded for permission to make a dash through Arab territory so as to meet the *Abbas* at Berber, and had been incensed when Wolseley held him back. The staff knew him as a diligent officer who was interested in archaeology, who spoke French, Arabic and some Turkish, and as a man who was indifferent to women. It was hardly Kitchener's fault that Gordon got more messages out of Khartoum than he received – men could always be found who were willing to leave the besieged city, but few wished to go there – and Kitchener ran exceptional risks in trying to maintain the correspondence; he ventured far into the enemy's ground, sometimes in Bedouin disguise and carrying with him a bottle of poison so that he could commit suicide if he was captured. When, about this time (November 1884), his exploits were revealed in the Press, an aura of romantic glamour attached itself to his name; it was the sort of reputation that was later to overtake Lawrence of Arabia.

So now, divining the importance of this young soldier whom he had never met, Gordon writes in his journal: 'Whoever comes up here had better appoint Major Kitchener Governor-General, for it is certain, after what has passed, *I am impossible.* (What a comfort.)'

Gordon now spent more and more of his time on the Palace roof. From that perch above the desert he could see into every part of his fortress, even as far as Omdurman Fort on the opposite bank of the river, and – what was just as important – his soldiers could see him. They were quite incorrigible, these soldiers, he reflected – not perhaps the Sudanese, but certainly the Egyptians. Unless they saw he had his eyes upon them sentries fell asleep at their posts, orders were forgotten, and every one lied. 'The North Fort hate my telescope; day and night I work them.' Yet still they found ways to circumvent him. 'I certainly claim to having commanded, more often than any other man, cowardly troops, but this experience of 1884 beats all past experiences. . . . A more contemptible soldier than the Egyptian never existed. Here we never count on them; they are held in supreme contempt, poor creatures. *They* never go out to fight; it would be perfectly iniquitous to make them.'

He packed off as many of them as he could in the steamers that he sent to Metemma and gave orders that, under no circumstances, were they to be brought back.

By November 12 the Mahdi had got his guns into position, those same guns that he had captured from Hicks, and the shelling of Khartoum began. It was erratic and did hardly any harm, but it had a demoralizing effect upon people who were now suffering from malnutrition, and presently events began to take a more ominous turn: one of the best of the steamers that had remained at Khartoum ran aground under the enemy shellfire and had to be abandoned. At the same time the Mahdi's forces closed in around Omdurman Fort and cut it off from Khartoum and the river. Gordon was still able to signal to the Egyptian commander there with bugle calls. But the Mahdi also had a bugler who knew the signals, and when Gordon sounded

'Come to us. Come to us,' from the Palace roof, he was answered ironically from the Arabs' camp, 'Come to us. Come to us.' There was, in any case, no hope for Omdurman Fort – unless of course the expedition arrived in time. Early in November there had been recovered a large haul of grain which had been stolen and secreted by merchants in Khartoum, and that gave the garrison a brief reprieve. But on December 13 Gordon estimated that they could hold out only another ten days.

Whenever he went out of the Palace now a crowd of women gathered round him calling out for food; every day the shelling and the rifle-fire grew a little heavier. The Arabs had a gun trained upon the Palace, and the shells crashed loudly but usually harmlessly on to the heavy stone walls.

Gordon's palace at Khartoum.

'One tumbles at 3 a.m. into a troubled sleep;' Gordon wrote. 'A drum beats – tup! tup! tup! It comes into a dream, but after a few minutes one becomes more awake, and it is revealed to the brain that *one is in Khartoum*. The next query is, where is this tup, tupping going on. A hope arises it will die away. No, it goes on, and increases in intensity. The thought strikes one, "Have they enough ammunition?" (the excuse of bad soldiers). One exerts oneself. At last, it is no use, up one must get, and go on to the roof of the Palace; then telegrams, orders, swearing, and cursing goes on till about 9 a.m.'

Somehow he kept the ship-building yard going and his engineers actually produced a new steamer to replace the one that had been lost. 'The town wanted to call it after me, but I said, "I have put most of you in prison and otherwise bullied you and I have no fear of your forgetting me".' The vessel was named the *Zobeir*. He could still occasionally be as light-hearted as this, could still refer to the Mahdi as 'his holiness', but then the frightful weight of uncertainty returned. '. . . There is not one person on whom I can rely. . . . I am weary of my life, day and night, day and night, it is one continual worry.'

'*Sir Charles Wilson, Major Slade and Mr Vandyke of the Intelligence Department are examining the Bedouin sent from Khartoum by General Gordon. The messenger is saying "Gordon Pasha then fired twenty-one guns in his joy at the approach of the British Army"*.' (The Illustrated London News.) *From a sketch by F. Villiers.*

The river was now beginning to fall and the drying mud-banks brought the enemy very near.

On December 13 he wrote, 'NOW MARK THIS, if the Expeditionary Force, and I ask for no more than two hundred men, does not come in ten days, *the town may fall*; and I have done my best for the honour of my country. Good-bye.

C. G. GORDON.

'You send me no information, though you have lots of money.   C. G. G.'

This was almost the last communication received from General Gordon. He bundled up the papers of his journal – the telegraph forms, the pieces of tissue paper, the little maps he had made and the pen and ink sketches – sewed them up in a cloth and wrote on the wrapper, 'Events at Khartoum. General Gordon's Journal. No secrets as far as I am concerned. To be pruned down if published. C. G. Gordon.'

The packages were handed to the captain of the *Bordein*, and on December 15 the vessel, under heavy fire, left for Metemma.

14

The Falling Nile

By the end of December 1884 the advance guard of the expedition had reached the Nile at Korti, midway between Debba and Merowe, and was in a position to start the final advance on Khartoum. It was decided that Gordon's plan should be adopted: one column was to follow the course of the river on its great eastward loop past Abu Hamel and Berber, while the other column, under Sir Herbert Stewart, marched directly across the desert to Metemma, where it was known that Gordon's steamers would be waiting. Wolseley had been forbidden by the British government to lead the advance guard, and remained behind at Dongola to assemble the bulk of his forces. There still appeared to be no cause for desperate haste. On December 30 one of Gordon's runners came into the camp at Korti with a message written on a piece of paper the size of a postage stamp. It said: 'Khartoum all right. 12.12.84. C. G. Gordon.' The runner, however, reported verbally that he had been instructed to say that the supplies of food in Khartoum were running very low and that the expedition should come on as quickly as possible. It must be remembered that up to this time no one had read the last batch of the journals, which were on board the *Bordein* at Metemma, 160 miles away.

On the morning of December 30 Sir Herbert Stewart began his advance with 100 British troops and 2,200 camels, and on January 2 he reached Jakdul Wells, 98 miles away. Here he gave orders for an outpost to be set up while he himself returned to Korto to bring on a further contingent of 1,600 men and 2,400 camels. On January 13 the whole column was united and the advance was continued until the evening of January 16, when it was reported that strong forces of Arabs lay ahead. They were encamped round the Abu Klea Wells and were clearly prepared for battle. Sir Herbert Stewart bivouacked for the night about three and a half miles away, and on the morning of January 17 he advanced to the attack. The Arab horsemen charged with the utmost recklessness, and succeeded in breaking into the British square where fierce hand-to-hand fighting took place among the camels. It was all over in five minutes. The Arabs drew off, leaving 1,100 dead on the ground, and the British casualties were under 200.

That same night the British took possession of Abu Klea Wells and at 4 p.m. on the following day the column resumed its march towards Metemma, 23 miles away. They continued all night, and soon after dawn on January 19 came within sight of the Nile. Their path to the river, however, was blocked by the enemy and once again the Arabs attacked out of the scrub and thick grass. The British soldiers had now been without sleep for more than forty-eight hours, but they managed to drive off the attack with a further loss of 111 men killed and wounded, and finally reached the bank of the river a little to the north of Metemma. Sir Herbert Stewart was mortally wounded in this skirmish, Burnaby, his second-in-command, had already been killed at Abu Klea, and thus the command of the column fell to Sir Charles Wilson, an officer of the Intelligence service who had not led troops in battle before.

On the morning of January 21 four of Gordon's steamers appeared, and the journals were now opened and read together with a letter dated December 14 in which Gordon declared that he expected Khartoum to fall within ten days. Still later news was brought in by a runner who carried another message written on a minute scrap of paper, and it read: 'Khartoum is all right. Could hold out for years. C. G. Gordon. 29.12.84.'; but Gordon apparently had sent this message simply as a gesture of confidence which, if intercepted by the Arabs, would deceive them. It was evident, therefore, that for at least three weeks Khartoum had been in the greatest extremity, and Wilson had every reason to push on without delay. Yet three days went by while the steamers' engines were overhauled and a reconnaissance was made along the river, and it was not until January 24 that he was ready to proceed. Wilson himself led the way in the *Bordein* with ten redcoats of the Royal Sussex regiment and 110 Sudanese troops. The *Tell Hewein* followed with ten more soldiers of the Royal Sussex, and 80 Sudanese, and she towed a lugger with a heavy cargo of maize and fifty more native troops. The crews were men of the Shaigiya tribe whom Gordon had sent down from Khartoum.

The Nile had now fallen very low, and the little convoy got into difficulties almost at once. One the second day out the *Bordein* struck a rock in the Sixth Cataract, and it was not until the morning of January 27 that the steamers were able to go on again. Further delays were caused when the firewood for the boilers ran out and more had to be gathered from the river bank. As the steamers neared Khartoum they were obliged to face an increasingly heavy rifle fire from the shore, and it seemed for a time that they would not get through. The Shaigiya tribesmen on board, whose families were in the town, wanted to desert to the Mahdi at one stage, and the captains of the two steamers agreed to go on only when they were promised a bonus of £100 apiece. On three separate occasions Arabs called out to the British from the bank that they were too late, that Khartoum had fallen and that Gordon was dead. But this was disregarded, and at last on the morning of January 28 the *Bordein* under incessant artillery fire steamed up to the junction of the Blue and White Niles and came within sight of the town. The help which Gordon had been calling for since March in the previous year had finally arrived.

At this point let us turn back and see what had been happening in Khartoum since Gordon had sent out his last messages in December. By the end of that month the supply of maize had failed almost entirely, and soon every living animal – donkeys, dogs, monkeys, even rats – had been eaten. Most of the women had long since sold their jewels for food. All that was now left for soldiers and civilians alike was palmtree fibre and a species of gum which contained very little nutriment and caused violent pains a few hours after it was eaten. Five thousand of the more disaffected citizens were sent out to the Mahdi with a message from Gordon that he should be merciful to them, but still the hunger increased; the dead lay in hundreds in the streets, and those that remained alive were too weak and too dispirited to bury them. On the barricades the soldiers, according to one witness, 'stood like pieces of wood' or went about their work in a sort of mechanical trance hardly knowing what they were doing any more. On January 5 the commander of Omdurman Fort signalled that he could hold out no longer, and Gordon was forced to agree to his surrender. The Arabs now closed in upon the town from every side.

Gordon as Governor-General of the Sudan in a uniform of his own devising.

Gordon still found means, however, to keep his people going. Rumours were spread about the town that messengers had come in from the expedition; it was due to arrive on the following day, and if not then, certainly it would come on the day after that. The soldiers were promised a year's pay for every day they hung on. Labourers on the docks were set to work preparing anchorages for the incoming steamers.

These measures were sufficient to keep a flicker of hope alive, but the town was now under continual bombardment through the day and night, and by the middle of January both Egyptian and Sudanese soldiers as well as civilians were deserting to the Mahdi. Gordon was approaching his fifty-second birthday, and there is a quality in the figure that emerges through these last days of the siege that seems rather to belong to legendary tragedy, to some incident of history as it is imagined in a fresco

or painting, than to life itself. The trim, alert officer vanishes, the crankiness evaporates, and now at last all inner uncertainties are resolved. He knows precisely what
he has to do, even though events may bring him to the breaking point. No doubt his
sense of guilt remained, but that was a secret thing, and it must have diminished
under hardship; it was his resolution, his complete acceptance of responsibility, that
his soldiers and the townspeople saw. To them he appeared to be a remote and
frightening figure, not unjust or rigid – he was too warm for that – but a man utterly
indifferent to ordinary weakness. He may have been respected, perhaps even venerated, by these thousands of dying Moslems at this desperate moment, but he was
also very much feared. Officials who called upon him were seen to tremble when he
came into the room, and there were some whose hands shook so badly they were
unable to light a cigarette.

Bordeini Bey, a Khartoum merchant who survived the siege, has given an intimate
picture of Gordon in his Palace at this time. 'In spite', he says, 'of all this danger by
which he was surrounded, Gordon Pasha had no fear. I remember one night some of
the principal men of Khartoum came to my house and begged me to ask Gordon
Pasha not light up the rooms of the Palace, as they offered a good mark for the enemy's
bullets. When I mentioned this to Gordon Pasha he became very angry, saying,
"Who has said Gordon was ever afraid?" A few evenings afterwards I was with
Gordon in the Palace, and . . . he brought a very large lantern which would hold 24
candles. He and I then put the candles into the sockets, placed the lantern on the
table in front of the window, lit the candles, and then we sat down at the table. The
pasha then said, "When God was portioning out fear to all the people in the world,
at last it came to my turn, and there was no fear left to give me; go, tell all the people
in Khartoum that Gordon fears nothing, for God has created him without fear."'

On January 20 the garrison was startled by a salute of 101 guns from the Mahdi's
camp, and it was thought at first that this was to celebrate a victory over the oncoming
expedition. But in fact the salute was a stratagem of the Mahdi's to cover up the
defeat at Abu Klea, and Gordon guessed as much when he saw through his telescope
the Arab women weeping on the opposite bank of the river. He now redoubled his
promises to the garrison that help was on the way, while in secret he laid a mine in the
arsenal so that it could be blown up if the town fell. The steamer *Ismailia*, which was
anchored below the Palace, was ordered to stand ready to take on board as many
passengers as she could. At a given signal she was to escape with them down the
White Nile to the south.

A meeting was then called of a group of the principal officials in the town, and was
informed by Gordon's secretary, Girgis Bey (Gordon himself did not attend), that
when the first of the expedition's steamers approached Khartoum they were to put
on their full uniform and come to the Palace. It was probable, Gordon said, that he
alone would be asked to go aboard the steamer, in which case the officials were to
protest violently to the British commander that they would not permit him to leave
Khartoum. Whether the expedition arrived in time or not, Gordon added, he had no
intention of going away.

It was one more attempt to keep the garrison firm, and it was not successful. By Saturday, January 24, all hope had been abandoned in the town.

Bordeini Bey gives this last picture of Gordon:

'At last, Sunday morning broke, and Gordon Pasha, who used always to watch the enemy's movements from the top of the Palace, noticed a considerable movement in the south, which looked as though the Arabs were collecting at Kalakala (one of the forts on the ditch to the south of the town). He at once sent word to all of us who had attended the previous meeting and to a few others to come at once to the Palace. We all came but Gordon Pasha did not see us. We were again addressed by Girgis Bey, who said he had been told by Gordon Pasha to inform us that he had noticed much movement in the enemy's lines, and believed an attack would be made on the town; he therefore ordered us to collect every male in the town from the age of eight even to old men, and to line all the fortifications, and that if we had difficulty in getting this order obeyed we were to use force. Girgis said that Gordon Pasha now appealed to us for the last time to make a determined stand, for in twenty-four hours' time he had no doubt that the English would arrive; but that if we preferred to submit, then he gave the commandant liberty to open the gates and let all join the rebels. He had nothing more to say. I then asked to be allowed to see the pasha, and was admitted to his presence. I found him sitting on a divan; and as I came in he pulled off his fez, and flung it from him, saying, "What more can I say, I have nothing more to say, the people will no longer believe me, I have told them over and over again that help would be here, but it has never come, and now they must see I tell them lies. If this, my last promise, fails I can do nothing more. Go and collect all the people you can on the lines and make a good stand. Now leave me to smoke these cigarettes" (there were two full boxes of cigarettes on the table). I could see he was in despair, and he spoke in a tone I had never heard before. I knew then that he had been too agitated to address the meeting, and thought the sight of his despair would dishearten us. All the anxiety he had undergone had gradually turned his hair a snowy white. I left him, and this was the last time I saw him alive.'

The Mahdi and his Emirs were very well aware of what was going on in Khartoum: deserters brought him the latest news of its ordeal every day. Yet still the Mahdi hesitated. He had an extreme fear of the British soldiers and Father Ohrwalder asserts that the mere appearance of twenty British redcoats at Khartoum would have entirely undermined his resolution. When the news of the defeat at Abu Klea reached Omdurman there was something like panic in the Arab camp. The Mahdi himself, Ohrwalder says, was in favour of retreating at once to Kordofan. The more aggressive of his Emirs, however, pointed out that the perfect moment for attack had arrived; the mud of the falling Nile had filled in a part of the ditch on the southern side of the town, and Gordon's soldiers were too weak to build new earthworks there. Let the tribesmen cross the White Nile by night and then rush this gap in the darkness. If they failed in this assault they could still retreat to Kordofan, while if they succeeded and the town fell the British expedition was bound to retire.

Throughout the third week of January there was a continuous council of war in the

Mahdi's camp, and January 25 – that same day that Gordon was making his final appeal to the garrison and Wilson in the *Bordein* was struggling up through the Sixth Cataract – the Mahdi overcame his anxieties at last. Orders were given for the assault to be made in the early hours on the following morning, and at once large parties of warriors began to cross the Nile. The Arabs went into the attack without the fear of death. In a final oration to his followers the Mahdi reminded them that paradise lay before them if they died, and no doubt they were not unmoved by the prospect of looting the richest town in the Sudan.

The moon set early that night. In silence some 50,000 Arabs crept up to the defences, especially concentrating at the point where the mud had filled in the ditch and a ridge of dry land opened a way into the town. It was found to be firm enough to bear their weight. At 3 a.m. on January 26 the town was awoken by a wild yelling on the lines, and the sound of heavy artillery fire. Those on the barricades who survived remember the Arabs rushing towards them crying 'Kenisa! Saraya!' – to the Church! to the Palace! – and then all was lost in confusion. The soldiers seem never to have had a chance of defending themselves. Before any sort of resistance could be organized the streets were filled with a tide of screaming fanatics who hacked with their spears at every human being in their path. No wild animals ever behaved as the Arabs did in that one short hour before the dawn; they killed their victims regardless of whether or not they surrendered, and without distinguishing between men, women and children. Most of the inhabitants naturally barricaded themselves in their houses, but the doors were soon bashed in, and fires, springing up everywhere, drove them into the streets again.

Barely three miles separated the Palace from the point where the defences were breached, and it was still dark when the first of the tribesmen came rushing into the Palace yard. Gordon, according to Bordeini Bey, had sat up writing until midnight on the previous night, and had then slept for two or three hours. He was woken by the sounds of the battle on the lines, and at once went up to the roof in his night clothes to try and make out what was happening. There was a gun on the roof and in the dawn light he began firing down on the thousands of Arabs pressing forward to the Palace. When he could no longer depress the gun at a sufficiently sharp angle to keep the mob back from the building he went to his room and changed into his white uniform. He then took up a revolver and a sword and went to the head of the stairs, 'standing in a calm and dignified manner, his left hand resting on the hilt of his sword'. The Arabs meanwhile had been hanging back, fearing that mines had been laid around the Palace, but now four men, bolder than the rest, rushed forward, and at once they were followed by hundreds of others. Some made for the roof where the Palace guard was stationed, and all were massacred. Others ran up the stairs to Gordon, and one of them called out, 'O cursed one, your time has come.' Gordon is said to have made 'a gesture of scorn' and to have turned away. Within a few seconds he was speared to death. It was just before sunrise.

Later his head was cut off and taken away in a handkerchief to Omdurman to be displayed before the Mahdi. The body remained all day in the Palace yard where

It was normal practice to display the heads of rebels as a deterrent.

Gordon's head shown to Slatin while still a prisoner of the Mahdi.

every passing tribesman jabbed his spear into it; and eventually it was flung into a well.

There are several other versions of the General's end – some witnesses asserted that he did defend himself and actually fought his way down into the garden before he was overwhelmed – but it is at least certain that the death did occur somewhere about the Palace in the very early hours of the morning, and Slatin, sitting in chains in Omdurman (he had been imprisoned when his correspondence with Khartoum had been discovered) saw the head being carried by to the Mahdi's tent later in the day. Afterwards the head was fixed to a fork in a tree, and all who passed by cursed it and threw stones at it.

The General's death was a disappointment to the Mahdi, for he had hoped to make a prisoner of Gordon, and to chain him like Slatin until he professed the true faith.

There was, too, a certain admiration for Gordon among the Arabs. According to Ohrwalder it was a common saying with them that, had he been a follower of their faith, he would have been a perfect man.

For six frightful hours the looting and the massacre went on until, in the end, some four thousand people were dead. Hansal, the Austrian Consul, was killed in his house. Numbers of women who had cut off their hair and put on men's clothes were captured, stripped and raped. Merchants and householders were flogged until they revealed the places where they had hidden their jewellery and their money, and in many cases servants saved their own lives by betraying their masters. The rage of the Arabs to destroy was just as great as their desire for loot, and so in every house mirrors and crockery were smashed, furniture was overturned and hangings were stripped from the walls and carried away. Human beings were the chief loot, but there was a great wastage of them at first. Men and women aliked were stripped naked and then taken across the river to Omdurman where they were herded into compounds. Many died of thirst there under the blazing sun. The more attractive women and young girls received better treatment: they were placed in three enclosures, one for un-married girls who were young and fair, one for married women who were still good-looking, and one for black slave girls. Under the rule of the Mahdi all loot, whether slaves or property, was placed in the *Beit-el-Mal*, the treasury of Islam, to be shared out according to each man's status and his prowess in battle. So now the Mahdi came to the women's enclosures and selected for himself all the younger and fairer girls of the age of five and upwards, and then it was the turn of the three Khalifas and of the Emirs.

In Khartoum meanwhile there was a confused scramble among the principal Arabs to obtain possession of the best dwelling-houses along the river. Gordon's garden was seized by Abdullah, the chief Khalifa, and before long every building of any size was the headquarters of some Emir and his retinue of wives and followers. For the moment all thoughts of austerity were forgotten, and in the midst of the shambles of Khartoum triumphal feasts and entertainments continued through the night. For two days the general pillaging of the town went on, and there was a constant passage of small boats carrying loot and prisoners across the river to Omdurman, but at length the Mahdi reasserted his authority; the workshops were re-opened, some attempt was made to clear the streets, and once more Khartoum began to resemble an armed camp, with Arabs instead of government soldiers manning the entrenchments and the guns. Here and there a fire still burned with a pall of smoke above it, and along the banks of the river the wrecked buildings lay deserted and roofless under the sun.

This then, was the situation in Khartoum on the afternoon of January 28, Gordon's 52nd birthday, when Sir Charles Wilson and his little flotilla appeared before the town. They were met by intense artillery and machine-gun fire from either bank, and when they came within sight of Government House they saw that no flag was flying on the roof. The ruined buildings and the enemy shooting from every side made it clear beyond all doubt that Khartoum had fallen, but to make absolutely sure Wilson ordered the *Bordein* to the bank, and here he heard from Arabs on the shore

OVERLEAF *Sir Charles Wilson and his flotilla appear outside Khartoum on January 28, 1885.*

that all the defences had collapsed. The steamers had now been under fire for four hours, and were in imminent danger of being sunk. Wilson gave the order to put about, and in the early evening they ran downstream under a furious barrage from either shore. Like most such retreats from disaster the return journey of the two boats has been very largely forgotten, but it was something of a miracle of its kind. Even after the British had cleared the limits of the town a hundred miles of hazardous navigation still lay between them and their base at Metemma, and now the Arabs, seeing them retreat, feared nothing from the redcoats and their guns. From dawn onwards they were harried by rifle-fire from the shore, and at one stage the *Bordein* was reversed, and lowered on winches, stern-first, through a gorge. Eventually both steamers stuck fast and were abandoned.

It was while the British were trying to extract themselves from this impasse that the Mahdi sent Wilson a message:

'In the name of God, the merciful, the compassionate, praise be to the bountiful Lord, and blessings be upon the Lord Mohammed, and on his family. From the servant who stands in need of God, and on whom he places dependence, Mohammed, the Mahdi, son of Abdullah, to the British and Shaigiya officers and their followers: God direct them to the truth. Surrender and be spared . . . as you have become a small remnant like a leaflet within our grasp, two alternatives are offered to you'; they could send an envoy to see for themselves that Khartoum was destroyed, and that Gordon was dead, and then offer their own surrender; or they could try to fight on and face inevitable death and torment in the next world.

They decided to go on. In the end, with the aid of the other steamers that Gordon had sent down the river they reached Metemma.

It seemed to Wolseley, when he heard the disastrous news, that his only possible course now was to advance on Berber and there build up his forces for a counter-attack in the autumn. But when he applied to London for permission to proceed with this plan he was ordered to return. The expedition fell back in some disorder down the Nile.

For some months prior to the fall of Khartoum Gordon's name had been a household word, not only in England but throughout the rest of the world as well, and it evoked the extremes of pity and admiration almost everywhere. From one end of Britain to the other the public had anxiously and eagerly followed the story of Wolseley's advance, and had debated Gordon's chances of holding out. Towards the end of January hopes had run very high. *Punch* had actually anticipated the rescue by publishing at the beginning of February a full-page cartoon which showed the General at the gates of Khartoum welcoming the expedition into the city. The caption was 'At last!' The following week the magazine was obliged to make a painful and humiliating retraction. It printed another cartoon showing an agonized Britannia with her arm over her eyes and in the background the Mahdi riding with his hosts into Khartoum. The caption this time was 'Too late!'

Queen Victoria's feelings have been described by Sir Henry Ponsonby, her private secretary: 'The Queen was in a terrible state about the fall of Khartoum, and indeed it had a good deal to do with making her ill. She was just going out when she got the telegram and sent for me. She then went out to my cottage, a quarter of a mile off, walked into the room, pale and trembling, and said to my wife who was terrified at her appearance, "Too late!"'

AT LAST!   "TOO LATE!"

The following letter in the Queen's handwriting reached Gordon's sister in Southampton:

'*How* shall I write to you, or how shall I attempt to express *what I feel*. To *think* of your dear, noble, heroic Brother, who served his Country and his Queen so truly, so heroically, with a self-sacrifice so edifying to the World, not having been rescued. That the promises of support were not fulfilled — which I so frequently and so constantly pressed on those who asked him to go — is to me *grief inexpressible*! Indeed it has made me ill . . . would you express to your other sisters and your elder Brother my true sympathy, and what I do so keenly feel, the *stain* left upon England, for your dear Brother's cruel, though heroic fate!'

Miss Gordon replied by sending the Queen one of Gordon's Bibles, and it was placed in a glass case in Windsor Castle.

There were some dissenting voices, however. Wilfrid Scawen Blunt was in the centre of a little party which, though sympathetic to Gordon himself, detested the whole conception of British aggression in the Sudan. These people believed that the Mahdi, like Arabi in Egypt before him, was the leader of a popular rising, and that the Sudan should have been left to work out its own destiny. Even as late as December 1884 Blunt and his friends were describing Wolseley and his men as 'butchers', and were agitating for peace negotiations with the Mahdi. The news of the fall of Khartoum reached London on February 5, 1885, and Blunt recorded the event as follows: 'Unexpected and glorious news of the fall of Khartoum . . . I could not help singing the way down [to the country] in the train.'

Most of Blunt's contemporaries, however, were absolutely and passionately opposed to him in this matter. The British public felt every bit as deeply as their Queen. Sir Philip Magnus, in his recent study of Kitchener, speaks of 'a mood of hysteria which lasted about three weeks, drew crowds every day to Downing Street in the hope that they might have a chance to hoot and jeer at the Prime Minister'. It was thought particularly unfeeling of Gladstone to have gone to the theatre on the evening of the very day the news of Gordon's death was received, and he was hissed by the crowd in St James's Street.

It was all very well for the House of Commons to vote a sum of £20,000 to Gordon's family; to the public it seemed that the General's death could not be compensated by money. The stain on England was ineffaceable and who was to blame for all the shilly-shallying and delay if not the Prime Minister himself?

There were other lesser scapegoats as well; had the soldiers in the relief column been resolute enough? Could they not have pressed on a little faster? When the details of the campaign came out and it was realized that the expedition could certainly have saved Gordon if it had got the steamers up to the town just two days sooner, there was a particular feeling of wrath towards Sir Charles Wilson. Why had he delayed three days at Metemma when he could have started in the *Bordein* for Khartoum on January 21 – five days before the garrison fell?

Wilson's reply to this was that he had questioned the Egyptian officers who had come down to Metemma from Khartoum and none of them had believed the town was about to fall, none had thought that there was any special need for haste. And so he had followed sound military principles by securing his base near Metemma and by reconnoitring the river before he proceeded. It had also to be remembered that his force consisted of only one battalion and that his orders were not to relieve Khartoum but merely to make contact with Gordon, pending the arrival of the full expeditionary force in March.

Before the end of the year Gordon's journals were handed over to his brother, Sir Henry Gordon, and were published in two volumes that became best-sellers overnight. Some of Gordon's more outrageous abuse of Granville was deleted, but most of the references to Baring remained. It was not until his retirement in 1907 that Baring, by then the Earl of Cromer, was able to make his reply in his *Modern Egypt*. It was a dignified performance. He pointed out that in 1885 a 'Gordon Cultus' took hold of England and silenced every criticism of him. Yet there was, in fact, a good deal to criticize. At Khartoum Gordon had forgotten all about his instructions, and, by remaining there, had forced the British government to send an expedition for his relief. Gordon, Baring said, 'was extremely pugnacious. He was hot-headed, impulsive, and swayed by his emotions. . . . He was liable to fits of ungovernable and often of most unreasonable passion. He formed rapid opinions without deliberation and rarely held to one opinion for long. . . . He knew nothing of English public life, or generally of the springs of action which move governing bodies. . . . In fact, except personal courage, great fertility in military resource, a lively though sometimes ill-directed repugnance to injustice, oppression and meanness of every description, and a considerable power of acquiring influence over those, necessarily limited in numbers, with whom he was brought in personal contact, General Gordon does not appear to have possessed any of the qualities which would have fitted him to undertake the difficult task he had in hand. . . . But, when all this has been said, how grandly the character of the man comes out in the final scene of the Sudan tragedy . . . no Christian martyr tied to the stake or thrown to the wild beasts of ancient Rome, ever faced death with more unconcern than General Gordon. His faith was sublime.'

Two major mistakes had been made, Baring concluded: his own in agreeing that Gordon should go up to Khartoum in the first place, and Gladstone's in not sending the expedition sooner. These were the arguments and admissions of an experienced administrator, and yet it seemed to most people in England that in a vague, confusing and most moving way, the truth still lay with General Gordon.

Little by little as the years went by it became apparent that, from start to finish, Wolseley's expedition had been based upon misapprehensions, and that Gordon had seen this more clearly than anyone. It was never a question of merely getting Gordon himself away from Khartoum. Had Wolseley reached the garrison in time he must have realized that the Sudan could not have been suddenly abandoned; some sort of government would have to have been established. He would have been bound either to defeat the Mahdi or to come to terms with him. It was neither an honourable nor a valid policy to 'let the Sudan stew in its own juice', to allow the country to sink back into chaos.

There was one other man in Africa in 1885 who foresaw all this almost as clearly as Gordon. The Anglican missionary, Alexander Mackay, whom we must presently meet, wrote from Buganda: 'He [the Mahdi] slew General Gordon as chief of the Turks, and stuck up the English hero's head to be ignominiously handled by the Arab rabble, whereupon the English army ran away home, forgetting that they came to do what Gordon came to do, viz. rescue the garrisons of the Sudan. Mark the logic. Because the General could not do that, without an army, therefore the army could not do it either, although it had another general!' Lupton, an Englishman, was still in the hands of the Mahdi, but no steps were taken by the expedition to discover whether he was dead or alive, let alone to rescue him. In the same way Slatin had been abandoned, and so had Emin, still holding out in Equatoria, and so had the Egyptian garrisons now awaiting their inevitable fate – massacre – in Kassala and Sennar.

'But the English,' Mackay goes on, 'to the amazement of all the Arabs, and the bitter disappointment of all the Europeans and Egyptians, turned tail, no man knows why, and ran home leaving all the garrisons to the mercy of the murderers.'

Gordon's death appeared to close a chapter that was by no means closed, but if England was in a mood for revenge it did not last very long. By April 1885 the public indignation was running down, and a new crisis on the North-West Frontier in India was filling the columns in the newspapers. Lord Salisbury, who defeated Gladstone in June and brought the Tories back into power, continued the evacuation policy in the Sudan. It seemed that the White Nile, like some recurring affliction that becomes acute and then, of its own accord, dies away, had vanished from British politics for the time being. But Gordon had raised issues in England that were fundamental, and emotions that were very deep. The struggle between Islam and Christianity was not ended, and Central Africa could not remain a void. A little group of Europeans still held on at the source of the river and they were determined not to fail.

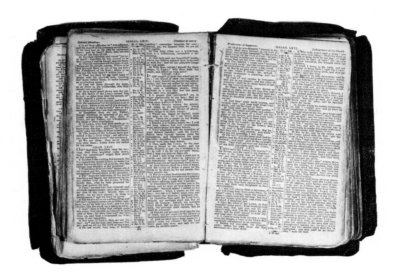

The Bible Gordon's sister gave to Queen Victoria.

The junction of the Blue and White Nile.

15

The Mahdi's Ghost

In February 1885, less than a month after the fall of Khartoum, the Mahdi retired across the river to Omdurman. He still professed his determination to conquer Egypt and the world, and as a first step in that direction he sent off a strong force of cavalry to harry Wolseley on his passage down to Wadi Halfa. Yet there was an extreme love of sensual pleasure in the Mahdi's character, and once the siege was over he seems to have abandoned himself to it altogether. If we are to believe the Europeans who were his prisoners at this time the life he now began to lead in Omdurman sounds like the Mohammedan idea of paradise. He had grown enormously fat in his late thirties, and in the privacy of his harem his concubines attended him as though he were some great, sleek queen-bee in the pulsating centre of a hive. Each day his body was anointed with sandalwood oil, and the patched *jibbeh* of the Arabs was exchanged for drawers and shirts of fine materials which were scented before he put them on. Antimony was painted round his eyes to give them an added lustre.

During the month of Ramadan, when an absolute austerity was enforced upon his followers, huge crowds gathered in Omdurman to await the Master's appearance at prayers. But they had little notion of what was going on inside the Mahdi's house. There he reclined on pillows of gold brocade with some thirty of his women taking turns to wait upon him: Aisha, the chief of his four legal wives, pitch-black negresses of the Nile tribes, copper-coloured Abyssinians and little Turkish girls, rather lighter in colour and hardly more than eight or nine years old. 'Almost every tribe in the Sudan,' Father Ohrwalder says, 'supplied its representative.' They squatted upon the Persian rugs spread over the sand, some of them fanning the Mahdi with ostrich feathers, others massaging his feet and hands, and thus in a trance of pleasure, interrupted only by short councils of war, the hot hours of the day went by.

When the crowd outside became importunate at the long delay the Mahdi would bestir himself at last. He was helped up, red shoes were placed upon his feet, drawers and shirt were replaced by his patched *jibbeh*, his girdle and his turban; and so attired he proceeded through the shouting and adoring crowds to the mosque. As he went by women fell to the ground behind him and embraced his footprints, believing that by so doing they would cure their illnesses and ensure the quick and painless delivery of their children. At times he would cross the river with a part of his harem and remain for a day or two in Gordon's Palace, but he rarely moved from Omdurman.

Meanwhile in Khartoum a semblance of order was being re-established. After the first fury of destruction was over it was found that no great damage had been done

The Mahdi's tomb, Omdurman.

and soon the dockyards were working once again. The remnants of Gordon's little fleet of steamers were salvaged and repaired, and at the arsenal the manufacture of cartridges and bullets went on as before. The lithographic press was put in order, and in the mint new pieces of gold and silver were struck with the Mahdi's imprint upon them. Huge magazines were established on the river bank to house the goods that had been seized from the inhabitants, and markets were set up for the sale of the grain and the cattle that were once again brought in from the surrounding country. The town, in fact, might even have had a prosperous look but for the utter misery of the conquered people. Many of them succumbed to an epidemic of smallpox soon after the siege, others died of starvation and maltreatment in the gaols, and every day new victims were brought for trial before the Mahdi's courts. It was enough for a man to be pronounced a 'Turk', an infidel, and any trumped-up charge then served to have him convicted, flogged and imprisoned. Hordes of spies and informers made any sort of life except that of abject obedience quite impossible.

Yet still great numbers of tribesmen and their families kept arriving in Khartoum and Omdurman from the outlying districts along the White and Blue Niles, and through the hot months of March, May and June the exaltation of victory continued in the air. Messengers kept bringing news of the British retreat and of the weakening of the last two Egyptian strongholds that were holding out at Kassala and Sennar. The *jibbeh* was now not only a symbol of spiritual faith but of military infallibility as well. Primitive sheikhs who a year before had counted their wealth in flocks of goats now dreamed of leading armies into battle and of taking whole provinces under their control.

In the midst of these excitements the Mahdi died. There are several different accounts of his end. According to one story he was given poison by a woman he had outraged, and he is said to have lingered on for a week in agony before he died. Others assert that typhus or smallpox was the cause of his death, and no doubt his long months of debauchery left him little strength to resist disease, especially in such an insanitary place as Omdurman. Whatever the cause, it is certain, however, that he died there on June 22, 1885. He had survived Gordon by just five months.

Long before this the Khalifa Abdullah had been chosen, in preference to the members of the Mahdi's own family, as his successor. He was a member of the Ta'aishi branch of the Baggara tribe, one of the poorest yet one of the fiercest of the nomadic groups in the West Sudan; a tall, imperious-looking man with a dark chocolate-coloured complexion much marked by smallpox, a long prominent nose and a short beard turning grey. In later years every possible epithet was attached to the Khalifa by those few of his European prisoners who were lucky enough to escape down the Nile to civilization: he was sly, suspicious, vain, quick-tempered, unbelievably cruel and despotic. Yet all agree that he possessed a certain ruthless charm, and there is no doubt whatever that he was an exceptionally shrewd and energetic man. It is said that he could neither read nor write, and he knew next to nothing about the outside world – he once asked Slatin if France was a tribe – but he was the kind of man who finds his way in politics through common sense. That

The Khalifa's house and harem in Omdurman.

he was brave goes without saying – all the Mahdists were brave – but he never succumbed to luxury as the Mahdi did. He lived grandly enough in the only two-storey
house in Omdurman with a personal bodyguard and a retinue of eunuchs, and he was
much addicted to harem life, but he continued to wear his greasy *jibbeh* and with the
utmost punctiliousness he presented himself at the mosque five times each day to lead
the tribes in prayer. He had joined the Mahdi when he was aged about 35, and from
the first had been one of his most unswerving supporters.

Abdullah moved very shrewdly through the early days of his rule. He made no
attempt to diminish the Mahdi's name, but rather he sought to enhance it and to use
it as a cover to strengthen his own hold on the tribesmen. He dreamed dreams in
which the Mahdi appeared before him, exhorting him to continue with the holy war,
and these dreams were recounted as though they were divine inspirations, direct
commands from the Prophet himself.

The reputation that the Mahdi established for himself in his own lifetime was
nothing compared to what his successor was able to do for his ghost. A tomb was
built in Omdurman with materials brought over the river from Khartoum, its 80-foot
dome visible from three days' journey away, and there the holy relics lay, perfumed

with incense and surrounded by candles in a cool gloom. It was held to be a holier thing for a Moslem to visit this place than to go on a journey to Mecca. Before long pilgrims began to arrive in Omdurman from as far away as Samarkand and Bokhara in Central Asia, and even from Mecca itself.

Abdullah appears to have divined by instinct the first principles for establishing a tyranny. A threatened rising of the two rival Khalifas was quickly put down and the Mahdi's family was submitted to a steady and increasing humiliation. Others who might have disputed the succession were dispatched with fresh troops to the out-skirts of the empire. At Omdurman itself the Khalifa concentrated his resources. Soon almost every post of importance was held by a member either of Abdullah's family or of his tribe. They were loathed, of course, but they were also feared, and their very unpopularity had the effect of binding them more closely to the Khalifa.

All state wealth was gathered into the *Beit-el-Mal*, which now became a kind of universal storehouse for specie, arms and ammunition, booty captured in battle, grain, livestock and even slaves, who were chained like horses in a long line on the river bank awaiting sale. Slavery, of course, had been revived throughout the Sudan during the Mahdi's lifetime, and it was now expanded into a major industry. On any day in the Omdurman market some fifty or sixty women and rather fewer men might be seen being offered up for sale. Women slaves were more in demand than men, and a black skin was preferred to copper-coloured. From 50 to 100 dollars (approxi-mately £10 to £20) would be paid for a pretty young concubine, who would be obliged to undress and submit to the usual handling before she was purchased. It seemed to the European prisoners in Omdurman that most of the slaves accepted subservience as a domestic animal accepts it. They expected to live out their lives in captivity; now that the influences of the outside world had receded from the Sudan they had no other horizon. Father Ohrwalder noticed that women owners were more cruel to their retainers than men; it was no uncommon thing, he says, to see a dis-obedient slave gashed with a knife. Equally fierce punishments were meted out by the courts to the Arabs themselves when they offended against the Mahdist law, and the only appeal against a judgment was to the Khalifa, who was not often ready to intervene; a great part of his personal wealth came from the confiscation of prisoners' property. In all important cases, such as mutiny, the Khalifa himself decided what the penalty should be (usually death by beheading) before the evidence was given to the court.

Ohrwalder estimated that, besides himself and the four surviving nuns of his ruined mission, there were about eighty Europeans or near-Europeans held prisoner in Omdurman, many of them Greeks who had been captured in the *Abbas* when Stewart was murdered. Some, like Martin Hansal, the son of the Austrian Consul, were taken in Khartoum; others, like the German, Charles Neufeld, were merchants who had hoped to trade in the Sudan and were engulfed by the Mahdist tide. Many of them pretended to be followers of the Moslem faith in order to save their lives, and were allowed to earn a living by manufacturing small articles of commerce and selling them in the bazaar. But it is surprising that any of them survived. Both Lupton and

Slatin were kept in chains for months at a time and were constantly threatened with death. Eventually Lupton was put to work in the dockyards at Khartoum, and there he died, worn out by starvation and illness, in 1888. Poor Lupton. He was barely 30. More than any of the other Europeans in the Sudan he gives the impression of being overwhelmed by events which were much too big for him. Emin, who knew him as

Father Ohrwalder with Sister Catterina Chincarini, Sister Elisabetta Venturini and the slave girl Adila.
From a photograph taken in Cairo.

governor of the Bahr-el-Ghazal province, describes him as 'a mere figurehead'. Yet he was brave, and within his limits he was steady and unpretentious. He was survived by an Abyssinian wife and two daughters, who vanished at once into the precarious anonymity of harem life in Omdurman.

Slatin was more fortunate because he was useful to the Khalifa as an interpreter and as a kind of aide-de-camp in the Khalifa's entourage. Abdullah liked to play a cat-and-mouse game with him, sometimes throwing him into prison and sometimes treating him as a privileged intimate. The latter experience was almost as bad as the former, since Slatin, when he was in favour, was obliged to sleep outside the Khalifa's tent, run beside his horse at military parades and sit cross-legged before him during the interminable services at the mosque. When he eventually escaped Slatin remembered the cramp in his legs as one of the severest trials he had to undergo.

The nuns attached to Father Ohrwalder's mission were at first distributed among the Emirs and savagely tortured when they refused to become Moslems. Later on they were permitted to live with the Greek community and they managed to eke out a living by sewing *jibbehs* for the tribesmen. Naturally it was the dream of all the Europeans to escape one day, but they were divided by hundreds of miles of desert from the Egyptian outposts and nothing could be done without camels and guides which were almost impossible to obtain.

Omdurman, after the fall of Khartoum, developed into a considerable city. It stretched for six miles along the bank of the Nile; a great dun-coloured honeycomb of flat-roofed huts and filthy narrow streets that led on haphazardly to the central meeting-place beside the Mahdi's tomb, and the population is estimated to have risen to 150,000, perhaps even more. There was a constant stir of movement in the city; men and women of some fifty different tribes mingled in the streets, and caravans were continually arriving along the great trade routes that led in from Kordofan in the west and Berber in the north. Except for a line that ran under the river from Khartoum to Omdurman the telegraph was destroyed, and messages from the outlying provinces were delivered by camel-post. Beside the Mahdi's tomb a space about 1,000 yards long and 800 yards broad was set aside as a mosque. It was roofed over by enormous mats held up by forked sticks which gave the place the appearance of a forest, and here each day the followers assembled in thousands, sitting cross-legged with downcast eyes, to hear the Khalifa describe his dreams and inspirations. No Emir or sheikh of any standing dared be absent from these services; the Khalifa liked to have them all under his eye and a man's presence at prayers was a proof of his loyalty.

Khartoum was not allowed to continue for long as a rival to Omdurman. When Ohrwalder visited the city in April 1886 he found that most of the damaged houses had been repaired and some of the Emirs and richer merchants were living there in comparative luxury. A few months later, however, the Khalifa gave orders that the city should be evacuated, and the inhabitants were allowed just three days to get out. Gangs of slaves then fell upon the empty houses and levelled them to the ground. Gordon's Palace and the Austrian Mission Church were the only buildings of any size that were left standing, and the only industries that were permitted to survive were those being carried on in the dockyard and the arsenal. Khartoum after this became a ghostly and forbidding place with bushes growing out of the ruined walls and the desert sand took possession of the empty streets.

Now, once again, austerity was the rule. Money, the Khalifa declared, distracted men's minds from heavenly considerations and was an offence against the Prophet. This, however, was not a principle that applied to the Khalifa himself, for he soon grew very rich indeed. Five hundred men rode behind him in his bodyguard, and by the same process of despotic inflation some four hundred women were added to his harem. As his power grew the Khalifa could endure only flattery. People coming to see him were obliged to advance on all fours, looking at the ground, and if they were wise they accorded him the same reverence that had been given to the Mahdi.

Abdullah never left Omdurman; he sat there in the centre of his political web with his Emirs around him, and he was kept very well informed by a spy-system that spread outwards from the city to the most distant provinces. Each day was like the last. He rose at dawn and proceeded to the mosque for prayers. He then returned to his house to sleep for two hours, and after a conference with his Emirs he rode forth in procession to review his soldiers on the outskirts of the town, his great black flag in front and his escort following behind. Like the Mahdi before him he was growing very fat, and a huge negro was required to lift him into the saddle. Friday was regarded as a special day, and then as many as 50,000 horsemen would gallop towards the black flag brandishing their spears and shooting their rifles in the air. Breakfast followed, and after midday prayers the Khalifa spoke again in the mosque. Two o'clock found him back again behind the high walls of his house or conducting business in the *Beit-el-Mal*, and then more prayers at sunset, more speeches and announcements in the mosque. The evening meal was followed by the fifth and final meeting for prayers, and finally the Khalifa retired to his harem to be seen no more until dawn the following day.

It was theocracy of the crudest and most rigid kind, and no one can say it was entirely cynical. After all, the Arabs could now claim that they had killed five British commanders and had defeated two full-scale expeditions that had been sent against them. The most modern European weapons had failed to hold them back. They felt invincible and they can hardly be blamed if they believed that there was a divine providence behind it all.

Then, too, the Khalifa was helped by his isolation. After Wolseley fell back to the Egyptian border (where his army was broken up and replaced by a defensive frontier force) very little news of what was going on in Omdurman and the White Nile provinces filtered through to the outside world. Of the 30,000 odd men in the Egyptian garrisons in the Sudan only a few thousand managed to return to the Delta. Major F. R. Wingate, whose star was rising as a brilliant young officer in charge of army intelligence in Egypt, gathered together such threads of information as were available from the statements of escaped prisoners and from captured letters and documents. But as yet no reliable European witness had found his way down to Wadi

Halfa, and the British and Egyptian outposts there stood like lifeguards on the edge of a hostile sea where no ship ever sailed and where very little debris was cast up on the shore. Rumours of revolts and upheavals in Omdurman and the outlying provinces came in from time to time, but nothing was known for certain. The interior of the Sudan was almost as remote as Tibet.

In Europe at this time, and especially in England, there was a general disposition to regard the Mahdist state as an implacable evil – as evil as ever Lenin's Bolshevism was regarded in the nineteen-twenties or Hitler's Nazism or Mussolini's Fascism in the nineteen-thirties and nineteen-forties. It was not only a question of Victorian power and self-righteousness smarting from a sense of unavenged defeat: it was felt that the Christian faith itself was defied by these murderous fanatics in the Sudan, and the Anti-Slavery Society in England lost no opportunity of spreading every fresh report of the Khalifa's brutalities. This was the atmosphere of war, when all things tend to become exaggerated and touched by propaganda. It was scarcely possible for any man, particularly if he was a public figure, to take a detached view, or to argue a case for the Arabs; to have done that would have meant being branded not as a liberal, not as a realist, but as a traitor. It is true that men like Slatin and Ohrwalder tried to give correct accounts of their experiences when they eventually escaped from the Sudan, but as prisoners-of-war they were hardly likely to have discovered virtues in their gaolers or to have known all that was going on. When they came to write their books the memory of their own sufferings was very vivid in their minds. Even such authorities as Wingate were inevitably affected by these feelings, and in subsequent years works of fiction like A. E. W. Mason's *Four Feathers* continued to spread the notion that Mahdism was all savagery and unrestrained barbarism.

That the Mahdists were, by our standards, incredibly primitive, cruel, obsessed and ignorant is impossible to deny. Yet it must be admitted that the Khalifa did succeed in erecting a much more coherent state than his Christian contemporaries would allow. If this state had been governed entirely by greed, by inhumanity and by crude emotions it would not have continued as long as it did; the bulk of the people were not crying out for liberation as the Europeans liked to imagine they were. Towards the end of the Khalifa's reign there was no exodus of refugees from the Sudan; the general run of the people had a bearable existence which was certainly no worse than life had been under the Egyptians. Had the Europeans not intervened the Sudanese would almost certainly have continued to accept the Khalifa's rule.

Even as early as 1887, two years after the fall of Khartoum, the Khalifa could count himself reasonably secure. The Egyptian garrisons at Kassala and Sennar had been starved out and obliterated; on the Red Sea the British still had a tenuous hold on the port of Suakin, but all the rest of the Sudanese coast almost as far as Massawa had fallen to Osman Digna; and in the north the Emir Nejumi with an army of some ten thousand men was penetrating into Egypt in the neighbourhood of Wadi Halfa. The Khalifa now controlled an empire greater even than the Mahdi's; it was half the size of Europe. He dispatched a letter to Queen Victoria in England, summoning her to Omdurman, where she was to offer her submission and become a Moslem.

'Know that God is mighty and great,' he wrote, and he went on to remind the Queen of the fate that had overtaken Hicks, Gordon, and the other British generals in the Sudan: '. . . Thy soldiers thought only of retreat from the Sudan with discomfiture and defeat, whereof they have had more than enough . . . Thus hast thou erred in many ways, and art suffering great loss, wherefrom there is no refuge for thee save by turning to God the King, and entering among the people of Islam and the followers of the Mahdi, grace be upon him. If thou wilt do thus . . . then shalt thou achieve thy desire of perfect felicity and true repose . . . the like of which eye has not seen, nor ear heard, or heart of man conceived. But if thou wilt not turn from thy blindness and self-will . . . thou shalt be crushed by the power of God and his might, or be afflicted by the death of many of thy people, who have entered on war with the people of God, by reason of thy Satanic presumption.'

Similar messages were sent to the Sultan of Turkey and the Khedive of Egypt.

The four Arab envoys bearing these letters presented themselves at the Anglo-Egyptian lines at Wadi Halfa and were sent on to Cairo where they were received by the Khedive. After some delay the documents were handed back to them with the verbal message that none of the three monarchs deigned to make a reply, and they returned to the Sudan.

The Khalifa's pretensions may have been absurd, and yet through these years Britain, Turkey and Egypt showed no signs of wishing to invade the Sudan again. There was even a very real fear in Cairo that the Mahdists might yet overrun the Delta, and by the summer of 1888 Nejumi, in fact, had advanced sixty miles into Egyptian territory. Nor was this all. The Khalifa was preparing to advance southwards as well. Emin, the last of Gordon's governors to hold out, had retreated up the White Nile almost as far as Lake Albert, and in June 1888 the Khalifa decided to crush him. The *Bordein* and two other steamers with a line of barges in tow and a force of four thousand Arabs on board was dispatched from Khartoum with orders to ascend the rapids as far as Dufilé, and then continue to Buganda at the headquarters of the river. The last phase of the Moslem re-conquest of the Nile had begun.

16

Paradise Reformed

———

Affairs had been taking a strange course in Buganda through these years. All communications with the north had been cut off by the Mahdist rising, and the few scraps of news that reached the east coast at Zanzibar were mostly supplied by Christian missionaries. They had arrived at Buganda at the end of the eighteen-seventies in response to the letter which, it will be recalled, Stanley had written to the *Daily Telegraph* in 1875, and they had found Mutesa still securely on his throne.

Mutesa had become an extremely interesting man as he had grown older. He remained at heart a savage, and he was still capable at any moment of giving way to the most vicious and childish excesses: this was still Central Africa in all its fantastic primitiveness, and it was not possible for any petty chieftain to escape from its crushing limitations. Yet by 1877 when the missionaries arrived he had been for twenty years on the throne, and he had learned a great deal from the Arab traders at his court; he professed to believe in their religion, he spoke Swahili and some Arabic, he had adopted Arab dress, and had even acquired a semi-literate secretary who wrote his letters for him.

Important visitors were now conducted to the throne room through a bodyguard of soldiers dressed in red tunics and white trousers, and Mutesa himself on these occasions was to be found reclining among linen cushions on a Persian carpet, a jewelled sword at his side, and his Arab gown bound about his waist with a belt of silver and gold braid. He was a much quieter man, however. Self-indulgence had undermined his health and he now drank very little beer, never smoked, and allowed no one else to do so in his presence.

The Arabs had warned him about the real meaning of the Christian invasion. The missionaries, they said, would appear to be very humble at first, but presently they would ask him to confine himself to one wife, to liberate his slaves and pay them wages, and to desist from plundering women and cattle. If Mutesa refused to obey them the missionaries would call into Buganda other white men, politicians and administrators; and if these in turn were defied soldiers would arrive who would force the King to submit and perhaps depose him as well. All in all it was not such a bad forecast of the future, and Mutesa was intelligent enough to understand it.

Yet he needed the help of the Christians; he needed all the firearms and the modern devices they could bring, and at the same time he saw that the missionaries at his court would serve as hostages, as guarantees against an armed invasion, whether from the Sudan in the north or from Zanzibar in the east. His best plan, therefore, was to make a show of friendship towards both sides, to play off the Arabs against the Christians, and thus he hoped to maintain his independence.

The missionaries were delighted with their reception. They presented their gifts (among other things they had brought letters from Queen Victoria and Stanley), and Mutesa professed the most lively interest in Christianity. Before long Bible-readings were being given regularly at the palace, and there was every sign that the King was breaking away from Islam. Mutesa did not actually agree to emancipate his slaves or reduce the number of his wives (who were now counted in thousands), but he did say he was perfectly willing to observe the Sabbath day, and he made no objection when the missionaries began to hold daily services in the little two-storey mission house they had built for themselves. The Baganda flocked to this new entertainment, and they were quick to learn. A printing press was set up to run off religious tracts in Swahili, and presently some of the younger pages at the court were making headway in reading. At the palace itself, meanwhile, Mutesa agreed to eject his witch-doctors and to submit to the missionaries' treatment for his illness (probably it was syphilis). He was an excellent patient and was soon able to walk again, a thing he had not been strong enough to do for many months. He also indicated to the missionaries soon after their arrival that there was nothing in the world he desired so much as a white wife, who would displace all the others, and that he was very ready to dispatch an ambassador to Queen Victoria in England, whom he acknowledged as a potentate quite equal to himself.

It was all most encouraging.

One must pause here for a moment to consider the magnitude of the work the missionaries were undertaking. It was not only paganism they were attempting to displace, but the Moslem faith as well, and Islam was entrenched in Central Africa by this time. It had strong attractions for the primitive tribesmen, since it could be understood and practised by the simplest mind. It was enough to declare 'There is no God but God and Mohammed is his prophet', and the pagan illiterate was accepted into a faith that offered him all kinds of advantages; he became a socially superior person inside the tribe, he received the protection of the Arab slave-traders, he was provided with a new code of living which did not greatly disturb his habits and which offered him the most dazzling pleasures after death. Perhaps it was a little galling for the African to give up alcoholic drink – his daily gourd-full of *pombe* – but no one pressed him too closely on that score, and the other obligations of Islam, the avoidance of certain sorts of meat, the fasts, the daily prayers, hardly constrained him.

The status accorded to women by Islam also suited the Africans very well, since they were accustomed to polygamy; Mohammed allowed a man four wives who were all inferior to him, and divorce was easy. Best of all, perhaps, was Mohammed's paradise, for it contained just those sensual delights that preoccupied the Africans here upon earth: a cool water-garden inhabited by beautiful women, the gratification of every physical want, and, by night, four houris to attend him in his square tent (it being understood that no one houri would be aware of the others' presence). This was just the sort of heaven that savage man might have imagined for himself.

As for slavery itself (which the Africans had always practised), it was condoned by Islam. Mohammed made it a virtue to liberate slaves and he laid it down that Moslems should not make slaves of other Moslems, but there was no general condemnation of the practice.

Compared to these easy-going doctrines, Christianity presented a hard, uncompromising front, and its prohibition of slavery and polygamy seemed to the tribesmen to be flying in the face of nature. The ethereal Christian heaven had very little appeal when contrasted with the sensuous Moslem paradise, and even the outward forms of Christianity were somewhat incongruous in this hot climate: the severe lines of Christian architecture were alien to Africa and even the western (and therefore Christian) clothes the missionaries wore – the tight jackets and trousers – must have seemed absurd to the Africans when compared to their own semi-nudity or the cool and comfortable Arab gown.

There was another obstacle before the Christians in Africa, and it was fundamental. Unlike the Moslems, who were all Sunnites, they were divided against themselves. Nothing is more strange in ecclesiastical history than the bitter conflict that developed between the Roman Catholics and the Protestants in Buganda through these years. Even the briefest glimpse of the careers of the Church Missionary Society representative Alexander Mackay and of his rival Père Lourdel, of the French White Fathers, gives one a startling insight into the tremendous religious fervour of the mission-workers of the time, their bravery, their bigotry and their utter determination. Mackay was a Scot, a blue-eyed little man with a genius for improvisation and for practical mechanics, and his faith in his God possessed him absolutely. Père Lourdel, who arrived in Buganda soon after the Protestants, was also a man of remarkable tenacity, and he was every bit as dedicated as Mackay was.

Mutesa quickly appreciated the advantages of this situation, and he seems to have enjoyed himself very much indeed. He liked to summon Mackay and Lourdel together to the court, and to provoke them into argument. The band of drums and harps was silenced, the wives and the courtiers gathered round, and all listened intently even if they did not understand. Then the Arabs would be brought in to put the case of Mohammed, and they contrived to vex Mackay tremendously. 'Terrific conflict with the Mussulmans again,' he writes. 'They blasphemed terribly against the assertion that our Saviour was Divine.'

Thus, even as early as 1879, and in these bizarre circumstances, three rival camps were forming in Buganda. The Arabs in the main were in favour of things continuing as they were. They were getting about a thousand slaves out of the country every year, and they were not at all appalled by Mutesa's brutalities. They continued to warn him privately that there could be only one end to the Christian invasion; the Europeans were 'land-eaters', sooner or later they would swallow him up. Mackay and Lourdel, on the other hand, continued to weaken themselves by acting independently; each built up his mission as rapidly as he could, each encouraged his followers to look upon the rival Christian faith as heretical and vile. This was a dangerous business among primitive people; they were liable to translate their hatred into action.

As their novelty wore off, Mutesa found that he liked his Christian guests less and less: just as the Arabs had predicted, they were forever trying to reform him and to prevent him from enjoying the exercise of his natural instincts – especially his instinct for human slaughter. He was also shrewd enough to see that, for the moment, the danger of his country's being invaded by white men was diminishing, and that therefore he was no longer bound to treat the missionaries gently.

Suddenly orders were issued that there were to be no more Bible-readings or Christian services at the palace; witch-doctors were re-admitted into the court and it was not long before their savage influence was felt. Executioners were posted on the highways leading into the capital. Like the thugs in India, they fell upon any un-suspecting man who happened to pass by, secured him in a forked stick through the night, and murdered him at dawn. On one particularly horrible day two thousand victims were tortured and then burnt to death as an offering to the spirit of Mutesa's father, Suna.

Mackay was crushed and disillusioned. 'Every day,' he wrote in his journal, 'there is a wanton slaughter going on of innocent victims. It is dark about 10 p.m. All is quiet, the last drum heard being the executioner's across the small valley, announcing that he has secured his victims for the day, and will spill their blood in the morning. Suddenly a sharp cry in the road outside our fence, then mingled voices; an agonizing yell again, followed by the horrid laugh of several men, and all is still as before.'

Could this be the same man who had so impressed Stanley, who had been so affable when the missionaries first arrived? He was 'a monster', 'a murderous maniac'.

Mackay and the other missionaries who had joined him now found themselves half-starved at Rubaga, Mutesa's capital, and the Roman Catholic priests were no better off. In their common adversity the two missions became more friendly, but they were practically banned from the palace during Mutesa's more violent outbursts of blood-lust, and the months went by in a steadily deepening atmosphere of super-stitious gloom. To make matters worse, the war with King Kabarega, who was still ruling in Bunyoro, was resumed more fiercely than ever.

In 1884 the young Scottish explorer Joseph Thomson made his brave journey through Masailand and reached the north-eastern shore of Lake Victoria. Then in October of the same year Mutesa died. Both these events might reasonably have been regarded as a good augury for the beleaguered missionaries in Buganda. Thomson had opened up a direct route from the Zanzibar coast, and it was now possible to reach Buganda in half the time taken by the roundabout journey along the southern and western shores of the lake; and presumably any successor to Mutesa would be an improvement. In fact, however, only evil was to follow. Mwanga, the 18-year-old boy who followed Mutesa as King, was an utter barbarian, who added sodomy and the smoking of *bhang*, or hemp, to his other vices. Mackay likened him to Nero.

It is interesting to compare the portraits of Mutesa and Mwanga which can still be seen in the royal burial ground at Kampala. Mutesa has a thin and nervous face, and it is dominated by his large, liquid, sensitive eyes. There is nothing sensitive at all about Mwanga, his features are dark and coarse, and there is something about him –

Bishop Hannington.   *Alexander Mackay.*

a certain air of swashbuckling authority and of passion – which indeed makes one think of the Roman emperors at their worst. And yet it is only fair to remember that the young King was surrounded by a bewildering number of rival factions at the court; from every direction foreign forces were closing in on him. It was only natural that he should regard the missionaries and the slave-traders as the agents of these forces, and that he should have taken his revenge upon them.

Bishop Hannington was the first victim. Hannington had been sent out by the C.M.S. to take charge of the gradually expanding chain of mission stations in East Africa, and he decided to follow Thomson's route up from the coast. Mackay tried unsuccessfully to warn him that this was very dangerous; there was a tradition in Buganda that the country would one day be overwhelmed by foreigners entering the country from the east. Directly he heard of the Bishop's approach Mwanga gave orders that he should be stopped and killed. Hannington had barely reached the north-eastern corner of Lake Victoria when the local tribesmen murdered him and obliterated his caravan.

After this, Mwanga and his advisers appear to have lost all control of themselves. It was the Arabs who provoked him to commit his worst atrocities. They had taught him to practise sodomy in the first place, and Mwanga burst into a furious rage when he found that Mackay's younger followers, most of them pages at the court, refused to submit to his perversity. Early in 1884 three of these children were tortured and murdered by the King's orders, and in 1886 there was a holocaust. The pages were assembled at the palace, and those who had become 'readers' at Mackay's mission were asked to step forward. Some thirty or more acknowledged that they were Christians, and were asked to renounce the faith. They refused and were burned alive in one great funeral pyre outside the capital.

It is astonishing that Mackay and his fellow-missionaries should have been able to arouse such heroic faith. At Gondokoro the Austrian Fathers had worked for eleven years among tribes that were only a little less civilized, and they had failed to convert even one man to Christianity. Yet here in Buganda, where Mackay and Lourdel had been established only since 1879, Christians could already be numbered in hundreds, and for many of them their religion was more important than life itself. Even the massacre of the pages failed to undermine their faith; they still came secretly by night to Mackay and Lourdel to receive their teaching and to pray with them.

But it was not a situation the missionaries could withstand for long. One after another they were ejected from Buganda, and temporarily took refuge on the southern shore of Lake Victoria. By the summer of 1888, when the Khalifa dispatched his steamers up the Nile from Khartoum, events in Buganda had degenerated into the wildest confusion. Mwanga was not the kind of man who could keep the three hostile political groups – the followers of Mohammed, the Roman Catholics and the Protestants – under control. Indeed he rather tended at first to throw in his lot with a fourth party – the pagans and the witch-doctors.

This, then, was the chaotic situation on the Upper Nile at the end of the 1880s: the Khalifa's expedition was pressing southward up the river from the Sudan, Buganda was moving rapidly towards civil war, and in Equatoria Emin, the last of Gordon's governors, was still helplessly waiting to see what the future would bring.

Mutesa's grave.

17

The Waters of Babylon

Even before Khartoum fell Emin had been called on by the Arabs to surrender, and in 1884, like Slatin and Lupton, he had decided to obey. Nearly two years had passed since he had been visited by a steamer from the north, and only the vaguest rumours reached him from Khartoum; it was reported that Gordon with 'a large army and elephants' had entered the town, but of the actual progress of the siege he knew nothing whatever. In 1884 Emin had still hoped to escape down the Nile, or at any rate to make contact with the Egyptian garrisons in Bahr-el-Ghazal and Darfur, but as the months went by a steadily deepening atmosphere of despondency settled upon his little headquarters at Lado. His correspondence with Frank Lupton in Bahr-el-Ghazal faltered and then ceased altogether. 'It is all up with me here,' Lupton had written in his last message, and soon after this runners came in with definite news that the Englishman had been taken prisoner, and that one of the Mahdi's Emirs was now marching on Equatoria.

Emin's prospects of retreating southwards into Buganda were hardly better than his chances in the north. He had a large and unwieldy garrison with him (it numbered about 10,000 Egyptians and Sudanese, many of them women and children), and it was scattered over a score of outposts on the Upper Nile, and the rare letters he received from the English missionaries in Buganda did not hold out much hope of his being able to get through to the east coast at Zanzibar.

Emin was not entirely alone with his soldiers and their families. Dr Junker, the German-Russian explorer, fled southward from the Arabs and reached Lado early in 1884; and presently they were joined there by another traveller, an Italian captain of the Bersaglieri, Gaetano Casati. These men, together with the educated officers on Emin's staff, formed a little oasis of civilized living at Lado, and they were not altogether unlike a group of survivors who had been shipwrecked on a desert island. 'We all of us dreamed of nothing but the steamer from Khartoum,' Junker wrote later on.

At first the situation was not really critical. The Arabs delayed their advance. Lado with its brick buildings and its neat streets remained quiet, and Emin and his staff, dressed in white uniforms, went about their work each day as though nothing had happened. But gradually the lack of supplies from the north began to take effect. A fire in Lado had destroyed most of the equipment which had been left there by Gordon and Baker, and there was an increasing shortage of ammunition. It was in these circumstances that Emin, in 1884, with the agreement of his Egyptian officers,

One of Stanley's lecture slides showing the Emin relief expedition. 'Zanzibar is somewhat changed during my eight years' absence. There is a telegraphic cable, a tall clock tower, a new Sultan's palace, very lofty and conspicuous with wide verandahs. . . . There are horses and carriages and steam rollers, and lamp posts at convenient distances to light the road when His Highness returns to the City from a country jaunt.' (Stanley)

decided to surrender. But then he changed his mind. After all, he still had his two steamers, the *Khedive* and the *Nyanza*, stationed above the rapids at Dufilé, and the Arabs, preoccupied with Khartoum, could hardly hope to overrun his whole province, especially if he moved his headquarters further up the river. Early in 1885 he left Lado with Junker and Casati, and journeyed some two hundred miles south to Wadelai. 'This is to be our headquarters until better times,' he wrote, and at once he began converting the fort into a habitable town. Here at last, in 1886, a year after the fall of Khartoum, he received letters from Kirk in Zanzibar and Nubar Pasha in Cairo informing him of Gordon's death and the abandonment of the Sudan. He was instructed to get his garrison out to the east coast as best he could since the Egyptian government could do no more for them.

But this was still an impossible proposition: Buganda was at war with Kabarega in Bunyoro, and even if this was not enough to block his path to the coast there was still no means of transporting his garrison across the thousand odd miles of virtually unexplored territory that divided him from the Indian Ocean. Unless help was sent to them in the form of ammunition, porters and transport animals they could not move. Junker, however, was eager to make the journey by himself, and with the assistance of Mackay in Buganda he actually succeeded in reaching Cairo via Zanzibar at the end of 1886. For the first time since the fall of Khartoum – indeed, since Emin had been cut off three years before – the outside world had authentic news of the strange little outpost of civilization that was still holding out in the centre of Africa. Up to this point Emin and his men had been conveniently forgotten in Europe, but now there was an immediate stirring of interest, and perhaps a certain feeling of guilt at the abandonment of Gordon had something to do with it. All at once the Press, the politicians and the geographic and missionary societies were eager for news. Who was Emin? How had he managed to hold out when all others had been submerged by the tide of barbarism that had swept along the Nile? Could he be rescued? The more the story came to light the more fascinating it appeared to be.

Emin, it seemed, was an extraordinary man, this German eccentric who had been brought up as a Protestant in Germany, but who changed his name in the Middle East and became a Moslem. Even Burton (now living out his last years in Trieste) hardly mastered such a range of accomplishments: Emin was a doctor of medicine, a botanist and ornithologist, a linguist who spoke French, German, English, Italian, Turkish, Arabic, Persian, demotic Greek, and several Slavonic languages. Gordon had recognized his exceptional gifts as an administrator and had promoted him from the post of medical officer to Governor of Equatoria at a salary of £50 a month. By carefully cultivating the ivory, coffee and cotton trade in his province Emin had converted an annual deficit into a profit of £8,000. The museums and scientific societies of Europe, it now appeared, knew him very well; before he had been cut off he had sent out thousands of carefully prepared skins of birds and animals, thousands of specimens of plants, and these collections had been accompanied by the most precise and scholarly notes. In his neat microscopic handwriting Emin had recorded all kinds of hitherto unknown facts about the migrations of birds on the Upper Nile and its

Emin Pasha – also from one of Stanley's lantern slides. 'From Dr Junker I learn that Emin Pasha is tall, thin, and exceedingly shortsighted; that he is a great linguist, Turkish, Arabic, German, French, Italian and English being familiar to him; to these languages may be added a few of the African dialects.' (Stanley)

tributaries, about the languages and customs of the tribes, about the rainfall and the geology of the country. He spoke, for example, of 'the great python africanus', which the women in some tribes befriended, keeping it as a pet in their huts, rubbing it with fat, and pouring fat down its throat; and elsewhere there were other tribes where poisonous snakes were caught and secured by a cord passed through a hole bored in their tails. These snakes were then placed near waterholes so that they would bite the antelopes coming down to drink and thus provide meat for the tribes.

There was nothing that did not interest this methodical and inquiring mind. He was forever on the move about his province, and his journeys were recorded in his journal with the precision of a chronometer: '15 August. Monday. Time: 5 hours, 21 minutes a.m. started off. Crossed Luri. Break from 9 hours 18 minutes a.m. to 9 hours 47 minutes a.m. – Arrived Lado 10 hours 48 mins. outward march 4 hours 38 mins. (against 4 hours 58 mins. for the return journey).'

In 1886 Emin had been twelve years on the Nile and he was aged 46. Junker described him as 'a slender, almost spare man, rather above the middle height, with a thin face surrounded by a dark beard and deep-set eyes which look observingly through his spectacles. The shortness of his sight compels him to strain his eyes and concentrate them on the person before him, and this imparts a hard, and at times almost furtive expression to his gaze.' His 'undeniably Oriental stamp', Junker went on, was of considerable assistance to Emin in posing among the Egyptian officials as a Turk. 'Every Friday he was seen to visit the mosque, where he repeated the prayers enjoined – and on these and all other occasions he preserved an almost painful punctiliousness and great care in his dress.' Yet Emin was probably not a devout Moslem. 'Don't be afraid,' he had written to his sister in Germany long before. 'I have only adopted the name [Emin]; I have not become a Turk.'

Not everyone liked Emin. His own soldiers seem to have treated him with the mocking and half-insolent respect that unruly schoolboys give to a weak and hesitating master. He did not give commands; he cajoled, he temporized, he entered into arguments. The soldiers obeyed him because it was the custom, because there was no one else to organize their lives. If they cared nothing for his scholarship and his superior cast of mind he was still a recognizable figurehead, and he had an Oriental acceptance of hardship that prevented him from breaking down.

Some of Emin's contemporaries found him very difficult. Casati was to write later that he had a prickly kind of pride and was never able to reach a clear decision. Gessi thought him 'a man full of deceit and without character, pretentious and jealous . . . a hypocritical person, ridiculously complimentary and cringing in his manner, and capable of deceiving the astutest man in the world'. In view of what was about to happen these criticisms are revealing. For the moment, however, they were hardly to the point. The important fact was that this singular and persistent man, by some strange means, was keeping a little flame of civilization alight in the centre of Africa, and now he needed help. Junker in 1886 had been able to send him a caravan of supplies from Rubaga, and he still very occasionally managed to correspond with Mackay in Buganda, but for the rest he was even more isolated than Gordon had been in Khartoum. The latest news to come out indicated that the Arabs were still threatening to invade Equatoria. When Emin had gone south to Wadelai the tribes had risen in revolt behind him, and in Lado a small Egyptian garrison was being besieged. In a letter from Wadelai dated July 22, 1886, Emin declared, 'I am still waiting for help and that from England.'

Gaetano Casati.

After the failure of the Gordon expedition the British government was naturally reluctant to involve itself. Salisbury, the Prime Minister, took the view that since Emin was a German it was up to the Germans to assist him. But there were other forces in Britain outside the government which were deeply interested in the matter. William Mackinnon, the Scottish ship-owner who had founded the British India Steam Navigation Company, saw here an opportunity for combining philanthropy with business. An expedition going to the rescue of Emin could very well explore the possibilities for trade as it went along. Mackinnon may not have completely committed himself to this project when he agreed to become chairman of the Emin Relief Committee, but he and his business friends certainly had it in mind, and they set about raising money with great vigour. Some £20,000 was collected (including £10,000 from the Egyptian government) and at the end of 1886 the committee was casting about for a suitable man to take charge of the expedition. One possible choice was Stanley. He was widely known, and his name would attract a good deal of support for the expedition. In the end it was decided that he should be sounded out.

Stanley at this time was lecturing in America, but he returned to England directly he received a cable from Mackinnon and agreed at once to go. From this moment the

Maxim automatic gun. From In Darkest Africa *by Stanley.*

plans went forward rapidly. Stanley himself contributed £500 to the funds, and offered to raise further sums by sending back dispatches to his newspapers in England and America. Once again the appointments were upon a lavish scale: the best of stores were ordered from Fortnum and Mason, and a Maxim machine-gun, the latest thing in modern weapons, was added to a heavy cargo of rifles and ammunition. Stanley was embarrassed by the number of young gentlemen-volunteers who wanted to accompany him, and who were ready to pay for the privilege, and eventually nine men were selected. Junker and Schweinfurth, who met the party at Cairo on its outward journey, at the beginning of 1887, thought that it more resembled a staff embarked upon a military conquest than a private expedition into the interior. And indeed there was a great deal more involved here than the simple rescue of Emin. The full extent of Stanley's commitments has never been entirely revealed, but it is certain that he was under instructions from King Leopold as well as Mackinnon. For Mackinnon he was to open up a trade route to Buganda, and to prepare the ground for a British East Africa Company. For Leopold he was to explore the possibilities of annexing Equatoria to the Congo. Emin was to be offered posts with both these enterprises; either he could join the British East Africa Company and build up a new trading station on Lake Victoria, or he could continue to govern Equatoria on Leopold's behalf. Then there was the question of the £60,000 worth of ivory which was said to be at Wadelai – it would come in very usefully as an addition to the expedition's funds. Finally there was Stanley's own share of the proceeds: in addition to his newspaper dispatches he planned to write a book about the journey. Business as well as politics had entered into African travel.

One cannot altogether blame Stanley for doing the best he could for himself. After all he was risking his life once more, and the writing of travel books was his trade. Yet there was a flaw in all these calculations and it was sufficiently important to cast an air of unreality over the whole adventure. That flaw was concerned with Emin himself. When Emin heard from Mackay in Buganda that a relief expedition was on its way he wrote: 'If . . . the people in Great Britain think that as soon as Stanley comes I shall return with him, they greatly err. I have passed twelve years of my life here, and would it be right of me to desert my post as soon as the opportunity for escape presented itself? I shall remain with my people until I see perfectly clearly that both their future and the future of the country is safe. The work that Gordon paid for with his blood, I will strive to carry on, if not with his energy and genius, still according to his intentions and in his spirit . . .

'If England really wishes to help us, she must try, in the first place, to conclude some treaty with Uganda and Bunyoro . . . A safe road to the coast must be opened up, and one which shall not be at the mercy of the moods of childish kings or disreputable Arabs . . . It is therefore out of the question for me to leave, so I shall remain . . . Evacuate our territory? Certainly not.'

In other words this was Gordon all over again; it was not 'rescue' that Emin wanted, but the political and military support which would enable him to remain where he was.

The letter was published in 1888 in a book called *Emin Pasha in Central Africa*, which was edited by Schweinfurth, but by then Stanley and his men had vanished into the interior and were completely out of touch.

There were other strange aspects about the expedition, and none of them boded very well for the future. To most people who consulted a map at the time it seemed obvious that the best path in Equatoria was the one that led directly inland from the Zanzibar coast. But Stanley wanted to follow an enormously roundabout route; he proposed to sail down to Zanzibar from Egypt, and having there picked up his porters, continue with them by sea around the Cape of Good Hope to the mouth of the Congo River on the west coast of Africa. He then planned to cross the entire continent from west to east, picking up Emin on the way. The reasons he gave for preferring this route appeared to have a certain validity, at all events on paper. His Zanzibar porters, he said, were bound to desert him if he marched them directly inland away from their homes, whereas if he landed them on the west coast they would realize that their only hope of survival was to remain with him until he reached Zanzibar. Like horses returning to their stables they would quicken their pace. Then,

The interior of Emin's house.

too, he could transport his men in boats for a thousand miles up the Congo River and this would bring them within 350 miles of Lake Albert, where he hoped to make contact with Emin.

A little reflection shows that there was not much merit in these arguments. The desertion of porters had not prevented other explorers (including Stanley himself) from getting through to the lakes from Zanzibar. It seems more likely therefore that Stanley's real reason for wanting to take the roundabout route was political. By coming through the Congo he pleased Leopold and furthered his own interests there. The Congo was his special field in Africa and he was determined to return.

Not unexpectedly he had his way. In February 1887 we find him very busy in

Zanzibar. He visits the Sultan Barghash on Mackinnon's behalf and gets his approval of the British plans in East Africa. On behalf of Leopold he seeks out the notorious Tippu Tib, who by now had become the virtual ruler of all the area between the Congo and Lake Tanganyika. Stanley made him just such an offer as Gordon would have made to Zobeir in the Sudan: Tippu Tib was to become Leopold's Governor on the upper waters of the Congo, and at the same time he was to supply Stanley with porters from Central Africa who would carry ammunition in to Emin and then bring out the £60,000 worth of ivory. It required but three days for Stanley to complete these arrangements, and on February 25, 1887, he embarked on the *Madura* with 620 Zanzibaris and Somalis, his British staff and his new business partner, Tippu Tib. Three weeks later they all landed at the mouth of the Congo on the west coast, and the most ghastly of all Stanley's journey's began.

Like Gordon in Khartoum, Emin was aware in a general way that help was coming, but he was very much in the dark as to precisely where or when it would arrive. Like Gordon too he was heavily involved in his own affairs. He succeeded in raising the siege of Lado, and even managed to re-occupy a dozen of his forts and stations which had been abandoned to the Arabs, but in Wadelai there were further disasters. The fort took fire one day, and although the ammunition was saved it was necessary to rebuild the entire settlement. Emin's daughter, Ferida, was still with him, but his Abyssinian wife had died and his own health was failing. One of his eyes had grown steadily weaker, and he was now obliged to hold a book within an inch or two of his glasses before he could read. In a letter to a friend he wrote, 'We have hung our harps upon the willows, and sit by the waters of Babylon.'

Despite all this, Emin's situation was not nearly so desperate as Gordon's had been in Khartoum; he had food in abundance, space to manœuvre, and his soldiers were seldom heavily engaged. But the long aimless days of waiting were destroying discipline in the garrisons, and it was clear that his little empire was beginning to disintegrate. In February 1888, twelve months after Stanley had left Zanzibar, Emin went south to Lake Albert in one of his steamers in search of news, but heard nothing definite. He returned to Wadelai and the long silence settled over the wilderness again.

It was broken suddenly and dramatically at the end of April 1888: one of Stanley's lieutenants, Mountenay Jephson, appeared in a steel boat at a station of Emin's on Lake Albert, and he had tremendous news. Stanley had actually been on the south end of the lake in December and had just missed Emin there. He was now camped on the shore barely a day's journey away. Emin set sail at once in the *Khedive* to meet his rescuer.

The history of the European pioneers on the White Nile is very largely a theme of conflicting personalities – of Burton's opposition to Speke, of Stanley's to Kirk and of Gordon's to Baring. Even the alliances that are made, such as that between Stanley and Livingstone, have often an odd and fortuitous character. But nothing could have been stranger than the meeting that now took place in the gathering darkness on the western shore of Baker's lake.

There was hardly a single quality that these two men had in common. Emin was

passive, subtle, studious, indecisive, evasive, meticulous, fatalistic and full of compromise. Before him stood a man who had no patience with fine shades of meaning,
who openly proclaimed his contempt for collectors and scholars, who knew only one
way of life and that was to march unflinchingly upon his set objectives. Emin, one
feels, was the sort of character who would have been given the worst table in a
restaurant, while Stanley, presumably, would have been led at once to the best
place in the room. Stanley's world was compacted into a straight line, an arrow in the
blue. Emin described a series of faint spirals in the dust. It was the conflict of ambition
and of a bull-like strength with a precise and cautious intelligence, and the issue
between them was doubly complicated at this moment since their normal roles were
reversed: Stanley, for once, was the one who stood in need, and Emin, the man he
had come to rescue, was the stronger of the two.

Stanley had had a frightful time. Even his original journey down the Congo in
1876 could hardly match the horrors that had overtaken him since he had left the
coast. His men were scattered over 700 miles of lethal jungle and half of them were
dead. Nothing in the way of starvation, of sickness and of calamitous accidents had
been spared them. For many months they had groped about like dying insects in the
gloom of the Ituri forest where daylight scarcely ever penetrated, and the pygmies
had taken a terrible toll among the bare-footed porters by planting poisoned arrows
in the ground. One by one Stanley had seen all his plans go wrong, and his white
officers had come to hate him. Those that survived were to give lurid accounts later
on of their leader's violent rages, of how he called one man a 'God-damned son of a
sea-cook' and rushed upon him shouting, 'I'll give you a bellyful' (while Tippu Tib
and the Africans looked on). Floggings of 300 lashes that were sometimes fatal had
been a common punishment for delinquents along the march. And now, his hair
turned white and barely recovered from a month of illness, Stanley had struggled up
to the lake with the remnants of his expedition. Except for a little ammunition he had
nothing to give Emin and no means whatever of rescuing him – indeed, he was
actually dependent upon Emin for food and other supplies in order to keep his men
alive.

Already, too, Stanley was beginning to have dark misgivings about the man he had
come to rescue. Why had Emin not been waiting to receive him when he had reached
the lake in the previous December? He had driven the expedition forward at a
murderous pace, believing that every day was vital; but here was the Governor of
Equatoria looking very spry and apparently in no real difficulty whatsoever.

Yet their first meeting on April 29, 1888, passed off very well. Stanley describes
the scene in his *In Darkest Africa*: 'At eight o'clock, amid great rejoicing, and after
repeated salutes from rifles, Emin Pasha himself walked into camp accompanied by
Captain Casati and Mr Jephson, and one of the Pasha's officers. I shook hands with
all, and asked which was Emin Pasha? Then one rather small, slight figure, wearing
glasses, arrested my attention by saying in excellent English, "I owe you a thousand
thanks, Mr Stanley; I really do not know how to express my thanks to you."'

Five half-pint bottles of champagne were opened and they had a two hours' talk.

OPPOSITE *The meeting of Stanley and Emin Pasha.* OVERLEAF *Stanley's scouts discovering the pygmies
carrying away a case of ammunition. From one of Stanley's lecture slides.*

Next day Stanley handed over the thirty-one cases of Remington ammunition he had brought and Emin, with his Sudanese soldiers parading smartly on the shore, conducted his guest aboard the *Khedive*. They then cruised pleasantly up the lake, and Emin, it seemed, was willing to talk about anything but the business in hand. 'I am unable to gather in the least what his intentions may be . . .' Stanley wrote in his diary, '. . . but the Pasha's manner is ominous. When I propose a return to the sea to him, he has the habit of tapping his knee, and smiling in a kind of "We shall see" manner. It is evident he finds it difficult to renounce his position in a country where he has performed vice-regal functions.'

There was some truth in this. Emin was carefully calculating his position. It seemed to him that no great future was awaiting him on his return to Cairo, whereas in Equatoria he was still master of the scene, or at any rate nominally so. Could he not, with Stanley's help, set himself up in Equatoria as an independent ruler, more or less? Why should he abandon to the Khalifa this green and flourishing land where he had worked so long?

On the whole, Emin thought, there was an excellent case here for delay. He did not reveal the weakness of his own position to Stanley, but instead raised doubts about Stanley's ability to get the garrison – all ten thousand of them with their wives and children – down to the coast.

Stanley said he could do it, but Emin still hesitated. It was perfectly clear that once they were on the march to Zanzibar Stanley would be ruthless in pressing onwards. Everyone in Africa knew what happened to stragglers on his journeys.

All through the first three weeks of May the argument dragged on, and in Stanley's account of it in *In Darkest Africa* there is a rising note of irritation. Yet he could not afford to be too brusque with Emin at this stage, since the *Khedive* was constantly bringing supplies and clothes into his camp from Wadelai. He sought to put an end to the discussion by coming out with his two propositions for Emin's personal future: would Emin like to govern Equatoria on behalf of the King of the Belgians at an annual salary of £1,500, with £10,000 to £12,000 administrative expenses? Or would he like to go with his garrison to the north-east corner of Lake Victoria and there set up a new colony for the British East Africa Company? Even these offers failed to pin Emin down. He flatly rejected the Belgian offer, saying that after so many years of service with the Egyptians he could not change sides. The British offer he found more alluring, but still he would not commit himself.

In the end it was decided that while Emin, Casati and Jephson remained behind and sounded out the garrison on whether they wished to go or stay, Stanley should make the fearsome 700-mile journey back to the Congo River to gather up his rearguard. On May 24 he set off.

Even now it is hardly possible to read Stanley's account of this gruesome march without recoiling. It is like some dark Germanic legend in which all nature is twisted into monstrous shapes, horror is piled upon horror, and the gnomelike little figures of the pygmies dart in and out of the nightmare as upon a canvas painted by Hieronymus Bosch. There is a perpetual twilight in the forest, and in the matted foliage

A typical glimpse of the jungle through which Stanley travelled.

monkeys and parrots scream and chatter out of sight. Below, in the fierce heat of the slimy, gloomy undergrowth, trees grow horizontally for fifty feet or more in their hopeless struggle towards the light, and wasps' nests hang among long creepers from their trunks. Every man is an enemy in this submerged world. The African savage, suddenly surprised, raises his weapon instinctively, stands staring for an instant, and then vanishes like a ghost.

The picture that Stanley, perhaps unwittingly, gives of himself is of some wild and dangerous beast crashing through the vegetation, and that, no doubt, is the actual impression he did make upon the pygmies and the animals living there. The porters that Emin had loaned him had known hitherto only the bright landscapes of the lakes, and now their dark skins turned bluish-grey, a fatal colour for a negro since it indicated death; and they did die in scores as the march went on.

Stanley's determination in the face of these disasters was tremendous, but he confesses that when he finally reached his rearguard on the Aruwimi River, a tributary of the Congo, he felt that he was going mad. A year before he had left here a party of several hundred men under the command of five white officers, who had instructions to follow him to Lake Albert as soon as Tippu Tib supplied the porters he had promised. But this rearguard had scarcely moved. Tippu Tib had naturally failed to produce the porters directly Stanley was out of sight, and now Barttelot, the leader of the party, was dead, murdered by one of his own men, another white officer had been invalided home to England, a third had vanished down the river, and Jameson, the second-in-command, was supposed to be drawing up somewhere in the rear. Jameson, it appeared, had actually been sending back to the west coast stores that he judged to be unnecessary, and among those stores had been Stanley's personal kit and his private hoard of delicacies from Fortnum and Mason. Stanley dashed off a furious letter to him saying that he was a demented idiot, and ordering him to report at once. There was no response; by now Jameson, having been made delirious with malaria, was also dead.

This left Stanley with Bonny, his one remaining white officer of the rearguard, and the remnants of his Zanzibari porters, most of whom were sick or half-starved. However, he managed to collect four or five hundred men who were able to walk, and half of these were still alive when he got back to Lake Albert in December 1888 after a six months' absence.

Here an entirely new crop of misfortunes was awaiting him. There was no sign of Emin, Casati or Jephson, and presently letters arrived from them saying that they too had been overtaken by disaster while Stanley had been away. At Dufilé, the most northerly of the remaining garrisons, Emin's Egyptian soldiers had risen in revolt, apparently with some vague idea of capturing Stanley and his provisions on his return to Lake Albert and of setting themselves up as an independent force. Emin and his two companions had been seized and kept in close confinement for three months.

It was the Arabs who had brought the mutineers to their senses. All this time the Khalifa's steamers had been making their way up the White Nile from Khartoum. Early in October 1888 they had arrived at Lado, and soon afterwards three Arab envoys appeared at Dufilé with a demand that the Egyptian garrison should surrender. A violent panic had ensued. The three envoys had been murdered, Emin and his companions had been hurriedly released, and the mutineers, all thoughts of mutiny forgotten, had fled southwards, abandoning Dufilé and a dozen other posts to the enemy. The three white men were now slowly making their way back to Lake Albert in the hope of meeting Stanley there. Emin was still unable to say what his ten thousand soldiers and their families intended to do; half of them were now loyal to him and presumably in favour of escaping with Stanley to Zanzibar, half were still against him, and there was no real authority anywhere.

Stanley says he was shocked and disillusioned when he heard this news. Emin had given him the impression that he was in perfect control of his garrison, and was well able to withstand the Arabs in the north. Now it was apparent that he could do nothing of the kind. Equatoria as a coherent state in the centre of Africa had ceased to exist, and Emin himself was in no position to prevaricate or to dictate terms any longer. Stanley sent Emin a letter saying that he would give him just twenty days to get to the south end of the lake and then they would march for Zanzibar.

Emin replied that since Stanley would not wait, then goodbye. Nevertheless, he did turn up in Stanley's camp in February, and there was a reconciliation of a kind between the two men: Stanley agreed to wait a few more weeks until such of Emin's followers as wished to escape from Equatoria had joined them.

During March these people straggled down to the south end of the lake, and this perhaps for Stanley was the most maddening time of all. He had been prepared to accept women and children and even concubines as well, but their luggage he considered excessive. They brought with them grindstones, beer-jars, bedsteads, all their last pathetic movable possessions, and Stanley's Zanzibari porters were obliged to carry these bulky packages up the cliffs, 2,000 feet high, that divided his camp from the shores of the lake. The camp itself was soon seething with discontent, and bitter quarrels broke out between the Zanzibaris and the Egyptians. Emin, it seemed to Stanley, only added to the confusion; he occupied his days with the 'frivolity' of his plant and bird collections. Jephson showed ominous signs of falling under Emin's listless influence, and Casati, surrounded by his household of native women, was plainly demoralized.

It is not difficult to imagine Stanley's frantic desire to break free from this coil that was steadily closing round him, and early in April the Egyptian officers gave him his opportunity. They were foolish enough to imagine that they could still overwhelm the white men and seize control of the expedition for themselves, and were actually stealing arms for this purpose when Stanley burst in upon them. The conspirators were assembled, disarmed and threatened with death – a sentence Stanley would certainly have carried out if he had been given the slightest provocation – and orders were given for the march to start at once.

By now some six hundred of Emin's people had arrived, and to these were added about a thousand of Stanley's men. The long column marched south towards the Equator, paused for a month when Stanley and Jephson collapsed with malaria, and

OVERLEAF *The expedition under attack. From one of Stanley's lecture slides.*

Some of Emin's people.

then trudged on again. It was at this time that Stanley beheld the sight that he had only glimpsed some twelve months before: the perpetual snow on the crests of the Ruwenzori Range, the so-called Mountains of the Moon. The bank of clouds that hangs forever round the upper slopes (the Ruwenzori is one of the wettest ranges in the world), rolled back just long enough for him to see the topmost peaks rising to close on 17,000 feet into the sky, and that was one more landmark he added to the African map. On Lake Albert the two steamers, the *Khedive* and the *Nyanza*, and the remainder of Emin's followers were abandoned.

All things considered the 1,500-mile journey down to the coast was less disastrous than might have been expected. By August the column had rounded the south-western shore of Lake Victoria, and at Usambiro they found the British missionary, Alexander Mackay, waiting to receive them with a quantity of stores that had been sent up from the east coast. Here they rested in the mission houses for nearly three weeks, and in October they pushed on again, leaving Mackay behind them. The Maxim gun cleared their way through belligerent tribes.

It is plain from Stanley's book that his relations with Emin had by now become almost impossible. Emin, hating the whole idea of being rescued, but unable to resist, was in a fretful and suspicious mood. On the march he would take only a small cup of coffee in the morning and fast all day until the evening. He avoided Stanley as much as he could and instead devoted himself to Ferida, his small half-Abyssinian daughter, who was carried in a hammock just ahead of the donkey which he himself rode. No doubt he made the most of his small advantages; after all, he was the chief trophy of the expedition, and Stanley could hardly afford to abandon him. Stanley's own feelings were a curious mixture. He seems to have been both irritated and attracted by Emin; he goes on and on about him in his book, he cannot leave him alone. Here, he says, is a highly intelligent man, a kind of Eastern *Guru* full of courtesy and acceptance. But what a weakling! How his subordinates bully him, how he hesitates and delays! A pathetic man with that Mohammedan fez on his head and the cataract in his eye. And in the end how ungrateful!

It is a pity that, except for a few brief notes and some cautious letters, we do not have Emin's account of this journey, especially in its later stages, for its conclusion is a strange imbroglio of vanity and wounded pride. Near the coast the column was met by a German expedition that had come out to look for them, and Emin was at first dazed and then delighted to discover that he had become a celebrity. On December 4, 1889, 2 years and 10 months after the expedition had left the mouth of the Congo, Stanley and Emin, accompanied by a group of German officers, rode on horseback ahead of the column into Bagamoyo to find the township bedecked in their honour, and four British and German warships in the harbour. A German garrison had now established itself at the port, and at 7.30 that evening the two travellers sat down to a champagne banquet, with a band from one of the German cruisers in attendance. It was an emotional and lively occasion, for both Stanley and Emin had long since been given up for lost, and now the great news of their arrival was about to break upon the world. Stanley indicates that he drank a great deal and feasted on the delicacies placed before him, and no doubt the others followed suit. Emin, delighted to be among Germans again, and overwhelmed at receiving a personal telegram from the Kaiser, made two speeches. He then got up and left the room.

It was thought that he might be feeling unwell, but some little time elapsed before a search was made for him. It was then discovered that, with his poor eyesight, he had lost his footing on a balcony and had fallen fifteen feet to the ground. The German hosts rushed out and threw water over him, but his skull was cracked and he lay unconscious through the night. Stanley waited a day while Emin was treated at the Bagamoyo hospital, and then on December 6, with the remainder of his men, crossed in a flotilla of warships to Zanzibar. From Zanzibar he sent to inquire about the patient, and Parke, the expedition's physician, remained in Bagamoyo to treat him. But Parke's attentions were not welcome in the hospital, and Stanley received no word from Emin – indeed, he never heard from him again.

There was, however, very little time for Stanley to brood on this unhappy parting, for by now the news of his safe arrival had spread around the world, and it was the rescuer and not the man he had rescued whom the public wanted to acclaim. He arrived in Cairo on January 16, 1890, to find the world was ringing with his name. Telegrams from Queen Victoria, the Kaiser, Leopold, the Khedive and the President of the United States. Warm letters from Mackinnon and his committee in London.

Invitations to banquets innumerable. In a word, kudos galore. Stanley very wisely resisted it for the moment. He found 'a retired house' in Cairo, the Hotel Villa Victoria, and there on January 25 he began to write the account of his journey. Proceeding at the rate of twenty printed pages a day he completed two volumes in precisely fifty days, and then sailed off to the welcome awaiting him in England. He was now 50.

In Darkest Africa was published later in 1890 and was an immediate success in six languages. Then followed in the same year Stanley's marriage to the artist, Dorothy Tennant, the conferring of honorary degrees upon him by the Universities of Oxford, Cambridge and Edinburgh, the purchase of a house at Furze Hill, near Pirbright (where the names Stanley Pool and the Mountains of the Moon were given to a pond and a hillock in the garden), and later his lecture tours, his entry into Parliament, and finally, in 1899, his knighthood. The hunter was home from the hill, and the waif from Wales had found his place at last.

Critics were not wanting, of course. They pointed out that nearly half of Stanley's original force of 700 Zanzibaris and Somalis were dead, that but 260 of the Equatoria garrison of ten thousand had managed in the end to reach Cairo, and that Emin, the principal object of the expedition, had been abandoned with a broken skull in Bagamoyo. Even the £60,000 worth of ivory was reported to have been lifted from Equatoria by an Arab trader before Stanley had arrived there – at all events Stanley never mentioned it. In the light of these facts the expedition could hardly be said to have succeeded at all.

Three of the surviving white officers wrote books about their experiences, and the journals and letters of two of the dead men, Barttelot and Jameson, were also published. Not all the authors drew very friendly pictures of Stanley – it was his ruthlessness that was chiefly remembered, the touch of megalomania. Casati, the Italian, in after years was observed to clench his fists at the very mention of Stanley's name, and Emin, slowly recovering in Bagamoyo, broke off all connection not only with his rescuer but with the British was well. No one, moreover, was much disposed to admire Stanley's dealings with the slaver, Tippu Tib.

But these were small voices in a tempest of applause. The hazards of the journey had been very great; Stanley, it was thought, was the only man who could have brought the expedition through, and in 1890 he stood forth as incontestably the greatest of all living explorers, the chief discoverer of Central Africa. In the face of his achievements one could afford to overlook, at any rate for the time being, the fact that the White Nile, along its entire length, from Khartoum to the Great Lakes, had returned once more to the barbarism in which Speke and Grant had found it nearly thirty years before.

The tower at Bagamoyo.

PART FOUR

──

THE CHRISTIAN
VICTORY

18

The Open River

Stanley's expedition was the last of the great private journeys to the Nile. By 1889 events in East and Central Africa were no longer controlled by individuals but by European governments, and the undisguised contest for new colonies had begun. Barghash's shadowy empire that stretched in theory from Zanzibar almost to the White Nile may perhaps be likened at this time to some old-fashioned family business which has managed to keep going for years with its assets under-valued and its methods increasingly out of date. Sooner or later resolute intruders were bound, as it were, to buy up a controlling interest in the company, and then eject its helpless directors into a comfortable and humiliating retirement. Something of this process at all events occurred when Germany, under Bismarck, decided to penetrate the East African mainland which the British and the Zanzibar Sultans had left uncultivated for so long.

In 1884 Karl Peters, who in many ways is the German counterpart of Stanley in Africa, made his celebrated raid into Barghash's dominions. Travelling inland from the Zanzibar coast towards Kilimanjaro he persuaded a group of native chieftains to accept the protection of his recently formed German Colonization Society. It was, as Professor Coupland has pointed out, cynical, farcical and effective; the chieftains could neither read nor write and they had very little idea of the real nature of the treaties they signed with their crosses. Peters alone was nothing in the world, but when Bismarck, like some powerful banker, decided to support him it was an entirely different matter. Barghash and Kirk in Zanzibar might protest that this was hardly less than a hostile invasion of an independent ruler's country, but they were powerless without the support of the British government; and this they did not have. The British had no wish to thwart the Germans; Khartoum had just fallen, Egypt was not yet settled, and England needed Bismarck's backing in her quarrel with the French in Africa. Gladstone professed himself to be very little disturbed when he heard of Peters's exploits in 'the mountain country behind Zanzibar with an unrememberable name'. 'If Germany becomes a colonizing power,' he declared, 'all I can say is "God speed her".'

The speeding in fact was done by Bismarck's warships. In August 1885 Commodore Paschen, commanding *Storch*, *Gneisenau*, *Prinz Adalbert*, *Elizabeth* and *Ehrenfels*, drew up his ships in line off Zanzibar, ran out his guns, and informed Barghash that within twenty-four hours he must acknowledge the Peters treaties on the mainland and enter into an agreement with Germany. Kirk, under instructions from London, was unable to interfere; indeed, he was obliged to lend his services to the Germans in conducting the negotiations, and by the end of the year an agreement was signed.

After this it did not take Britain and Germany very long to come to an amicable agreement for the carving up of the Sultan's empire. The Germans took the view that Barghash was entitled only to those areas where his authority was acknowledged, and those areas, they decided, included only the three islands of Zanzibar, Pemba and Mafia, and a strip of the mainland coast ten miles in depth and 600 miles long. The rest of the great East African plateau that swept for a thousand miles into the interior was described as a legitimate 'sphere of influence' for the European powers to divide amongst themselves.

Colonel Kitchener, the British representative on the boundary commission (he had come south to Zanzibar from the Sudan), was almost as indignant as Kirk at this cynical appraisal of the situation, but he was instructed to accept it on behalf of the British government, and an official settlement was made in London in 1886.

Barghash was allowed to keep his three islands and the coastal strip, and the rest of the territory that had been nominally under his control was divided roughly into halves – the area known as Tanganyika falling to the Germans and Kenya being allotted to the British. The western boundaries of this huge appropriation were left undefined; Buganda (or Uganda) for the moment appeared to be anybody's game.

Kirk had now been twenty years in Zanzibar, and his policy had collapsed entirely. He had persuaded Barghash that, in return for the suppression of the slave-trade, he could rely upon the British to maintain his independence, and now that independence had gone forever. He had tried to induce the British to develop East Africa before the other European powers arrived, and nothing had been done. He had striven to keep the peace between Africans, Christians and Moslems, and now the Arabs everywhere were arming against the Europeans, and men like Peters, who for sheer ruthlessness put even Stanley in the shade, were teaching the Africans to hate white men as they had never been hated before. Even the slave-trade, profiting by the general confusion, showed signs of reviving. The last known slave dhow in East African waters was captured in 1899, but the traffic was not entirely abolished in Zanzibar until 1907, and in Tanganyika until 1922.

Early in 1886 Kirk was awarded a G.C.M.G., and in July he left on leave for England. No doubt he had a premonition that he would not be asked to return to Zanzibar, and in London this was confirmed. If he felt bitter he made no great parade about it. He settled down to life in England and a directorship of the Imperial British East Africa Company which now, belatedly, was formed by William Mackinnon and his friends as a rival to the German company.

Barghash did not survive Kirk's departure for very long. It is scarcely surprising that these events had left him disillusioned and listless. He grew increasingly unwilling to conduct public business, and in March 1888 he died at the early age of 51. His younger brother, Sayyid Khalifa, succeeded to a throne that hardly counted in the new pattern of affairs in Africa, for by then the great European land-grab had begun. Essentially it was a race for the interior between Germany and Britain, and Buganda (which had been left out of the 1886 agreement) was the prize. By 1890 the essential point was decided: in July of that year representatives of the German and British governments, meeting in London, agreed that the whole of Uganda should be ceded to the British as a sphere of influence.

Emin from a late photograph. He was actually 5 feet 6 inches in height. A ceremonial uniform which Stanley had brought from Cairo for him proved to be so big that 6 inches had to be lopped off the trousers

Emin played a strange part in these events. He remained for four months in Bagamoyo recuperating from his fall, and his accident seems if anything to have increased his eccentricity and his deviousness. For a time no one could make out what it was he wanted to do – to return to Egypt or Europe, where he was loaded with honours from universities and learned societies, or to stay and finish his work in Africa. There was, however, no real doubt about the outcome. After so many years of exile and of living the life of a Moslem it had been an overwhelming thing for him to speak his own language again and to be honoured by his own countrymen. He was deeply touched by the telegram he received from the Kaiser, and when this was followed by the award of a medal, the Second Class of the Order of the Crown, with a Star, he was stirred by all the pride and the patriotism of the colonial official who suddenly, after many years of obscurity, finds himself mentioned in the Honours List. Now at last he was not alone; the weight of personal responsibility which he had borne for so long in Equatoria was lifted, and he had a powerful protector behind

Fort Bagamoyo.

him. When he had still not completely recovered from his accident – he was partially deaf in one ear and he had difficulty in swallowing – it was announced that he had joined the Germans and would lead a new expedition for them into the interior. Among the British there was a good deal of bitterness when this news was announced; after all they had not rescued Emin merely in order to make his services available to the Germans. But Emin could now afford to ignore his opponents. He was soon entrenched in the German camp at Bagamoyo, and his letters reveal that he shared in the general feeling of hostility towards the British there.

He bought an estate outside Bagamoyo, settled his daughter in the town under the protection of a guardian who was instructed to teach her German, and by the end of April 1890 he was ready to lead his expedition inland. A German zoologist, Dr Franz Stuhlmann, three German officers, and some seven hundred Africans were placed under his command, and he was generously equipped with guns and ammunition. His instructions were 'to secure on behalf of Germany the territories situated south of and along Lake Victoria up to Lake Albert'. He was 'to make known to the population there that they were placed under German supremacy and protection, and to break and undermine Arab influence as far as possible'. In other words, he was to seize Uganda and the sources of the Nile before the British could get there.

Soon after he had left the coast, however, he was informed of the new agreement by which Uganda had been allotted to the British, and he was now ordered to confine his activities to Tanganyika. But Emin decided to go on. Who knows what visions were agitating his tired and failing mind? Perhaps, like so many others before him, he was driven onward by an obsession for the vast unexplored spaces of Africa itself. At all events, having founded the town of Bukoba, on the western shore of Lake Victoria, he pushed on to the north, ignoring repeated orders to return to the coast. In 1891 he actually succeeded in making contact with his old soldiers at the south end of Lake Albert, but most of them refused to acknowledge him as their leader any more. Many of the men and their families were now dressed in the skins of wild animals, and had been reduced to a squabbling and disorderly rabble. After some weeks of useless parleying, Emin abandoned them and went on into the Congo. The Germans by now had disowned him, and the last months of his life are the pitiful story of a man possessed. He seems to have formed the fantastic notion that with the remnants of his little column he could cross Africa to the Cameroons on the west coast, and like Livingstone before him he held on doggedly to his scientific work, believing that, in the end, it would justify all his actions and compensate every hardship.

'Caught a red mouse at last!' runs one of the final entries in his diary. 'Collected twenty-five fresh species of birds; shot a young crocodile.' When smallpox broke out in his camp Stuhlmann was sent back to Lake Victoria with such of the men as could walk, and it was understood that Emin was to follow as soon as the sick had recovered. But it is doubtful if he would ever have turned back. In October 1892, two and a half years after he had left Bagamoyo, he kept his inevitable appointment with death in the depths of the Congo, some eighty miles south of Stanley Falls; a group of Arab slavers rushed him in his tent and cut his throat. He was aged 52. Another year elapsed before definite news of Emin's fate reached the outside world, and his murderers were hunted down and executed by Belgian officers in the Congo. The bulk of his estate (£5,200 had been paid to him by the Egyptian government for his work in Equatoria) was left to his daughter, and she was taken into the care of his relatives in Germany.

Emin's certainly was the most intelligent brain in Central Africa since Burton's time. Harry Johnston, arriving in Uganda as British administrator some years later, rated him as one of the greatest of African explorers in the sense that he tried to

The last view of Emin, August 17, 1890, from a photograph taken by F. Stuhlmann.

understand Africa and the teeming life he found there, rather than to treat the country merely as a blank space to be 'discovered' and delineated on a map.

At all events, he belongs to that small group of adventurers who opened up the White Nile to civilization, and among the mass of new men who were now advancing on the river only a few like Lugard could match their stature. These new arrivals were soldiers and administrators rather than explorers. They moved in groups and teams and wore the uniforms of European governments. They did not know to the same extent as their predecessors the crushing and yet captivating weight of loneliness in Africa.

The early pioneers were vanishing very quickly at this time. The two missionaries, Mackay and Lourdel, were buried in Central Africa within six months of one another in 1890 (neither of them having ever returned to Europe), and in that same year Burton died in the British Consulate at Trieste. A large map of Africa hung above his truckle bed together with an Arabic inscription: *All things pass.* Grant was buried in Scotland in 1892, and in the following year Baker died among his sporting trophies at his house near Newton Abbot. His wife, however, lived on for many years, a spartan and determined old lady who would permit no fires in the house from May to October. The nephew, Julian Baker, who had taken part in the Gordon relief expedition, eventually rose to the rank of admiral in the British navy. Stanley alone among the great explorers survived into the present century. He died at his home in England in 1904.

One feels that all these people, with the exception of Lourdel, would have approved very much of the final settlement of Uganda under the British in the eighteen-nineties. Lugard, the chief architect of the modern state, was a man after their own hearts: he perceived his objects with the utmost clarity and proceeded towards them with an astounding energy. Yet he was still only a young unknown officer of 32 when he reached Uganda as an employee of the British East Africa Company – by then established in offices at No. 2 Pall Mall, London, with a capital of £250,000 – at the end of 1890. Within two years he had built a chain of stations from Mombasa to the Nile (the true route into Uganda, as Gordon long ago had foreseen), had signed a firm treaty with Mwanga, had settled the religious wars between the Moslems and the Christians, had defeated Kabarega in Bunyoro to the north, and had carried out the work that both Emin and Stanley failed to do, namely the evacuation of the garrison from Equatoria.

It was an extraordinary achievement. Speke from his grave must have looked on with admiration. Then too, Lugard was an even better propagandist than Gordon. When the Company wished to withdraw from the territory he had conquered for it on the grounds that the expense of its administration was too great, Lugard returned to England and raised a public outcry. In letter after letter to *The Times*, in public speeches up and down the country, he declared that the garrisons he had left behind in Uganda could not be abandoned, and that the valley of the Upper Nile could not be allowed to return to its former chaos: the British government must step in and take over the administration. Gladstone, once more in office, and with the memories of Gordon and the Wolseley expedition vividly in his mind, recoiled from the idea, but once again he had the public, the Church and the Queen against him. In 1891 Victoria wrote to Rosebery, the Foreign Minister: 'The fate of Gordon is not, and will not be, forgotten in Europe, and we must take great care what we do. The difficulties are great, doubtless, in Uganda, but the dangers of abandoning it are greater.'

In the end she had her way. In April 1894 the government announced that Uganda was to become a British protectorate. By the end of the eighteen-nineties the Mahdists, who had advanced as far as Wadelai, were driven out, a mutiny of Emin's former soldiers was put down, and Mwanga, who had gone over to the Moslems, was finally defeated with Kabarega. This was the end of all serious opposition to the British at the headwaters of the Nile.

In looking back over the forty-odd years that had elapsed since Speke and Grant had first breached the defences of these primitive kingdoms, one is struck by the personality of Kabarega. If he has been neglected in these pages it is because the explorers' records of him – almost the only records available – are sparse and almost invariably hostile. No missionaries ever resided at Kabarega's camp; not even Emin, his one apologist, continued for long in friendship with him. Yet Kabarega rises

F. D. Lugard.

Kabarega in old age.

above all others in Uganda as a guerrilla fighter, and as a brave and determined defender of African independence. He is the one man who continues on the scene from first to last: as a young warrior he saw Speke and Grant march into his father's capital near Masindi; he fought Baker, Gordon, Stanley and Lugard as well as Mutesa. He was nearly always defeated and yet he never gave up so long as there was the ghost of a chance of rousing his men to resistance. It was a hopeless struggle, of course, but he did not think it so. And thus it is a little sad that one Sunday in April 1899 the British should have tracked him down in his last stronghold in a swamp north of Lake Kyoga, and that both he and Mwanga, who had joined him in adversity, should have been captured and deported to the Seychelles. Their durance on the island was more prolonged than that of Archbishop Makarios in recent times. Mwanga died there in 1903, but Kabarega still lived on, and there is a photograph taken of him in his old age that shows him standing with a walking stick and wearing a frock-coat with a stiff white collar and a handkerchief tucked neatly into his pocket – a caged lion. Yet still the gaze of the eyes is direct and fearless, and it is a fine and indomitable head such as one might expect to see cast in heavy bronze.

When Kabarega reached the age of 80, and it was judged that he could make no more disturbances for the white men in Africa, he was allowed to come home from the Seychelles. However, he succeeded only in reaching the source of the Nile at Jinja and there he died. The body was carried up to Bunyoro and entombed close to the battlefield where he fought Baker in 1872. The modern traveller passing by on the main road will discover it very easily; a grass and reed hut surrounded by trees and a hedge. It is somewhat dark inside, but one can descry upon the grave a dusty covering made of the traditional bark-cloth and the skins of leopards – the fierce and untamable animals which are the symbol of the royal kings of Uganda.

In the Sudan also the old pattern had collapsed, and the new era of European domination – and of European vengeance – had begun. One might take the year 1889 as the turning of the tide against the Khalifa. In early August Nejumi was routed and killed with all his chief Emirs at the Battle of Toski, sixty miles inside the Egyptian border. With this the Mahdist threat to Cairo vanished forever. Meanwhile on the Red Sea Osman Digna was falling back under a new British assault, and there were heavy casualties among the Khalifa's men in a third campaign that was being fought against the Coptic Christians in Abyssinia.

These defeats might have been fatal to the Khalifa had he not been protected by the deserts of the Sudan, and there were other dangers threatening him as well. The country was becoming depopulated. Slatin, at a later stage, estimated that, of the original nine million inhabitants, about 75 per cent were exterminated during the Khalifa's rule. The continual wars and the slave-trade destroyed many thousands every year, diseases such as smallpox and syphilis were endemic, and now in 1889 the country was overwhelmed by famine. Great areas of cultivatable land had been left idle while the Arabs went off to war or congregated in the capital, and in the province of Darfur, where the Khalifa had put down a revolt with the utmost brutality,

wild animals had taken possession of the empty plains. And now there appeared out of the blue one of those periodic plagues of African locusts which turn the land into a desert overnight. The insects arrived in such myriads along the Nile they blotted out the light of the sun, and the little grain they left in the ground was devoured by another plague – this time of mice.

The catastrophe naturally fell heaviest upon the overcrowded inhabitants of Omdurman. People became so desperate with hunger they turned cannibal and ate young children; hundreds of emaciated bodies were to be seen lying in the streets or floating down the Nile.

It says something for the force of the Khalifa's character, and also for the virility and toughness of the Arabs themselves, that they were able to survive these disasters and to continue to rule the Sudan for another eight years. But after 1889 it was a process of gradual retrenchment. In 1891 Father Ohrwalder escaped to Egypt with two of the surviving nuns, and Slatin managed to follow him four years later. From these and other witnesses a fairly precise picture was built up of the Khalifa's dwindling defences, and the Egyptian army began to take heart again. It was now commanded by an enthusiastic group of British officers who had learned the tactics of the desert.

Meanwhile in England there was a rising agitation for another campaign in the Sudan. Revenge for the death of Gordon and the defeat of the Hicks and Wolseley expeditions was, of course, a leading motive. International politics also pushed the British into action: in the general scramble for territory in Africa they supported the claims of Germany and Italy against the French, and it was feared (with good reason) that France was preparing to move into the Sudan. Early in 1896 the Italians were defeated by the Emperor Menelik of Abyssinia at Adowa, and it seemed possible that they might be driven out of Africa altogether, unless the British created a diversion on the Nile. To all this was added the old (and empty) fear that the Khalifa might renew his attack on Egypt and the Suez Canal. Thus the conditions for an imperialistic war were very nearly everywhere fulfilled. Perhaps too, from somewhere out of the past the voice of Gordon could be heard: 'The Mahdi must be smashed up . . . Remember that once Khartoum belongs to Mahdi the task will be far more difficult; yet you will, for the safety of Egypt, execute it . . .' You will 'be forced to enter a far more serious affair'.

By 1896 the British were ready to enter into this far more serious affair: Messrs Thomas Cook's fleet of pleasure steamers on the lower Nile was requisitioned, some ten thousand Egyptian soldiers and their British officers were assembled on the Sudanese border, and even Sir Evelyn Baring was eager for the fray. His protégé, General Kitchener, now aged 48, was appointed to the command of the expedition, and he had with him a group of young men who were already making a name for themselves in the world: Wingate, with his excellent intelligence service, Slatin, now a senior officer in the Egyptian army, the young sailor, David Beatty, and later, the young soldier, Winston Churchill.

The ascent of the Nile from Egypt was a long business – not the few months that

A plague of locusts near El Djebelein.

The Rameses *; one of Thomas Cook's pleasure steamers.*

Wolseley required, but two years. This time there was to be no haste and no mistake. Only one battle of any importance was fought before Omdurman. In April 1898 the Emir Mahmoud, one of the most aggressive of the Khalifa's surviving generals, advanced down the Nile as far as Atbara to meet the oncoming expedition. On Good Friday Kitchener fell upon him with all the force of his modern artillery, and to the music of Scottish pipes, English flutes, drums and brass, the British and Egyptian soldiers stormed the Arab barricades. No quarter was given to the enemy during the assault, and before long some 2,000 of them were dead. Churchill relates that after the battle Kitchener 'rode along the line, and the British brigades raising their helmets on the dark, smeared bayonets cheered him in all the loud enthusiasm of successful war. For almost the only moment in the course of this story he evinced emotion. He was, said an officer who watched him closely, quite human for a quarter of an hour! And indeed, if anything could break this stern man's reserve, it should have been the cheers of the soldiers who had stormed the Atbara *zeriba*; for this was the most memorable day in all his life that had yet run out.'

A victory parade was held in the neighbouring town of Berber, and Kitchener rode forward on a white horse to take the salute. At the head of the parade came the defeated general, Mahmoud, a proud and handsome young man in his early thirties. Chains were riveted round his ankles, a halter was passed round his neck, and his

RIGHT *Mahmoud in his bloodstained jibbeh after his capture at the Battle of Atbara.*

hands were bound behind his back. In these bonds he was made sometimes to walk, sometimes to run, and when he stumbled his guards drove him on. The inhabitants of Berber and the camp followers of Kitchener's army jeered at the prisoner and pelted him with rubbish.

It was a barbarous incident and there was worse to follow. To be fair, however, one must remember that much harsher treatment would have been meted out to the British and the Egyptians had they been captured by the Arabs, and that colonial warfare in the nineteenth century with all its savagery never achieved quite the same refinement of cruelty that was practised upon many prisoners in the last world war.

Kitchener's attitude to these matters was a complex one, and Sir Philip Magnus has gone a long way towards explaining it by pointing out that, at this time, he was an extremely reserved and unpopular man – as unpopular as only driving personal ambition could make him. He was unmarried. Mary Baker, the 16-year-old daughter of Baker's brother Valentine, had fallen in love with him in Cairo in 1883, but whether or not he might have married her is unknown since she died in the following year while Kitchener was in the Sudan with the Wolseley expedition. In Cairo he was regarded as a snob; it was known that he frequented the great houses on his trips to England (and he dashed back there to get political support more than once during the campaign), but in Egypt he avoided the provincial homes of his officers and their wives, and preferred instead to meet wealthy Jews and Turks. He had no use for married men on his staff, and was ruthless in cutting pay and allowances. No excuse, however genuine, was accepted from his subordinates for even the slightest failing. Ordinarily his manner was surly. He showed no interest in the welfare of his soldiers and seldom spoke to them. As an economy measure he allowed very few doctors to accompany the expedition, and his attitude to the wounded Arabs was, to say the least, one of indifference: they were left on the battlefield to die. Yet it is also clear that Kitchener towered above his men in a way that few field commanders have ever done. He was greatly feared and admired as a man of dispassionate, machine-like efficiency. His drill sergeants paid him the compliment of growing 'Kitchener' moustaches which were long, thick and martial. His officers never dared to question his decisions. The General's private doubts and hesitations were revealed only to his superiors such as Baring, and with Baring Kitchener very carefully watched his step.

So now, stimulated by success, eager for loot and more battle honours, the expedition pressed on towards Omdurman. Early in the summer of 1898 they reached Metemma and there they found the trenches and graves that had been dug by Wolseley's soldiers when they delayed in their advance to Khartoum thirteen years before. By September 1, 1898, Kitchener was before Omdurman with a force of more then twenty thousand, which included many British soldiers as well as gunboats of the Royal Navy, 100 guns, and a vast supply column of camels and horses. It had rained heavily in the night, and through the clear air the soldiers saw the great dome of the Mahdi's tomb rising in the sky, and beneath it, on the uneven surface of the desert, a long shadowy line that looked as though it might be a *zeriba*, a defence-work made of thorns and the branches of trees.

Churchill describes the scene: 'Suddenly the whole black line which seemed to be the *zeriba* began to move. It was made of men, not bushes. Behind it other immense masses and lines of men appeared over the crest; and while we watched, amazed by the wonder of the sight, the whole face of the slope beneath become black with swarming savages. Four miles from end to end, and, as it seemed, in five great divisions, this mighty army advanced – swiftly. The whole side of the hill seemed to move. Behind the masses horsemen galloped continually; before them many patrols dotted the plain; above them waved hundreds of banners, and the sun, glinting on many thousand hostile spearpoints, spread a sparkling cloud.'

It was not thought that the Khalifa stood much of a chance; many of his 50,000 warriors were armed with nothing better than spears, his guns were obsolete and Baker's old steamers, *Bordein* and *Ismailia* (which blew up when she was laying crude mines in the river near Omdurman), were not really a match for the British gunboats – and in the event this optimism was perfectly justified. Had the Khalifa attacked at night or had he chosen to make his stand in the desert out of the range of the British gunboats it might have been another story. But he did neither of these things. Allah, he declared, had ordered that he must fight at Omdurman.

The Arabs were very brave. They attacked *en masse* at dawn on September 2, rushing straight into the British artillery fire, and Kitchener's rifles completed the

OPPOSITE *Some of Gordon's belongings: a drum belonging to the 11th Sudanese Regiment; Gordon's camel saddle, compass, revolver, headrest and Bible; the Sultan of Darfur's helmet captured after his death in battle in 1879; medals struck by Gordon at Khartoum and those he won in the Crimea.* OVERLEAF *The Battle of Omdurman, Friday, September 2, 1898.*

work. 'No white troops,' G. W. Steevens, the war correspondent, wrote, 'would have faced that torrent of death for five minutes. It was not a battle but an execution.' Except on the left flank, where the 21st Lancers made a gallant, disastrous and pointless charge, the Arabs never succeeded in reaching the invader's lines; the dead and wounded piled up in mounds on the desert, and within an hour or two there were some ten thousand bodies lying there, while many thousands of others who were wounded, or simply demoralized, streamed back in a rout to Omdurman. Kitchener's casualties were about 400. The General watched the action on horseback, with his staff around him and the great red banner of the Egyptian army flying over his head. 'At half-past eleven,' Churchill says, 'Sir H. Kitchener shut up his glasses, remarking that he thought that the enemy had been given "a good dusting".'

There was a break then for lunch, and afterwards Kitchener, who had now added the Khalifa's black flag to his own, rode into Omdurman. Very little resistance occurred. Most of the tribesmen who had survived the massacre had decamped, and a great wave of joy spread through the city when it was announced that the inhabitants who had stayed behind (mostly women) were not to be killed. Slatin, who must have spent a grimly exultant day, was recognized and cheered. In the early afternoon Kitchener made his way through the mangled corpses and the dead animals (the British artillery bombardment had been very heavy and lyddite was used for the first time) to the Mahdi's tomb in the centre of the town, and here an accident occurred. Four British shells, fired in error, fell almost at the General's feet, and Hubert Howard, *The Times* correspondent, was killed. Pressing on further through the maze of crooked streets in search of the Khalifa Kitchener arrived at last at the prison, and here he released Charles Neufeld, the German trader who had been captured twelve years before, and about thirty others who were shackled in chains. He then returned to the mosque, where he set up his headquarters. Slatin brought him word there in the evening that the Khalifa had escaped; on returning to Omdurman from the battlefield he had rested for two hours and had prayed at the Mahdi's tomb. Then at 4 p.m., the very moment that Kitchener had entered the town, he had mounted a donkey and had ridden away with one of his wives, a Greek nun (who was to be used as a hostage), and a few attendants. About 30,000 fugitives, including Osman Digna, who had come up from the Red Sea for the battle, had gone with him. British cavalry through the following days pursued the Khalifa for a hundred miles south of Khartoum before they turned back empty-handed. The Khalifa by then was well on his way to El Obeid.

In Omdurman Kitchener proceeded to establish the honours of victory. The Mahdi's tomb had already been damaged severely by the bombardment, and now the body of the Mahdi himself was dug up and flung into the Nile – not, however, until the head was severed, and this was purloined by Kitchener as a trophy of war. He appears to have had the notion that he might have used the skull for an inkstand or a drinking cup, or alternatively that it might have been forwarded as a curiosity to the Royal College of Surgeons in London, and it was sent down to Cairo. There was an outcry about this matter when it became known to the public, and

The 21st Lancers charging at Omdurman, by R. Caton Woodville.

not even the General's popularity in England (where he was idolized after Omdurman) was able to protect him from it. Queen Victoria was deeply shocked – she thought the whole affair 'savoured too much of the Middle Ages' – and Kitchener was obliged to write her a mollifying letter. Baring in Cairo meanwhile quietly possessed himself of the skull, and sent it up to the Moslem cemetery at Wadi Halfa, where it was secretly buried by night.

But these events were to follow later as part of the disillusionment and sense of anti-climax which usually succeeds a victory. In Khartoum during these first days of exaltation after the battle Kitchener had another function to perform which was much more to the public's taste. Not many relics of Gordon remained; the earthworks he had caused to be dug were still visible, the *Bordein* was captured, and the telescope through which he had gazed so often from the Palace roof was recovered in perfect condition from the arsenal. But at this moment Gordon's memory was very bright. On September 4 a picked guard of soldiers was drawn up in a square before the ruins of the Palace, and four chaplains conducted a funeral service. Gordon's favourite hymn, 'Abide with Me', was sung, the British and Egyptian flags were broken out from poles erected on the rubble of the roof, and after the two national anthems had been played, three cheers were raised for the Queen and three more for the Khedive of Egypt. The gunboats crashed out a salute from the river. Kitchener, standing in the centre of the square, was deeply moved. Eye-witnesses declared that his shoulders were observed to be shaking with sobs, and that, turning away, he was obliged to ask one of his officers to dismiss the parade. Afterwards he walked for a long time in the Palace garden below the stairs where Gordon had been killed. 'Surely he is avenged,' the Queen wrote in her diary when she heard of the ceremony. This was true of course. Yet one cannot help feeling that Gordon himself was the last man in the world who would have wished to be avenged, and that he would have obtained a much deeper satisfaction from the college that rose in his name when Khartoum was rebuilt – that same college which has trained the Africans who rule and administer the Republic of Sudan at the present time.

There remained one other score for Kitchener to settle on the White Nile, and it was urgent. Shortly before the battle he had received from England sealed orders which he was not to open until Khartoum was reconquered. On reading these orders now he discovered that he was to proceed upstream from Khartoum at once, for it was believed that a party of Frenchmen led by a Captain Jean-Baptiste Marchand had crossed Africa from the west coast and put themselves astride the river. They were to be dislodged.

It had been known for some time that the French had been planning this *coup* – and indeed the British had contemplated sending an expedition north from Uganda to head them off – but nothing had been heard of Marchand for many months. Now, however, within a day or two of opening his orders, Kitchener received first-hand evidence that the French party had actually arrived. On September 9 Gordon's old steamer *Tewfikia*, manned by unsuspecting Arabs who knew nothing of the fall of Omdurman, arrived at Khartoum from the White Nile and was immediately captured.

A drawing of Kitchener outside the Mahdi's tomb, by R. Caton Woodville.

The crew had an arresting story to tell. They declared that they had gone south a month before in company with another steamer, the *Safia*, to collect grain. Approaching the old Egyptian post at Fashoda, about four hundred miles up the river, they had been fired on from the shore by black troops commanded by white officers under a strange flag, and had lost forty of their number killed and wounded. They had at once retreated, and the *Tewfikia* had been sent back to Omdurman for reinforcements. In support of their story the Arabs pointed to the bullets that were imbedded in the plates of the *Tewfikia*: they were nickel-plated and of a small bore known only in Europe.

Marchand's 3,000-mile march across Africa had been a *tour de force*. Setting out two years before from Brazzaville with a dozen French officers and something over 100 Senegalese he had made his way past fantastic obstacles in the interior, and had arrived at Fashoda in July 1898, six weeks before the Battle of Omdurman. His objects were entirely political. He proposed to seize the valley of the Upper Nile in the name of France, to join hands with the Emperor Menelik in Abyssinia, to drive off or come to an agreement with the Khalifa, and above all to forestall the Kitchener

The arrival of the Anglo-Egyptian flotilla at Fashoda in 1899.

expedition that was advancing up the river. Hardly anything more provocative, more hopeless of accomplishment or more audacious could have been imagined. Yet it was done, and the French government was prepared to back the enterprise almost to the point of war – not war between Marchand's hundred-odd men and Kitchener's army on the Nile, since that would have been ridiculous – but war against Britain in Europe. No such dangerous crisis was to occur again until the actual outbreak of hostilities in 1914, and by then France and Britain were allies against Germany.

Just why Marchand should have chosen Fashoda as his goal, describing it as a vital point of communications on the Nile, is something of a mystery, for there were half a dozen other places up and downstream that would have done equally well. It was a miserable collection of square, flat-roofed houses on the river bank, and perhaps its only claim to fame was that it was the headquarters of the priest-kings of the Shilluk tribe. The climate was hot and malarial and for a long time the Egyptians had used the place as a kind of Devil's Island for life prisoners.

Kitchener lost no time in setting out. On September 10 he sailed up the river with five steamers, two battalions of Sudanese, one hundred Cameron Highlanders, a

RIGHT *Captain J.-B. Marchand.*

battery of artillery and four Maxim guns. Once again he was taking no chances. Three days later he came up with the *Safia*. The Arabs on board opened fire and were quickly shelled out of the river. On September 18 the British flotilla was approaching Fashoda, and Kitchener sent a messenger on ahead with an invitation for Captain Marchand to come on board the following day.

Up to this stage of the campaign we have seen Kitchener in a harsh and uncompromising light. Nothing, however, could be more admirable than the way in which he handled the explosive and delicate situation he now found before him. It was fortunate, of course, that he spoke French so well, and he was doubly fortunate in having to deal with a man of Marchand's stature and good sense; but even apart from this the General's performance was a model of diplomatic skill. He did not provoke

The meeting between Kitchener and Marchand on board the Dal.

the French by wearing British uniform, but appeared instead in an Egyptian army fez and under the Egyptian flag.

The opening round of courtesies was extremely well done. Marchand congratulated Kitchener upon his victory at Omdurman and welcomed him to Fashoda in the name of France. Kitchener congratulated Marchand on his splendid achievement in reaching the Nile, and added that he was bound to protest against his presence there. What did Captain Marchand propose to do? The Frenchman said he would fight if he was attacked and that he and his companions would die at their posts; and this would probably mean war between France and England. He would agree to nothing until he had further instructions from France. Kitchener replied that he himself had his instructions already, and they were perfectly clear: he was to take possession of the Upper Nile. But he was quite ready to leave Marchand undisturbed until he had communicated with the French government, and all facilities would be given by the British to enable him to do so.

It was a fair proposition and Marchand agreed to it. After an amicable lunch on board Kitchener's gunboat he went back to his camp, and there, in the afternoon, Kitchener returned his call. A Colonel Jackson who also spoke French, and who was given the title of 'Military and Civil Commandant of the Fashoda District', was landed with a contingent of men who raised the Egyptian flag and immediately began to set up camp alongside the French. Kitchener made a short reconnaissance up-stream to the mouth of the Sobat River, where he established another garrison, and then sailed away.

It was now up to the two governments at home to settle the issue, but nothing could have looked less like a settlement than the fury of indignation that swept over France and England directly the news from Fashoda became known. It seemed to the British that the French had attempted to rob them of their victory by an underhand trick. Captain Marchand, they protested, would have been wiped out by the Mahdiists if Kitchener had not won the Battle of Omdurman. What was this insignificant detachment of French adventurers compared to Kitchener's army? Salisbury described Marchand as 'an explorer in difficulties upon the Upper Nile'. (This was not strictly true. Marchand was surprisingly well provisioned and equipped. His men were provided with such things as mosquito nets which were unknown in the British army, they had cultivated a flourishing vegetable garden, and when they eventually evacuated Fashoda they left with the British a quantity of champagne and other wine.)

To the French it seemed that this was one more instance of British greed and British bullying. The British had abandoned the Sudan after the fall of Khartoum in 1885. Marchand by his courageous march had taken possession of a part of the empty space, and now it belonged to France by right of prior occupation. The French had got there first, and if for the moment they were weak in Africa they were not weak in Europe. The French nation would fight for its rights.

Throughout the first weeks of October 1898 the French and British Press attacked one another with an extreme virulence, and Kitchener, returning home at the end of the month, provided an additional outlet for the fierce patriotism that was raging through England. A special train bore him from Dover to London, and Charing Cross Station was bedecked in his honour. He stayed with Salisbury in the country and then went on to the Queen at Balmoral. The public was delighted to see him honoured – it was part of their defiance of the French.

Fashoda itself continued for a time to be the quiet centre of this maelstrom. Marchand and Colonel Jackson, though vigilant, got along with one another very well, and the two camps exchanged provisions. In the middle of October 1898, Marchand was summoned by the French government to Cairo, and he was cour-teously received by the British at Khartoum; they gave him a banquet, showed him over the battlefield, and then sent him on his way to Egypt.

Conditions at Fashoda deteriorated immediately after his departure. Captain Germain, who had been left in charge of the French expedition, was a less accommodating man than his chief. In defiance of the agreement that had been made between the two sides he occupied the country of the Dinka tribe on the right bank of the river, and prevented the Dinka chiefs from making contact with the British. The French boat, the *Faidherbe*, was dispatched up the river beyond the limits that had been agreed with Kitchener. Jackson, with two gunboats under his command and much stronger forces, held his hand but protested repeatedly. By the time Marchand returned a situation that was reminiscent of Mackay and Lourdel and the rival British and French factions in Buganda had developed, and hostilities were almost on the point of breaking out. Marchand quietened the scene. At Cairo he had learned with bitterness – a bitterness so deep that in after life he never again referred to Fashoda – that the French were giving way.

Indeed they had never had a real choice. It was apparent by now that the Abyssinians did not intend to come to their help on the river – they had a loathing of those hot and foetid swamps – and no matter what happened in Europe the French position at Fashoda was clearly untenable. Then too, France herself, and the French army in particular, were ruinously divided over the Dreyfus case at this time. The British, on the other hand, were absolutely united upon the Fashoda issue.

At a Lord Mayor's banquet given for Kitchener in London on November 4, 1898, Salisbury was able to announce that the crisis was over; the French were willing to withdraw.

Early on the morning of December 11, 1898, the French lowered their flag at Fashoda to the accompaniment of a roll of drums and a flourish of bugles. There was a moment of slight tension when one of the French officers, in a passion of hurt pride, stepped forward and flung the flagpole to the ground. However, a communal breakfast of the two garrisons followed, and later in the day the British fired a salute as the French steamed away on their long journey home through Abyssinia (they preferred not to take the easier, shorter route down the Nile through British territory). The British flag was not raised until they were out of sight, and as a further gesture, the hated name of Fashoda was erased from the map. The village that exists today near the original site of the outpost is called Kodok. Marchand was given a tremendous reception on his return to France, but he was seen no more in Africa. He went on to China to play his part in the Boxer rising, and died in 1934 after a distinguished career in the First World War.

On March 21, 1899, in London, Salisbury and Cambon, the French Ambassador, signed an agreement by which the Nile valley was reserved to the British and the Egyptians, while the French were to be given a free hand to the west of the river. That same month a further agreement was signed between Britain and Egypt by which the two countries undertook to rule the Sudan together. Kitchener, as Gordon had suggested so long before, was appointed Governor-General.

By now the General was back in Khartoum and honours were falling thick upon him: a step up in the army list, a grant of £30,000 from Parliament and a vote of

Kitchener being fêted at the banquet given for him at the Mansion House on November 4, 1898.

LORD LANSDOWNE
RESPONDING
FOR THE
ARMY

THE
MARQUIS OF
SALISBURY
PROPOSING "THE
HEALTH OF THE
SIRDAR"

SIR W. HARCOURT
PROPOSING
"THE HEALTH
OF THE
ᴿᴰ MAYOR"

THE SIRDAR
REPLYING

thanks from both Houses. Five thousand workmen began to rebuild Khartoum and seven thousand trees were planted to relieve the bareness of the new city. Kitchener was determined that the new Palace which was rising from the ruins of the old should be worthy of his office. Workmen were instructed to scour Khartoum for suitable materials. 'Loot like blazes,' Kitchener wrote to Wingate, 'I want any quantity of marble stairs, marble pavings, iron railings, looking-glasses and fittings; doors, windows, furniture of all sorts.' He also let it be known to the cities which were anxious to honour him in England that he needed no more ceremonial caskets or ornamental swords; he had enough already and would prefer plate, furniture and pictures for a private house that he intended to buy. Early in 1899 Baring came up to Khartoum for the first time, and he laid the foundation stone of Gordon College, for which Kitchener had raised £120,000 by public subscription in England. Soon afterwards a statue of Gordon himself, mounted on a camel, was placed in the principal square behind the Palace.

Both Baring and Slatin, who had been so much in Gordon's mind during the last months of his life, lived on into distinguished old age. Baring, elevated to the title of the Earl of Cromer, returned to England in 1907 and became a strong opponent of women's suffrage. He was chairman of the committee inquiring into the disastrous campaign at Gallipoli when he died of influenza in 1917, aged 76.

Slatin was awarded a knighthood after Omdurman and became Inspector-General of the Sudan. Later, as head of the Red Cross in his native Austria, he was warmly regarded for his humanity to Allied prisoners in the First World War.

Zobeir was allowed to return to the Sudan in 1899 and he lived on to an extreme old age on his estates to the north of Khartoum.

Affairs in the Sudan, however, were not quite settled by the Battle of Omdurman: the Khalifa was still at large. A number of unsuccessful attempts were made to track him down in the wild country to the south of El Obeid, but it was not until October 1899, more than a year after the battle, that spies brought in definite news of his whereabouts. They declared that Abdullah, with all the principal Emirs who had survived, had established a camp near Jebel Gedir, some 400 miles south of Khartoum, and 80 miles to the west of the White Nile. This was the Baggara country where the Khalifa had been born, a place of dry hills and forests: a little to the north lay Abba Island, where the Mahdi had first declared his holy mission.

Kitchener dispatched a force of 8,000 men to Kaka, the nearest point on the river, and in November Wingate arrived to take command. In bright moonlight on November 21 he marched westward from the Nile with a flying column of 3,700 picked men, and on the following day caught up with an Arab caravan that was taking grain to the Khalifa's camp. It was annihilated within a few hours, and Wingate pressed on rapidly through a thick forest. On November 23 his scouts brought him word that they had found the enemy camp at a place called Um Diwaykarat, about a dozen miles away.

It seemed probable that the Khalifa would stand and fight: his supply of grain had been captured, his pursuers blocked his escape-route to the north, and to the south and west lay nothing but waterless scrub. Wingate decided to attack at dawn. With the camel corps scouting on the flanks and the cavalry in front, the column moved off shortly after midnight, making as little noise as possible. At many places it was necessary for the men to hack their way through the forest, but by 3 a.m. the cavalry were within a mile of their objective and the infantry was now ordered to advance in fighting formation. In the distance they heard drums and horns sounding a warning in the Khalifa's camp, but these noises soon died away and the soldiers gained the grass on the rising ground without interference.

'At 5.10 a.m.,' Wingate wrote later in his report to Kitchener, 'in the uncertain light preceding dawn, our infantry picquets were driven in, and the indistinct forms of advancing Dervishes became visible.' The British machine-guns opened fire, and it was another Omdurman on a smaller scale. When the cease-fire sounded an hour later it was found that for the death of three of his men and the wounding of twenty-three others Wingate had gained a remarkable prize: a thousand Arabs were dead or wounded, and among the ten thousand-odd prisoners were 29 important Emirs, the Khalifa's eldest son and intended successor, and many women and children.

But it was on the battlefield itself that Wingate came upon a really awesome sight: '. . . only a few hundred yards from our original position on the rising ground, a large number of the enemy were seen lying dead, huddled together in a comparatively small space; on examination these proved to be the bodies of the Khalifa Abdullah,

The dead Khalifa.

the Khalifa Ali Wad Helu [another of the original three Khalifas chosen by the Mahdi], Ahmed-el-Fedil, the Khalifa's two brothers, Sennousi Ahmed and Hamed Mohammed, the Mahdi's son, Es-Sadek, and a number of other well-known leaders.

'At a short distance behind them lay their dead horses, and, from the few men still alive – amongst whom was the Emir Yunis Eddekin – we learnt that the Khalifa, having failed in his attempt to reach the rising ground where we had forestalled him, had then endeavoured to make a turning movement, which had been crushed by our fire. Seeing his followers retiring, he made an ineffectual attempt to rally them, but recognizing that the day was lost, he had called on his emirs to dismount from their horses, and seating himself on his "furwa" or sheepskin – as is the custom of Arab chiefs who disdain surrender – he had placed the Khalifa Ali Wad Helu on his right and Ahmed Fedil on his left, whilst the remaining emirs seated themselves round him, with their bodyguard in line some twenty paces to their front, and in this position they had unflinchingly met their death. They were given a fitting burial, under our supervision, by the surviving members of their own tribesmen.'

Kitchener added these words to Wingate's report: 'The country has at last been finally relieved of the military tyranny which started in a movement of wild religious fanaticism upwards of 19 years ago. Mahdism is now a thing of the past, and I hope that a brighter era has now opened for the Sudan.'

As the last weeks of the century ran out it did indeed seem that a better future had opened up, not only for the Sudan but for the whole valley of the Nile. Hardly forty years had elapsed since all the upper reaches of the river and the source itself were an unknown wilderness ravaged by tribal wars and slavery, and now at every point the civilized world was reaching into the centre of the continent. The slave-trade, if not absolutely dead, was dying fast. The telegraph was restored, and in 1899 a permanent channel was finally hacked through the Sudd. By a new system of railways and steamers it was now possible for a traveller to make his unmolested way along the entire length of the river. Still another railway was being driven inland from the east coast of Africa to Lake Victoria.

There had been fearful ravages, of course. The population of the Sudan had dwindled to a bare two million, and in Buganda hardly a million inhabitants remained compared to the three or four millions in Grant's and Speke's day. In some areas rinderpest had entirely wiped out the herds of domestic cattle, and even worse plagues were soon to follow. For many hundreds of miles the banks of the White Nile were a desolation. In the light of this one was permitted to wonder whether the price paid for civilization was not too high. 'The Nile-land of today . . . ,' Harry Johnston wrote at the turn of the century, 'is much of it in sad contrast with its condition during Sir Samuel Baker's government of the Sudan, and even during the silver age of Emin. . . . It is sad to think that the people were possibly happier [then].'

But by 1899 the nadir had been reached, and the incredible virility of Africa was beginning to assert itself again. Gladstone, who had died shortly before the Battle of Omdurman, might turn restlessly in his grave at many of the things the British had done along the river, but on the eve of the new century Queen Victoria, then in her penultimate year, could survey the scene with satisfaction. She ruled the river from the Mediterranean to the Mountains of the Moon. Egypt, the Sudan, Uganda – all were hers in fact, if not in name, and the Nile, for the first time in its history, was an open highway from Central Africa to the sea.

Gordon's statue at the Gordon Boys' School, Woking.
It was previously in Khartoum.

Epilogue

The principal eye-witnesses of the events described in these pages are now dead. It is a great loss that this is so. How much one would have liked to have talked to Burton, Gordon, Emin and so many others, to have at least seen Livingstone with one's own eyes, and to have put so many questions to men like Kirk and Baring; to have asked poor Speke what really happened when he went out shooting on that autumn afternoon near Bath in 1864.

With such strong characters one is tempted to make comparisons and classifications. It might be suggested, for example, that some, like Livingstone and Gordon, were born great; others like Stanley and Kitchener achieved greatness, and others like the Khedive Ismail had greatness thrust upon them. But then there still remains another group – Burton and Emin are members of it – which fits into no category at all. A common hunger for adventure certainly bound them all to Africa, and one notes that so many of these men were Scottish, were the sons of clergymen, and were affected by, or took part in, the three great military events of the time: the Crimean War, the Indian Mutiny and the American Civil War. The desire to suppress the slave-trade and evangelize the African tribes, the profits to be made from ivory and the hope of discovering gold and other minerals, the collector's and the sportsman's instinct, the simple wish to be the first to break into new country – all these things drew the explorers on; and it has to be admitted that a great deal of effort was wasted on expeditions that set out to rescue men who did not particularly want to be rescued.

But this must not be allowed to diminish the splendour of the explorers' achievement in obtaining, within the space of twenty years or so, the answer to a geographical mystery which had baffled the world since the beginnings of civilization. It must be remembered that they *walked* to the sources of the Nile; the country then was just as primitive and hostile as it was in prehistoric times, the harsh climate had not altered, disease was probably just as prevalent, and their scientific knowledge of the region was hardly superior to that of the early Greeks and Romans. This was a sunburst of Victorian courage and imagination.

Central Africa, with its tremendous rainstorms and its forest fires, its earthquakes, droughts and plagues, is a mighty destroyer of the relics of the past, but such as remain have not been greatly overlaid by new civilizations, and it is still a rewarding experience to follow the explorers' route from Zanzibar into the interior and then descend the White Nile from its source to Khartoum. At every step of the way one is reminded of some phrase they recorded in their diaries, some old engraving or pen-

and-ink sketch that has survived, some moment of triumph or disaster in their wanderings, and a hundred years vanishes in an instant.

Tornadoes, naval bombardments and the simple corrosion of the tropical air have devastated the Zanzibar waterfront, and it has been much rebuilt, but the general outline remains the same. One can still see through Burton's eyes the Arab dhows that have been washed in from the Persian Gulf by the monsoon, the Sultan's palace and the grey coral walls of the fort adjoining. A tall square house standing somewhat by itself on the left may appear to be just another house, but the initiate will know that Livingstone lived there before he set out on his last journey; and on going ashore he will make his way through the narrow streets to the old British Consulate which is now the headquarters of an East African trading concern. Tippu Tib's house with its carved doorways lies only a little distance off, and in a grove of mangoes just outside the town the visitor will find the ruined walls of the harem that Barghash built for his wives shortly before he died. It must have been a grandiose place, but now there is a heavy monastic silence in the air, and it makes a pleasant contrast with the hot alleyways in the town where the rickshas still push through the crowd, and where, amidst a violent farrago of scents and smells, the exotic produce of the island – the pawpaws, sugarcane, limes, groundnuts, jackfruit, guavas, nutmegs, cloves, pineapples, coconuts and dried shark's fins – is still laid out for sale, precisely as it was a century ago.

Beside Barghash's ruined harem a warm transparent sea washes up on to the beach of powdered coral that is almost as white as snow, and beyond it the green plantations of the island spread away. For most of the year a steamy heat envelops Zanzibar, and no matter how blue the sky there is always the oppressive feeling of an approaching thunderstorm in the air. In the evening, when the crowds emerge on to the waterfront for a breath of air, hectic sunsets break across the ocean, and presently the Southern Cross appears low down on the horizon. In the gathering darkness the boats in the harbour leave a bright trail of phosphorus in their wake. All this is very much as Burton described it.

There is a little museum in the town, and here one can see portraits of the Sultans, a folio of letters written by Speke, Grant and Livingstone, and the usual display of local arts and crafts. It is a good museum, splendidly arranged, and yet, as one passes by the showcases, one is aware that something is missing: the relics of the slave-trade. True, there is more than one picture of Tippu Tib on the walls, and in one corner a heavy pair of wooden stocks, much worn by the human limbs they once imprisoned, has been laid upon the floor. But Zanzibar wishes to obliterate slavery from its civic memories. The jungle has now overgrown the underground caves where the slaves were herded awaiting export overseas, and hardly a trace remains of the old slave-market which Grant described as 'a triangular space surrounded by rickety huts thatched with coco-nut leaves where the naked slaves sat silent as death'. The open square is there but it has been changed beyond all recognition. Upon one side the Anglican Cathedral rises up, and the bell tower with its explicit British clock is a very definite impediment to the memory of the terrible and lurid past.

At Bagamoyo, on the mainland, one is shown the window from which Emin is thought to have fallen when he reached the coast with Stanley in 1889, and on the river nearby one can still enjoy, with Burton, 'the deep dead silence of the tropical night, broken only by the roar of the old bull-crocodile at his resting-time, the *qua-qua* of the night heron, and the shouts and shots of the watchmen, who know from the grunts of the hippopotamus, struggling up the bank, that he is quitting his watery home to pay a visit to their fields.' The old caravan routes leading inland have long since been abandoned, but here and there along the way one comes upon old men who remember the slaving days very well. At Mpwapwa, which was an important staging post, one of Stanley's unfortunate companions lies buried, and Africans from some twenty or thirty different tribes are living in the district. These people are the descendants of slaves or porters who, on their way down to the coast, deserted the caravans or were left behind because of sickness. Like seeds scattered casually by the wind, they have taken root and somehow managed to survive.

From Mpwapwa one can strike towards Lake Victoria across the Wembere Steppe, which is the route that Emin and Stanley followed, or take the more generally used road that leads to Tabora. The house where Livingstone and Stanley stayed at Tabora has been faithfully rebuilt and converted into a kind of museum, with Arab muskets and other trophies on the walls. Someone had the notion of obtaining facsimiles of the dispatches that Stanley wrote here for the *New York Herald* after the two men had returned from Ujiji on Lake Tanganyika, and it is very strange to read the excited headlines in these surroundings: 'Dr Livingstone Found'; 'The Famous Explorer in Good Health'. The words seem to arrest time for a moment, and it is not difficult to imagine Livingstone sitting under the mango tree which stands outside the front door, planning the journey that was to bring him to the source of the Nile at last, and being mercifully unaware that he would never reach it and that within nine months he would be dead.

Here too, or at any rate close by, Burton and Speke began their quarrel and Speke alone marched off to investigate the reports of a great lake in the north. Mwanza, the place at which he obtained his first sight of Lake Victoria, is now a modern port with European buildings on the shore, and villas and churches dotted about the rocky hills above, and there is a regular service of steamers to Uganda and Kenya in the north. Yet in the outlying villages nothing very much has happened since 1858: the mango trees originally planted by the slavers have now grown to a great height, and in their deep green shade the Arabs still sit cross-legged on the verandas of their black-brick huts. These are the thin, courtly, serious men with moist, brown eyes and a fringe of black beard round their faces, whom Burton liked so well. But once again the drama has gone; they trade no longer in slaves and ivory, but in such things as cotton cloth and plastic buttons and perhaps, occasionally, a little illegal rhinoceros horn, which is still regarded as a great aphrodisiac in the East.

From Mwanza gravelled and paved roads that roughly follow Speke and Grant's route lead on around the western shore of the lake to Karagwe, but of Bweranyange, Rumanika's old capital, little now remains. Of the reed palace where the King used

The Mountains of the Moon.

to meet Speke and Grant, and later Stanley, and the compound where they watched the war-dances in the moonlight, and the house of the fat wives, there is no sign whatever; these things, like the fictional scenes in a novel, have their reality now only in the records of the explorers. They were discovered only to be lost again.

Bukoba, the town that Emin founded on the western shore of the lake, is a green and cheerful place with quite a Corinthian reputation for lasciviousness; it is said that the women here are unusually kind and affectionate, and that there is a great demand for them among the native brothels of East Africa. Whether this be true or not it is a fact that the traveller here notices a certain lightening in the atmosphere: both men and women smile and wave as his car passes by, and the clothes they wear are brilliant billowing cottons. The dull scrub of Tanganyika is now replaced by wide green fields and plantations of bananas. The air is warm and damp – there are said to be two hundred thunderstorms a year at this end of the lake – and after the rain tropical butterflies make a patchwork quilt around the steaming puddles on the road. Presently jungles appear, splashed here and there by the scarlet flowers of the flame tree, and it is apparent that one has crossed one of the great migratory routes of the African birds – over a thousand species have been noticed – for they appear in myriads in the evening: great spiralling fleets of Abdin storks, egrets, fish eagles, pelicans, ducks and geese of many kinds, and the crested crane which cries as it flies, like a lonely Siamese cat. This is the threshold of Uganda.

Not much remains of Mutesa's capital at Rubaga. Its seven hills are now the city of Kampala, a world of Indian shops and cinemas, of railway yards and bus stations, of Christian churches and commercial crops of tea, coffee and bananas. Jet aircraft coming in from Europe will provide perhaps for their passengers a brief glimpse of the source of the Nile at Jinja, but Jinja is a place of bright brick bungalows like any other African colonial town, and the natural fall of the river from the lake is imprisoned in concrete.

One must go north from the source, following in the tracks of Speke, Grant, Emin and Gordon, and enter Bunyoro in order to see the river as they saw it. Even as late as 1959 it was difficult for a motor vehicle to follow the rough tracks into the Karuma Falls where the Nile begins its tempestuous westward course to Lake Albert. Samuel Baker and his wife, struggling back here after the disastrous Battle of Masindi, must have beheld the river with relief, for it is a lovely sight, a great white foaming rush of water past green islands. The hippopotamuses, rising to the surface in the whirlpools, look like knights in a disordered game of chess, and have not as yet been much disturbed by the new electric power station on the bank.

For fifty miles below this point the Nile is barely navigable, but at the foot of the Murchison Falls it broadens into a quiet and softly-moving stream, with millions of little green cabbages, the *Pistia stratiotes*, floating on the surface of the water. Here we are in the region of Gordon's and Emin's forts. Magungo, the first of these, lies on the left bank just above the junction of the river with Lake Albert, and has been much cut up by hippopotamus trails and by elephants coming down to the river to drink. But it is Wadelai, the capital of Equatoria under Emin's rule, that one chiefly

Sunset over the Nile.

wishes to see. There is no road to Wadelai; one must proceed there either by launch (following the river about forty-five miles downstream from Lake Albert), or by bouncing across country in a truck. Choosing the overland route in the month of December, the writer found himself cut off from the river by a thick wall of coarse grass some eight feet high, which made the going very slow. There was no sign of a track, and the last village had been left far behind. It was, then, a matter of some astonishment that a tall and nearly naked African now suddenly jumped up in front of the truck, and pointing with his black finger into the grass ahead, uttered a single, luminous cry: 'Emin Pasha'. No doubt this man's family had been here since Emin's time, and had somehow retained their memory of the name through nearly three-quarters of a century. Clearly too, he had reasoned that only some business connected with Emin or his ghost could have brought a white man to this outlandish spot. At all events it was both startling and pleasant to be reminded thus of the continuity of things and, sure enough, the green sheen of the river with fields of feathery papyrus on either bank soon broke into view. But where was Wadelai?

A cairn of stones marked the site of the town, and upon it was a plaque with the words:

WADELAI EGYPTIAN STATION 1879–89
HEADQUARTERS OF EQUATORIA UNDER EMIN PASHA.

But the town itself had returned almost entirely to the jungle. It is much the same with all the other stations on the river; only at Dufilé, a little further to the north, where Gordon and Gessi assembled their steamers above the rapids, can you easily trace, among the borassus palms that have since sprung up, the general outline of the fort.

Here too, another change overtakes the river. Its rapids rush on into the dry wastes of the Sudan, and the Arab influence begins to make itself felt. The Sudd can still be a slight ordeal for a traveller even though he now passes through it on the deck of a paddle steamer with wire netting around him to keep the mosquitoes at bay. By the end of the first day – and from Juba it takes nearly three days to reach the clear water above Malakal – he will understand very well how Baker came to write 'during the dead calms in these vast marches the feeling of melancholy produced is beyond description. The White Nile is a veritable Styx.'

To have been becalmed in this moist green wilderness must have been demoralizing; to have endured there the approach of death through starvation and fever as Gessi did, too horrible to contemplate. The papyrus reed when seen for the first time, or carved in stone upon some Egyptian monument, is a beautiful plant with delicate arching fronds making an hieratic pattern against the sky. But when it is multiplied to madness, hundreds of square miles of it spreading away like a green sea on every side, the effect is claustrophobic and sinister. The channels through which the steamer passes are often only forty or fifty yards wide, and so the passenger looks out upon interminable walls of interlacing stalks and they press upon him in imagination like the walls of a prison or a maze. Even the water in the channel itself is not clear, since within the last year or so that most prolific of aquatic plants, the water hyacinth, has taken hold upon the Nile. It reaches out from the banks in long floating filaments with a pretty purple flower, and although it is savaged and cut about by the steamers' paddles it never seems to die; rather, it strengthens its hold on the river from year to year and could, if unchecked, succeed in the end in blocking the stream once more as it was in Gessi's time.

At Khartoum, however, there is more evidence of the past. The Mahdi's tomb has been re-erected at Omdurman, and the Khalifa's house has been converted into a museum. From here it is but a short drive to the battlefield, which remains virtually as it was in 1898 – an uneven expanse of dry and rocky desert. The new city of Khartoum on the opposite bank of the river bears very little resemblance to the fortress Gordon knew. Even the General's statue has been removed in recent years, and one cannot be quite sure of finding the identical spot on the Palace stairs where he is supposed to have stood when he was stabbed to death. Yet from the roof the view is still much the same, and one sees more or less what Gordon saw: the low, mud-hut silhouette of Omdurman on the opposite bank, the desert spreading away on every side to become lost in mirages on the flat horizon, and at one's feet the Blue Nile coming in to join the White.

Here, more than anywhere, the river reveals its calm, slow, massive power. Already the main branch, the White Nile, has come two thousand miles from the centre of Africa, and it is so wide, so lake-like, so busy with barges and sailing boats, one finds it difficult to believe that the stream has still another two thousand miles to go before it reaches the sea.

But the Nile at Khartoum is something more than a great artery pumping life into the arid sand: it has a quality in time as well, something to do with the continuous movement of the water perhaps. One does not here feel so very distant from Wolseley's and Kitchener's soldiers making their way up from Egypt, or from the Khalifa's warriors, or from Speke taking pot-shots at the hippopotamuses in the reeds, or from Mrs Baker washing her yellow hair in this same water, or from the Mahdi praying on Abba Island, or from Livingstone, Gordon, Gessi and so many others who, in their different ways, gave their lives for the river, or from Burton and Stanley who staked their reputations upon it, or even from Herodotus and Nero's centurions. The river binds them all together. Each of them was drawn towards it by an irresistible attraction, and it makes very little odds whether we think of the stream as it is in this present century or as it was in the age of Ptolemy. The Nile seems to be impervious to change. It flows on now, as it has always flowed, perpetually renewing itself from year to year and from century to century, a never-ending flood of warm, life-giving water that spans half Africa from the Equator to the Mediterranean, and it is still the mightiest river on the earth.

Asolo, Italy, 1960

Chronology

460 B.C.
Herodotus ascends the Nile to Aswan

1st cent. A.D.
Legendary merchant Diogenes lands on the east coast and makes 25-day journey into the interior of Africa

c. A.D. 50
Nero sends an expedition to Nubia

2nd cent. A.D.
Ptolemy's map

1770s
James Bruce traces Blue Nile from its source to its junction with White Nile (Khartoum)

1811
Thomas Smee describes Zanzibar

1823
Anti-Slavery Society founded

1839
United States sets up a consulate at Zanzibar

1845
Sultan of Zanzibar forbids export of slaves

1848
Johann Rebmann reports having seen snow-capped peak (Kilimanjaro)

1849
J. L. Krapf claims to have seen snow-capped peak (Mount Kenya) to the north of Kilimanjaro

1850s
Lakes Ujiji, Nyanza, and Nyasa reported

1854
Baker and Speke meet on board ship between India and Aden
Burton and Speke meet at Aden

1855
Death of Seyyid Said, Sultan of Zanzibar
Tribesmen attack encampment of Burton and Speke in Somaliland

1856
Burton and Speke land on Zanzibar Island (Dec. 19)

1857
[Indian Mutiny breaks out in May]
Burton and Speke leave Zanzibar for African mainland (June 16)
Burton and Speke begin their African journey (June 25–27)
Burton and Speke reach Kazeh (Nov. 7)

1858
Burton and Speke reach Lake Tanganyika and explore it (Feb. 13)
[Indian Mutiny ends in March]
Burton and Speke back at Kazeh for refit (June)
Speke sets off without Burton (July 9)

Speke reaches Mwanza (Aug. 3); gets back to Kazeh mid-Aug.
Burton-Speke party sets out for east coast
Livingstone makes his Zambezi expedition

1859
Burton-Speke party reaches east coast near Dar-es-Salaam (Feb.)
Burton and Speke reach Zanzibar (March 4)
Speke leaves for England (mid-April)
Burton reaches England (May 21)
Speke's two articles published in *Blackwood's Magazine*

1860
Burton's *Lake Regions of Central Africa* published

1861
Speke and Grant reach Karagwe (Nov.)

1862
Speke sets out for the court of Mutesa, King of Buganda (Jan. 8)
Sir Samuel Baker and his wife reach Khartoum (June)
Speke and Grant leave Buganda (July 7)
Speke reaches the Nile at Urondogani (July 21)
Speke reaches the falls he names Ripon (July 28)
Speke and Grant reach Karuma

Falls in central Uganda (Nov. 19)

Speke and Grant reach Faloro (Dec. 3)

Bakers leave Khartoum for Gondokoro (Dec. 18)

1863

Speke and Grant leave Faloro (Jan. 10)

Bakers reach Gondokoro (Jan.)

Speke and Grant reach Gondokoro and meet the Bakers (Feb. 13)

Bakers set off southward from Gondokoro (March)

Speke, back in London, is given an ovation by the RGS, and the Founder's Medal (June 22)

Speke's *Journal of the Discovery of the Sources of the Nile* published

1864

Bakers reach Karuma Falls (Jan. 22)

Bakers leave Kamrasi's headquarters (Feb.)

Bakers reach 31°N. latitude (March)

Bakers catch sight of and name Lake Albert (March 14)

Meeting at Bath of the British Association for the Advancement of Science at which Speke and Burton were to debate (Sept.)

Death of Speke in England (Sept. 15)

Times leader on Speke (Sept. 19)

Bakers rescued by Arab slave caravan (Sept.)

Grant's *A Walk across Africa* and Speke's *What Led to the Discovery of the Sources of the Nile* published

1865

Bakers reach Gondokoro (Feb.)

Murchison delivers a eulogy of

Speke to the RGS (May 22)

Murchison asks Livingstone to go to Africa again

Livingstone sails from Folkestone (Aug.)

Bakers reach Suez (Oct.)

1866

Livingstone reaches Zanzibar (Jan.)

Livingstone lands at the mouth of the Rovuma river (March)

Baker's *The Albert N'yanza* published

1867

Baker's *Nile Tributaries of Abyssinia* published

1868

Livingstone discovers Lake Bangweolo (July 18)

1869

Gordon Bennett summons Stanley to an interview in Paris

Livingstone reaches Ujiji (March)

Cholera in Zanzibar

Bakers accompany British Royal tour of Egypt

Suez Canal opened (Nov. 17)

The Pethericks' *Travels in Central Africa* published

1870

Death of Sultan Seyyid Majid bin Said of Zanzibar

Death of Kamrasi, King of Bunyoro

Baker sails south from Khartoum (Feb. 8)

Baker establishes base camp near Malakal (April)

Baker sets sail again up the Nile (Dec)

1871

Baker stuck in the Sudd (March)

Baker reaches clear water and has a dam constructed (March 9)

Baker flotilla reaches Gondokoro (April)

Baker annexes to Egypt country surrounding Gondokoro and names it Equatoria (May 20)

Livingstone sees Africans shot down by Arab slavers at Nyangwe (July 15)

Stanley finds Livingstone at Ujiji (Nov. 10)

Livingstone and Stanley settle direction of flow of the Rusizi

Livingstone and Stanley walk from Ujiji to Tabora (Kazeh)

1872

Baker, his wife, and his nephew leave Gondokoro for Bunyoro which they reach mid-March (Jan. 22)

Livingstone parts from Stanley (March 14)

Bakers reach capital of Bunyoro (April 25)

Baker annexes Bunyoro to Egypt (May 14)

Stanley reports his meeting with Livingstone (May)

Battle of Masindi, Bunyoro (June 8)

Baker retreats from Bunyoro (June 14)

Baker reaches Foweira on the Nile (June 24)

Bakers back at Fatiko, Sudan (Aug.)

Livingstone sets off on his last journey

Gordon meets Nubar Pasha, Egyptian Prime Minister, in Constantinople

Burton's *Zanzibar* and Stanley's *How I Found Livingstone* published

1873

Bakers leave Fatiko (March)

Livingstone working round the south of Lake Bangweolo (April)

Livingstone found dead by his servants (May 1)

Zanzibar slave market closed (June)

Bakers reach Cairo (Aug.)

Susi and Chuma, Livingstone's servants, carrying Livingstone's body, meet Lovett Cameron at Tabora (Oct.)

Gordon is invited to succeed Baker as Governor of Equatoria

1874

News of Livingstone's death reaches England (Jan. 28)

Gordon sets off to take up his appointment in Equatoria

Livingstone's body brought to Bagamoyo on the east coast of Africa (Feb. 15)

Gordon chooses his party and reaches Khartoum (Feb.–March)

Gordon reaches Gondokoro (April)

Livingstone's body carried to London for burial in Westminster Abbey (April 18)

Stanley sails again for East Africa (Aug.)

Stanley sets out from Zanzibar (Nov.)

1875

Stanley sets sail on Lake Victoria and circumnavigates it (March 8)

Stanley meets Mutesa, King of Buganda (April 5)

Stanley back at Mwanza (May 6)

Stanley writes to the *Daily Telegraph* urging sending of missionaries to Buganda

Ismail Pasha, Khedive of Egypt, sells Suez Canal shares to Britain

1876

Gordon reaches Dufilé (Feb. 8)

Stanley launches the *Lady Alice* on Lake Tanganyika at Ujiji (June)

Gordon boards the *Nyanza* at Dufilé (July 20)

Stanley sets sail on the River Lualaba, to find that it joins the Congo, and goes on down river to the Atlantic (Aug.)

Gordon and Gessi go down to Cairo and back to England on leave

1877

Ismail Pasha telegraphs to Gordon in London (Jan. 17)

Gordon back in Cairo; appointed Governor-General of the Sudan (Feb.)

Gordon reaches Khartoum (May 4)

Stanley returns to Zanzibar

Christian missionaries arrive in Buganda

1878

Gessi returns to Egypt and is appointed Governor of Bahr-el-Ghazal province

Gordon brought by Ismail Pasha back to Cairo to preside over board of inquiry into Ismail's financial dealings, but resigns and returns to Khartoum

Stanley's *Through the Dark Continent* published

1879

Ismail Pasha deposed (June)

Gordon resigns his governor-generalship and goes to Abyssinia, but is expelled from that country, and returns to England (July)

Catholic and Protestant missionaries in Buganda in rivalry with each other and with Moslem Arabs

1880

Gordon back in Cairo (Jan. 2)

Gordon visits Leopold II, King of the Belgians, in Brussels

1881

Gessi reduced in rank by the Egyptians; dies

[French take Tunis, May 12]

Egyptian army officers march on the Abdin Palace in Cairo (Sept. 8)

The Mahdi proclaims a Holy War in the Sudan

1882

Egyptian government resigns, but is reinstated by a popular rising (May 27)

Anti-European rioting in Alexandria (June 1)

14,000 Europeans embark at Alexandria (June)

British fleet fires on Alexandria (July 11)

Sir Garnet Wolseley lands in Egypt (Aug.)

The Mahdi's men lay siege to El Obeid

Battle of Tel-el-Kebir: Arabs defeated by the British (Sept. 13)

Abd-el-kader is appointed Governor-General of the Sudan

1883

El Obeid falls to the Mahdi (Jan.)

Hicks Pasha advances up the Nile (Summer)

Hicks Pasha defeated 30 miles south of El Obeid (Nov. 5)

Gordon offered and accepts employment in the Congo

1884

Stanley writes to *The Times* suggesting sending to the Sudan a force commanded by Gordon (Jan. 1)

The Times publishes letter from Gordon on affairs in the Sudan (Jan. 14)

Gordon interviewed by Wolseley at the War Office, London (Jan. 15)

Gordon leaves London for Egypt (Jan. 18)

Gordon leaves Cairo for the Sudan (Jan. 28)

Gordon reaches Khartoum (Feb. 18)

Silence falls on the Sudan (March)

Announcement in London that an expedition is to go to the Sudan (Aug. 8)

More than 800 Egyptians killed in a skirmish outside Khartoum (Sept. 4)

Wolseley arrives in Cairo (Sept. 9)

The *Abbas* leaves Khartoum with dispatches from Gordon (Sept. 10)

The *Abbas*, disabled through striking a rock, is captured by the Mahdi (Sept. 18)

Bahr-el-Ghazal province falls to the Mahdi

The Mahdi moves to Omdurman: final stage of the siege of Khartoum begins (Oct. 21)

Mutesa, King of Buganda, dies (Oct.)

Shelling of Khartoum begins (Nov. 12)

The *Bordein* leaves Khartoum for Metemma carrying Gordon's papers and journals (Dec. 15)

A runner from Gordon reaches Korti. Sir Herbert Stewart begins his advance (Dec. 30)

Karl Peters raids the dominions of the Sultan of Zanzibar

1885

Omdurman Fort surrenders to the Mahdi (Jan. 5)

Stewart seizes Abu Klea Wells

(Jan. 17); is killed near Metemma (Jan. 19)

Sir Charles Wilson on way to Khartoum on the *Bordein* (Jan. 24)

The *Bordein* strikes a rock in the Sixth Cataract (Jan. 26)

The Mahdi orders assault on Khartoum; Khartoum falls and Gordon is killed (Jan. 26)

The *Bordein* reaches junction of Blue Nile and White Nile (Jan. 28)

News of the fall of Khartoum and Gordon's death reaches London (Feb. 5)

Death of the Mahdi; he is succeeded by the Khalifa Abdullah (June 25)

Gordon's *Journals* published

1886

Mainland empire of Sultan of Zanzibar divided between Germany and Britain

1889

Mahdiist forces defeated in Battle of Toski, Egypt (Aug.)

1891

Father Ohrwalder and two nuns escape to Egypt from the Mahdiists

F. R. Wingate's *Mahdiism and the Egyptian Soudan* published

1895

Slatin Pasha escapes from the Mahdiists

1896

[Emperor Menelik II of Abyssinia defeats the Italians at Adowa, March 1]

Kitchener appointed to command Sudanese expedition

J. B. Marchand leaves Brazzaville (French Congo) for the Sudan

1898

Battle of Atbara: Kitchener defeats Mahdiists (April 8)

Marchand reaches Fashoda, Sudan (July)

Battle of Omdurman; Mahdiists defeated and Khartoum freed (Sept. 2)

Funeral service held at Khartoum for Gordon. Mahdi's body dug up and thrown into the Nile (Sept. 4)

Kitchener sets sail from Khartoum for Fashoda (Sept. 9)

Anglo-Egyptian flotilla approaching Fashoda (Sept. 18)

French and British press attack one another with virulence (Oct.)

Marchand summoned to Cairo by the French government

French lower their flag at Fashoda (Dec. 11)

1899

Agreement signed in London reserving the Nile valley to the British and Egyptians, country to the west of the Nile to France (March 21)

Kabarega of Bunyoro and Mwanga of Buganda deported to the Seychelles

Anglo-Egyptian condominium of the Sudan established; Kitchener appointed Governor-General

Khalifa Abdullah defeated and killed, together with his chief followers, at the Battle of Jebel Gedir (Nov. 23)

Select Bibliography

Allen, Bernard Meredith. *Gordon and the Sudan*, Macmillan, London, 1931

Baker, Sir Samuel White. *The Albert N'yanza, Great Basin of the Nile, and explorations of the Nile Sources*, 2 vols, Macmillan, London, 1886

——*Ismailia: A Narrative of the Expedition to Central Africa for the Suppression of the Slave Trade*, 2 vols, Macmillan, London, 1874

Baring, Sir Evelyn (Earl of Cromer). *Modern Egypt*, Macmillan, London, 1908

Blanch, Lesley. *The Wilder Shores of Love*, Murray, London, 1954

Blunt, Wilfrid Scawen. *Secret History of the English Occupation of Egypt*, T. Fisher Unwin, London, 1907

—— *Gordon at Khartoum*, S. Swift & Co., London, 1911

Bourne, H. R. F. *The Other Side of the Emin Pasha Relief Expedition*, Chatto & Windus, London, 1891

Burton, Lady Isabel. *Life of Captain Sir Richard F. Burton*, 2 vols, Chapman & Hall, London, 1893

Burton, Sir Richard Francis. *First Footsteps in East Africa*, 2 vols, Longmans, Green, London, 1856

—— *The Lake Regions of Central Africa*, 2 vols, Longmans, Green, London, 1860

—— *Zanzibar, City, Island, and Coast*, 2 vols, Tinsley Bros, London, 1872

Burton, Sir Richard Francis, and M'Queen James. *The Nile Basin*, Tinsley Bros, London, 1864

Caix de Saint-Aymour, Robert. *Fachoda: la France et l'Angleterre*, Paris, 1899

Casati, Gaetano. *Ten Years in Equatoria, and the return with Emin Pasha*, 2 vols, trans. Mrs J. R. Clay, F. Warne & Co., London, 1891

Chaillé-Long, Charles. *Central Africa: Naked Truths of Naked People*, Sampson Low & Co., London, 1876

—— *The Three Prophets*, D. Appleton & Co., New York, 1884

—— *My Life in Four Continents*, Hutchinson, London, 1912

Churchill, Winston S. *The River War*, Longmans, Green, London, 1899

Coupland, Sir Reginald. *The Exploitation of East Africa, 1856–1890*, Faber & Faber, London, 1939

——*Livingstone's Last Journey*, Collins, London, 1945

Dearden, Seton. *The Arabian Knight: A Study of Sir Richard Burton*, Arthur Barker, London, 1936; revised edn, 1953

Delbecque, Jacques. *La Vie du Général Marchand*, Paris, 12th edn, 1937

Felkin, R. W., and Wilson, C. T., *Uganda and the Egyptian Sudan*, Sampson Low & Co., London, 1882

Fitzgerald, Percy H. *The Great Canal at Suez*, 2 vols, Tinsley Bros, London, 1876

Gessi, Romolo. *Seven Years in the Sudan*, trans. L. Wolffsohn and B. Woodward, Sampson Low & Co., London, 1892

Gordon, General C. G. *The Journals of Major-*

General C. G. Gordon at Khartoum, ed. A. Egmont Hake, Kegan Paul, London, 1885

—— *Letters of General Gordon to His Sister*, Macmillan, London, 1888

Grant, James Augustus. *A Walk Across Africa*, Blackwood, London, 1864

H., J. W. [Mrs J. W. Harrison]. *A. M. Mackay, by his Sister*, Hodder & Stoughton, London, 1890

Holt, Peter M. *The Mahdist State in the Sudan, 1881–1898*, Clarendon Press, Oxford, 1958

Johnston, Sir Harry Hamilton. *The Uganda Protectorate*, 2 vols, Hutchinson, London, 1902

—— *The Nile Quest*, Lawrence & Bullen, London, 1903

Junker, Wilhelm. *Travels in Africa 1875–1886*, trans. A. H. Keane, 3 vols, Chapman & Hall, London, 1890–2

Laufer, Jean-Jacques. *Stanley, Briseur d'Obstacles*, Paris, 1946

Livingstone, David. *Missionary Travels and Researches in South Africa*, 2 vols, Murray, London, 1857

—— *Narratives of an Expedition to the Zambesi and its Tributaries*, 2 vols, Murray, London, 1865

—— *Last Journals of David Livingstone in Central Africa, from 1865 to his death*, 2 vols, ed. H. Waller, Murray, London, 1874

Lugard, F. D. (Baron Lugard). *The Rise of our East African Empire*, 2 vols, Blackwood, London and Edinburgh, 1893 (see also under Perham in this list)

Magnus, Sir Philip. *Kitchener, Portrait of an Imperialist*, Murray, London, 1958

Middleton, Dorothy. *Baker of the Nile*, Falcon Press, London, 1949

Neufeld, Charles. *A Prisoner of the Khaleefa: Twelve Years' Captivity at Omdurman*, Chapman & Hall, London, 1899

Oliver, Roland Anthony. *The Missionary Factor in East Africa*, Longmans, Green, London, 1952

Perham, Dame Margery. *Lugard: I The Years of Adventure, 1858–1898*, Collins, London, 1956

Petherick, Mr & Mrs John. *Travels in Central Africa*, 2 vols, Tinsley Bros, London, 1869

Power, Frank. *Letters from Khartoum*, Sampson Low & Co., London, 1885

Schweinfurth, Georg. *The Heart of Africa*, trans. E. E. Frewer, 2 vols, Sampson Low & Co., London, 1873

Schweinfurth, Georg, ed. *Emin Pasha in Central Africa: His Letters and Journals,* trans. Mrs Felkin, George Philip, London, 1888

Schweitzer, G., ed. *Emin Pasha, His Life and Work*, 2 vols, Constable. 1898

Seaver, George Fenn. *David Livingstone: His Life and Letters*, Lutterworth Press, London, 1957

Slatin, Sir Rudolf Carl. *Fire and Sword in the Sudan, 1879–1895*, trans. Major F. R. Wingate, E. Arnold, London, 1896

Sparrow, J. W. G. *Gordon, Mandarin and Pasha*, Jarrolds, London, 1962

Speke, John Hanning. *What led to the Discovery of the Source of the Nile*, Blackwood, Edinburgh & London, 1864

—— *Journal of the Discovery of the Source of the Nile*, Blackwood, Edinburgh and London, 1863

Stanley, Henry Morton. *How I Found Livingstone*, London, 1872

—— *Through the Dark Continent*, 2 vols, London, 1878

—— *In Darkest Africa, or the Quest, Rescue and Retreat of Emin, Governor of Equatoria*, 2 vols, Sampson Low & Co., London, 1890

Steevens, George Warrington. *With Kitchener to Khartoum*, Blackwood, Edinburgh and London, 1898

Stisted, Georgiana M. *The True Life of Captain*

Sir Richard F. Burton, H. S. Nichols, London, 1896

Strachey, Lytton. *Eminent Victorians*, Chatto & Windus, 1918

Thomas, Harold Beken, and Scott, Robert. *Uganda*, Oxford University Press, London, 1935

Wingate, Major F. R. *Mahdiism and the Egyptian Soudan*, Macmillan, London, 1891

Wingate, F. R., ed. *Ten Years' Captivity in the Mahdi's Camp, 1882–1892 : from the original manuscripts of Father Joseph Ohrwalder*, Sampson Low & Co., London, 1893

Sudan Notes and Records, Khartoum, 1927

Tanganyika Notes and Records, Dar-es-Salaam, 1947, 1957

The Uganda Journal, Uganda Society, London, 1935, 1936, 1941, 1951

Illustration Acknowledgments

COLOUR PLATES

Dr John R. Baker: p. 93 (Photograph John Freeman)
Samuel White Baker, *The Albert N'yanza*: p. 170 (above and below) (Photographs John Freeman)
R. M. Bloomfield, Ardea: p. 57
Compagnie Financière de Suez et de l'Union Parisienne: pp. 148, 157, 158–9, 160 (Photographs Mme Simone Guiley-Lagache)
Daily Telegraph Colour Library: p. 169
Alistair Duncan, Middle East Archive: pp. 94, 352
Miss D. F. Goodrick, W. F. & R. K. Swan (Hellenic) Ltd: pp. 17, 58 (above)
Gordon Boys' School, West End, Woking: p. 331 (Photograph Derrick Witty)
Bernard W. Kunicki: pp. 58 (below), 111
James and Neil Maconochie: pp. 46–7, 48, 130, 313
Mansell Collection: pp. 18, 112, 230–1, 301
National Army Museum, London: pp. 332–3 (Photograph John Freeman)
National Portrait Gallery, London: pp. 187, 229, 314
Picturepoint Ltd: p. 232
Richmond upon Thames Borough Council: p. 35 (Photograph John Freeman)
Roger-Viollet: pp. 273, 274
Royal Geographical Society: pp. 36, 75, 76 (Photographs John Freeman)
Emil Schulthess: pp. 45, 304, 351
Captain Horace Smith, Parker Gallery: p. 334 (Photograph John Freeman)
R. M. Stanley: pp. 129, 147 (Photographs John Freeman); 291, 292, 302–3
Victoria and Albert Museum, Print Room: p. 188

MONOCHROME

T. & R. Annan & Sons Ltd: p. 80
Dr John R. Baker: pp. 91, 108
Samuel White Baker, *The Albert N'yanza*: pp. 14, 104 (Photographs John Freeman); 101, 102
Samuel White Baker, *Ismailia*: pp. 97, 163, 164, 165, 172, 173 (Photographs John Freeman)
Colonel C. Chaillé-Long, *Central Africa*: pp. 140, 141, 143, 144 (Photographs John Freeman)
Church Missionary Society: p. 288 (left and right)
Compagnie Financière de Suez et de l'Union Parisienne: pp. 153, 154–5 (Photographs Mme Simone Guiley-Lagache)
Thos Cook & Sons Ltd: p. 328
Crown Copyright: p. 87 (right)
Baron Carl Claus von der Decken, *Reisen in Ost-Afrika*: p. 24 (Photograph John Freeman)
G. Ebers, *Egypt*: pp. 180, 203, 263 (Photographs John Freeman)
General C. G. Gordon, *The Journals of Major-General C. G. Gordon at Khartoum*: pp. 240, 241 (Photographs John Freeman)
The Illustrated London News: pp. 79, 242, 244, 255, 343
Sir Harry Johnston, *The Nile Quest*: p. 13 (Photograph John Freeman)
Life © Time Inc.: pp. 88, 326 (Photographs Eliot Elisofon)
The Last Journals of David Livingstone, ed. H. Waller: Frontispiece, pp. 118, 119, 132 (left), 133 (Photographs John Freeman)
James and Neil Maconochie: pp. 125, 134
Mansell Collection: pp. 20–1, 40–1, 72–3, 96, 166, 195, 204, 206, 216, 248–9, 256, 264, 266–7, 269, 347
National Army Museum, London: pp. 211, 212, 234
National Maritime Museum, Greenwich: p. 22

The Reverend R. W. Pilgrim: p. 86 (Photograph D. J. Wheadon)
Radio Times Hulton Picture Library: pp. 23, 107, 215, 222, 223, 226, 323
Reproduced by gracious permission of Her Majesty the Queen: p. 272
Richmond upon Thames Borough Council: p. 84 (Photograph John Freeman)
Roger-Viollet: pp. 10 (above and below), 102, 338; pp. 101, 340 Collection Viollet; p. 339 Viollet Harlingue
Royal Commonwealth Society: pp. 245 (right), 277, 329 (Photographs John Freeman)
Royal Geographical Society: pp. 27; 117, 122–3, 136, 179, 295, 298, 310 (Photographs John Freeman)
Georg Schweinfurth, *The Heart of Africa*: p. 194 (Photograph John Freeman)
Rodney Searight: pp. 213, 337 (Photographs John Freeman)
Gerald Sparrow, *Gordon, Mandarin and Pasha*, Jarrolds: p. 259
John Hanning Speke, *Journal of the Discovery of the Source of the Nile*: pp. 38, 39, 54, 55 (above), 60, 65, 66, 67, 69 (Photographs John Freeman)
Henry M. Stanley, *In Darkest Africa*: pp. 190, 296 (Photographs John Freeman)
R. M. Stanley: pp. 139, 308–9
Franz Stuhlmann, *Mit Emin Pasha ins Herz von Afrika*: pp. 289, 319, 321 (Photographs John Freeman)
The Times: p. 87
UNESCO: pp. 55 (below) (Photograph J. H. Blower); 238 (Photograph A. Raccah)
F. R. Wingate, ed., *Ten Years' Captivity in the Mahdi's Camp: from the Original Manuscripts of Father Joseph Ohrwalder*: p. 279

Index